W9-COA-738

VISUAL QUICKSTART GUIDE

MAC OS 9

Maria Langer

 Peachpit Press

Visual QuickStart Guide
Mac OS 9
Maria Langer

Peachpit Press
1249 Eighth Street
Berkeley, CA 94710
510-524-2178 • 800-283-9444
510-524-2221 (fax)

Find us on the World Wide Web at: http://www.peachpit.com/

Peachpit Press is a division of Addison Wesley Longman

Copyright © 2000 by Maria Langer

Editor: Clifford Colby
Indexer: Maria Langer
Cover Design: The Visual Group
Production: Maria Langer, Kate Reber

Colophon

This book was produced with Adobe PageMaker 6.5 on a Power Macintosh G3/300. The fonts used were Kepler Multiple Master, Meta Plus, and PIXymbols Command. Screenshots were created using Snapz Pro on a Strawberry iMac, Power Macintosh G3/300, and PowerBook 3400/180c.

Notice of Rights

Notice of Liability

The information in this book is distributed on an "As Is" basis, without warranty. While every precaution has been taken in the preparation of the book, neither the author nor Peachpit Press shall have any liability to any person or entity with respect to any loss or damage caused or alleged to be caused directly or indirectly by the instructions contained in this book or by the computer software and hardware products described in it.

Trademarks

ISBN 0-201-70004-2

9 8 7 6 5 4 3 2 1

Printed and bound in the United States of America.

 Printed on recycled paper.

Dedication

To Tim Holmes, Eric Simenel,
and the rest of the Mac OS 9
development team

Thanks!

To Cliff Colby, for helping me fine-tune this fourth edition of my Mac OS VQS. I appreciate the way he gently nagged me to get an outline together, then sped up the production process when the book was ready to go to the printer.

To Victor Gavenda, for fielding my technical questions—even when he was as puzzled as I was. (No need to send me CDs this time around, Victor; aren't you glad I got that ISDN setup?)

To Nancy Ruenzel and the other powers-that-be at Peachpit Press, for continuing to put up with me, despite frequent crankiness and occasional whining. (I'm trying to behave. Really.)

To Kate Reber, for another great layout job. (We make a good team, don't we?)

To the rest of the folks at Peachpit Press— especially Gary-Paul, Mimi, Trish, Hannah, Paula, Zigi, Jimbo, and Keasley—for doing what they do so well. (I'm still waiting for all of you to come by for dinner one day. What you need is a "retreat" here in Wickenburg...)

To Apple Computer, Inc., for another great release of the world's best operating system.

And to Mike, for the usual reasons.

http://www.gilesrd.com/mlanger/

TABLE OF CONTENTS

TABLE OF CONTENTS

INTRODUCTION TO MAC OS 9

Introduction

Mac OS 9 is the latest version of the computer operating system that put the phrase *graphic user interface* in everyone's vocabulary. With Mac OS, you can point, click, and drag to work with files, applications, and utilities. Because the same intuitive interface is utilized throughout the system, you'll find that a procedure that works in one program works in virtually all the others.

This Visual QuickStart Guide will help you learn Mac OS 9 by providing step-by-step instructions, plenty of illustrations, and a generous helping of tips. On these pages, you'll find everything you need to know to get up and running quickly with Mac OS 9—and more!

This book was designed for page flipping. Use the thumb tabs, index, or table of contents to find the topics for which you need help. If you're brand new to Mac OS, however, I recommend that you begin by reading at least the first two chapters. In them, you'll find basic information about techniques you'll use every day with your computer.

If you're interested in information about new Mac OS 9 features and the components of Mac OS 9, be sure to browse through this **Introduction**. It'll give you a good idea of what you can expect to see on your computer.

START HERE

New Features in Mac OS 9

Mac OS 9, which was released in the autumn of 1999, is a major revision to Mac OS. This section provides a summary of some of its biggest new features.

✔ Tip

- Most of these features are covered in this book.

Searching Features

- Sherlock has a whole new interface (**Figure 1**) that includes more search sites, customizable channels, and special features for searching for e-mail addresses and shopping online.

- The File menu (**Figure 2**) now offers two search commands for using Sherlock's search capabilities:

  - ▲ Find enables you to find files on any mounted disk.

  - ▲ Search Internet enables you to search the Internet for information, e-mail addresses, or merchandise available online.

Security Features

- The File menu's new Encrypt command (**Figure 2**) launches the new Apple File Security application (**Figure 3**) so you can password protect files.

- The Keychain feature enables you to store frequently used logon information in one place. Unlock the keychain, and your computer can log onto servers and Internet sites automatically.

- The new Apple Verifier application can check a file's digital signature to make sure it comes from a source you trust.

Figure 1 Sherlock has a whole new interface. Now it's even more clever about searching disk, servers, and the Internet.

Figure 2
The File menu offers a number of new commands for accessing new or improved features.

Figure 3 You can now use encryption to secure individual files.

Figure 4 With Multiple Users enabled, more than one person can share a Mac, without security worries.

Figure 5 You can use voiceprint security to log in to a Mac with Multiple Users enabled.

Figure 6 The Panels interface is highly simplified—perfect for new users (like my sister).

Networking

◆ You can now use file sharing and program linking over a TCP/IP network connection. This means you can share files and programs over the Internet.

Multiple Users

◆ You can now set up your Macintosh so it can be accessed by multiple users (**Figure 4**), each with privileges and an interface that you define.

◆ Users can use voiceprint identification (**Figure 5**) to log in to a system set up for multiple users.

◆ The Panels interface (**Figure 6**), which is available as part of the multiple users feature, is highly simplified—perfect for new users or youngsters.

Interface Changes

◆ The Monitors & Sound control panel has been separated into two separate control panels: Monitors and Sound.

◆ The Keyboard control panel now enables you to map function keys to items such as files, folders, and network volumes. (This feature is only available on Macintosh models that support it.)

Updating Software

◆ The new Software update feature makes it possible to automatically check for, download, and install system software updates. All you need is an Internet connection.

NEW FEATURES IN MAC OS 9

Mac OS 9 Components

Mac OS 9 includes the following software components:

◆ **Mac OS 9** is the basic collection of system software files, including the System file, Finder file, control panels, and extensions. This is the foundation of Mac OS; its various parts are covered throughout this book.

◆ **Internet Access** enables you to connect to the Internet. I tell you about accessing the Internet in **Chapter 11**.

◆ **Apple Remote Access** enables you to use your modem to connect to another computer or establish a PPP connection to the Internet. I discuss Apple Remote Access in **Chapters 10** and **11**.

◆ **Personal Web Sharing** enables you to build your own Web server for sharing information on an intranet or the Internet. I tell you about Personal Web Sharing in **Chapter 11**.

◆ **Text-to-Speech** enables your computer to read text and alerts with a synthesized voice. I cover speaking text in **Chapter 7** and setting Speech options in **Chapter 15**.

◆ **Mac OS Runtime for Java** enables you to run Java applets from the Finder.

◆ **ColorSync** helps ensure color accuracy when working with color images.

◆ **English Speech Recognition** enables your computer to recognize and respond to human speech.

◆ **Language Kits** allows you to display and edit additional languages.

◆ **Network Assistant Client** enables your network administrator to manage your computer.

✔ **Tip**

■ The Mac OS 9 installer, which I discuss in **Chapter 1**, enables you to install any combination of these components.

SETTING UP MAC OS 9

Setting Up Mac OS 9

Before you can use Mac OS 9, you must install it on your computer and configure it to work the way you need it to. This is a three-step process:

1. Use the Mac OS 9 installer to install the components you want.

2. Restart your computer.

3. Use the Mac OS Setup Assistant, as well as other assistants, to configure the Mac OS 9 components you installed.

This chapter explains how to complete all three of these steps, so you can properly install and configure Mac OS 9 on your computer.

✔ Tips

■ Mac OS 9 offers many installation and configuration options—far too many to discuss in detail in this book. Although the figures and instructions in this chapter cover only the most common options, I think you'll find enough general information to help you complete virtually any combination of installation and configuration options.

■ I tell you how to use the Internet Setup Assistant in **Chapter 11**.

The Mac OS 9 Installer

Mac OS 9 comes with an installer application that makes software installation easy. Simply launch the installer and follow the instructions that appear on screen to select a destination disk, learn more about the software, agree to a license agreement, and select the Mac OS 9 components you want installed. The installer builds the System and Finder files for your computer and copies the software you specified to your hard disk.

The Mac OS 9 installer can perform two types of installations:

◆ **Standard Installation** lets you select the Mac OS 9 components you want installed. The installer copies all standard parts of each selected component to your hard disk.

◆ **Customized Installation** lets you select the Mac OS 9 components you want installed and then lets you select the individual parts of each component to be installed.

The first half of this chapter explains how to use the Mac OS 9 installer to perform both a standard and a customized installation.

✔ Tips

■ The installation instructions in this chapter assume you know basic Mac OS techniques, such as pointing, clicking, double-clicking, dragging, and selecting items from a menu. If you're brand new to the Mac and don't know any of these techniques, skip ahead to **Chapter 2**, which discusses Mac OS basics.

■ A standard installation of Mac OS 9 includes the following components: Mac OS 9, Internet Access, Apple Remote Access, Personal Web Sharing, Text-to-Speech, Mac OS Runtime for Java, and ColorSync.

Mac OS Install

Figure 1 To launch the Mac OS 9 installer, double-click this icon.

Figure 2 The Mac OS 9 installer's Welcome window appears when you launch it.

■ I tell you about the individual components of Mac OS 9 in the **Introduction** of this book.

■ You can click the Go Back button at any time during installation to change options in a previous window.

■ You can press (Return) or (Enter) to "click" a default button—a button with a dark border around it—such as the Continue button in **Figure 2**.

THE MAC OS 9 INSTALLER

Figure 3 Use the Select Destination window to select the disk on which to install Mac OS 9.

Figure 4 Choose a disk from the Destination Disk pop-up menu.

Figure 5 Turn on the Perform Clean Installation check box to create a brand new System Folder for Mac OS 9.

✔ Tips

- The destination disk is normally your internal hard disk but can be any disk that is turned on at startup.

- Only those hard disks and removable high-capacity media (such as Zip, Jaz, and SuperDisk disks) that appear on your Desktop are listed in the Destination Disk pop-up menu (**Figure 4**).

- A status area beneath the Destination Disk pop-up menu indicates the version of Mac OS that is installed on the disk, as well as the available disk space and the amount of disk space required for a basic installation (**Figure 3**).

To launch the installer

1. Start your computer from the Mac OS 9 CD-ROM disc.

   or

   Start your computer the usual way and insert the Mac OS 9 CD-ROM disc.

2. Locate and double-click the Mac OS Install icon (**Figure 1**).

3. After a moment, the installer's Welcome window appears (**Figure 2**). Click Continue.

✔ Tip

- To start your computer from the Mac OS 9 CD-ROM disc, insert the disc, choose Special > Restart, and hold down C until the "Welcome to Mac OS" message appears. This is the recommended way to start your computer when installing OS software.

To select a destination disk

1. In the installer's Select Destination window (**Figure 3**), use the Destination Disk pop-up menu (**Figure 4**) to select the disk on which you want to install Mac OS 9.

2. Click Select.

- To create a brand new System Folder for Mac OS 9, click the Options button. Turn on the Perform Clean Installation check box in the dialog box that appears (**Figure 5**). The old System Folder is renamed "Previous System Folder" and should be deleted after you move non-Apple control panels, extensions, and preferences files to their proper locations in the new System Folder.

To read important information about Mac OS 9

1. Read the contents of the installer's Important Information window (**Figure 6**). Click the down arrow on the vertical scroll bar to scroll through the entire document.

2. When you have finished reading the information, click Continue.

✔ Tips

- Read the information in this window carefully! It provides important, late-breaking news about installing Mac OS, including compatibility information and special instructions not included in this book.

- To save a copy of the information for future reference, click the Save button. Then use the Save As dialog box that appears to select a disk location and enter a name for the file. Click Save to complete the save. (I tell you more about the Save As dialog box in **Chapter 5**.)

- To print a copy of the information for reference, click the Print button. Then click Print in the Print dialog box that appears to send the document to your printer. (I tell you about printing and using the Print dialog box in **Chapter 9**.)

Figure 6 The Important Information window contains late-breaking news about installing Mac OS 9.

Figure 7 The Software License Agreement tells you exactly what you're allowed to do with Mac OS 9 software.

Figure 8 To complete the installation of Mac OS 9, you must click Agree in this dialog box.

To read and agree to the Software License Agreement

1. If desired, choose a language from the pop-up menu at the top-right of the Software License Agreement window (**Figure 7**).

2. Read the contents of the window. Click the down arrow on the vertical scroll bar to scroll through the entire document.

3. When you have finished reading the agreement, click Continue.

4. A dialog box appears, informing you that you must agree to the terms of the agreement you just read to continue (**Figure 8**). Click Agree.

✔ Tips

- To save a copy of the license agreement for future reference, click the Save button. Then use the Save As dialog box that appears to select a disk location and enter a name for the file. Click Save to complete the save. (I tell you more about the Save As dialog box in **Chapter 5**.)

- To print a copy of the license agreement for reference, click the Print button. Then click Print in the Print dialog box that appears to send the document to your printer. (I tell you about printing and using the Print dialog box in **Chapter 9**.)

- If you click Disagree in step 4, the installer returns you to its Welcome window (**Figure 2**).

READING THE LICENSE AGREEMENT

To customize an installation

1. In the Install Software window (**Figure 9**), click the Customize button. The window changes to the Custom Installation and Removal window (**Figure 10**), which displays a list of software components.

2. Toggle the check box settings to turn on only those for the components you want to install. Be sure to click the down arrow at the bottom of the vertical scroll bar to view all the options.

3. If desired, choose an installation mode from the pop-up menu beside each checked component.

    ▲ **Recommended Installation** installs the recommended parts of the component for your computer.

    ▲ **Customized Installation** displays a dialog box similar to the one in **Figure 11**. Use this option to specify which parts of the component should be installed, and click OK.

✔ Tips

■ If you change your mind about making a custom installation, click the Don't Customize button (**Figure 10**) to go back to the Install Software window (**Figure 9**).

■ To successfully use the Customized Installation option, you must be familiar with all parts of each component you want installed. This is a feature designed for Mac OS experts. If used improperly, it can cause erratic system behavior.

■ You can click the triangle to the left of an item (**Figure 11**) to display individual items within it (**Figure 12**).

■ You can click the info icon (or "i" button) to the right of an item to learn more about it (**Figure 13**). Click OK to dismiss the information dialog box.

Figure 9 Use the Install Software window to select the Mac OS components you want to install.

Figure 10 Use the Custom Installation and Removal window to select Mac OS 9 components for a custom installation.

Figure 11 Windows like these enable you to select the parts of a specific component that you want to install.

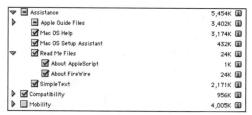

Figure 12 Clicking the triangle to the left of an item displays individual items within it.

Figure 13
When you click an item's "i" button, a window full of information about the item appears.

Figure 14 You can use this dialog box to set two additional installation options.

To set other installation options

1. Click the Options button in the Install Software or Custom Installation and Removal window to display a dialog box like the one in **Figure 14**.

2. To prevent the installer from attempting to update the hard disk driver of the destination disk, turn off the Update Apple Hard Disk Driver check box.

3. To prevent the installer from creating an installation log file, turn off the Create Installation Report check box.

4. Click OK.

✔ Tips

■ As shown in **Figure 14**, both of these options are enabled by default. If you're not sure how to set these options, leave them both turned on.

■ If you're not sure what to do in step 3, leave the check box turned on. The Mac OS 9 installer can only update the driver on an Apple-branded hard disk—one that comes with a Macintosh computer. It cannot affect a hard disk made by another manufacturer. If the installer cannot update your disk's driver, it will display a message saying so and provide additional information about updating your driver.

SETTING OTHER INSTALLATION OPTIONS

To complete the installation

1. In the Install Software window (**Figure 9**) or Custom Installation and Removal window (**Figure 10**), click the Start button.

2. A dialog box like the one in **Figure 15** may appear, informing you that other applications cannot be running during the install process and that you will have to restart your computer when it's finished. Click Continue.

3. The installer performs some maintenance tasks, then begins installing the software you selected. A progress window like the one in **Figure 16** appears to show you how it's doing.

4. When the installation is complete, a dialog box like the one in **Figure 17** appears. Click Restart.

✔ Tips

- The amount of time it takes to install Mac OS 9 depends on the components you selected (if you customized the installation), the speed of your computer's CPU, and the speed of your CD-ROM drive. A basic installation can take 15 minutes or more.

- To perform additional Mac OS 9 installations, click the Continue button in the dialog box that appears when installation is complete (**Figure 17**). This returns you to the Install Software window (**Figure 9**).

Figure 15 A dialog box like this may appear after you click the Start button.

Figure 16 The Mac OS 9 installer displays a progress window as it works.

Figure 17 A dialog box like this appears when the installation is complete.

COMPLETING THE INSTALLATION

Figure 18
To restart your computer, choose Restart from the Special menu.

Restarting Your Computer

To configure and use your newly installed Mac OS 9 software, you must restart your computer. This loads the new software into the computer's RAM and, if necessary, launches the Mac OS Setup Assistant.

To restart your computer

If you are not prompted to restart your computer at the conclusion of the installation process (**Figure 17**), choose Special > Restart (**Figure 18**).

✔ Tips

■ Do not restart your computer by turning off power and then turning it back on! This can cause file corruption. I tell you other ways to restart your computer in **Chapter 2**.

■ If you have more than one disk with Mac OS software installed on it, you may have to use the Startup Disk control panel to specify which disk's operating system should be loaded at startup. I tell you about the Startup Disk control panel in **Chapter 14**.

The Mac OS Setup Assistant

When you restart your computer after installing Mac OS 9, the Mac OS Setup Assistant automatically appears (**Figure 19**). This program uses a simple question and answer process to get information about you and the way you use your computer. The information you provide is automatically entered into the appropriate control panels to configure Mac OS 9.

Figure 19 The Mac OS Setup Assistant offers an easy way to configure Mac OS 9.

✔ Tips

- Your computer may automatically rebuild the Desktop file for attached disks when you restart after installing Mac OS 9. If so, a dialog box like the one in **Figure 20** appears. Do not stop this process. When it is finished, the dialog box will automatically disappear.

- If the Mac OS Setup Assistant does not automatically appear at startup, you can launch it by opening the Mac OS Setup Assistant icon in the Assistants folder on your hard disk. I explain how to work with files and folders in **Chapter 3**.

- I tell you about control panels and how you can use them to customize Mac OS in **Chapters 14** and **15**.

Figure 20 When you first start your computer after installing Mac OS 9, it may automatically rebuild the invisible Desktop files on attached disks.

Figure 21 Use the Regional Preferences window to select your language version.

To use the Mac OS Setup Assistant

1. Read the information in each Mac OS Setup Assistant window. Enter information or make selections when prompted.

2. Click the right arrow button or press →️ to continue.

   or

   Click the left arrow button or press ←️ to go back and make changes in previous windows.

✔ Tip

- The next few pages explain exactly how to enter information in each window that appears.

To select regional preferences

1. If you haven't already done so, click the right arrow button in the Introduction window of the Mac OS Setup Assistant (**Figure 19**).

2. Read the information in the Regional Preferences window (**Figure 21**) to learn how Mac OS 9 uses your language version.

3. Click the language you prefer to select it.

4. Click the right arrow button.

✔ Tips

- The languages that appear in this dialog box will vary depending on the language supported by your copy of Mac OS 9.

- You can set the keyboard layout for a language in the Keyboard control panel, which I discuss in **Chapter 14**.

To enter your name & organization

1. Read the information in the Name and Organization window (**Figure 22**) to learn how Mac OS 9 uses your name and company.

2. Enter your name in the What is your name? edit box.

3. Press [Tab] or click in the What is your company or organization? edit box to position the blinking insertion point.

4. Enter the name of your company or organization.

5. Click the right arrow button.

Figure 22 Enter your name and organization in these edit boxes.

✔ Tips

- You must enter a name in the What is your name? box. You may, however, leave the What is your company or organization? box empty if desired.

- You can also enter your name in the File Sharing control panel, which I tell you about in **Chapter 10**.

Figure 23 Use the Time and Date window to check and, if necessary, change the time or date.

Figure 24 To change the time (or date), click an incorrect number in the sequence to select it and then click the up or down arrow until the right number appears.

To set the time & date

1. Read the information in the Time and Date window of the Mac OS Setup Assistant (**Figure 23**) to learn how Mac OS 9 uses the time and date.

2. If daylight savings time is currently in effect, select the Yes radio button by clicking it.

3. If the time in the What time is it? box is not correct, change it. To do this, click an incorrect number in the time sequence to select it (**Figure 24**) and either type in the correct number or click the up or down arrow button beside the time until the correct number appears.

4. If the date in the What is today's date? box is not correct, change it. To do this, click an incorrect number in the date sequence to select it and either type in the correct number or click the up or down arrow button beside the date until the correct number appears.

5. Click the right arrow button.

✔ Tips

■ The time and date, which are tracked by your computer's internal clock, may already be correct. If so, no changes will be necessary.

■ You can also set the time and date in the Date & Time control panel, which I tell you about in **Chapter 14**.

SETTING THE TIME & DATE

To select your geographic location

1. Read the information in the Geographic Location window of the Mac OS Setup Assistant (**Figure 25**) to learn how Mac OS 9 uses your location.

2. Click the up or down arrow on the scroll bar until the name of a city in your time zone (preferably near you) appears. Click it once to select it.

3. Click the right arrow button.

✔ Tip

■ You can also set your geographic location or time zone in the Date & Time control panel, which I tell you about in **Chapter 14**.

To set Finder preferences

1. Read the information in the Finder Preferences window of the Mac OS Setup Assistant (**Figure 26**) to learn about the difference between the standard Finder and Simple Finder.

2. If you want fewer menu commands in the Finder, click the Yes radio button to select it.

3. Click the right arrow button.

✔ Tips

■ The standard Finder—*not* Simple Finder— is used throughout this book.

■ I illustrate both standard Finder and Simple Finder menus in **Appendix A**.

■ You can also set Finder preferences in the Preferences dialog box, which I tell you about in **Chapter 4**.

Figure 25 The Geographic Location window lists cities all over the world—including one near you.

Figure 26 Use the Finder Preferences window to turn Simple Finder on or off.

Figure 27 The Local Network Introduction window tells you a little about networks.

Figure 28 Use this window to enter a name for your computer and a password to protect your files from unauthorized network users.

To set network options

1. Read the information in the Local Network Introduction window of the Mac OS Setup Assistant (**Figure 27**) to learn more about networks.

2. Click the right arrow button.

3. Read the information in the Computer Name and Password window (**Figure 28**) to learn how Mac OS uses your computer's name and password.

4. To change the default name that the Mac OS Setup Assistant has assigned to your computer, type it in the top edit box. (The name should be selected as shown in **Figure 28** so it is not necessary to click in the box first; simply type to overwrite the contents of the edit box.) Then press (Tab) or click in the bottom edit box to position the insertion point there.

   or

   To accept the default name that the Mac OS Setup Assistant has assigned to your computer, just press (Tab) or click in the bottom edit box to position the insertion point there.

5. In the bottom edit box, enter a password you want to use to protect your computer from unauthorized access by other network users.

6. Click the right arrow button.

7. Wait while the Mac OS Setup Assistant validates the computer name and password.

8. Read the information in the Shared Folder window (**Figure 29**) to learn what a shared folder is and how it is used.

9. If you do not want a shared folder on the network, select the No radio button by clicking it. Then skip to step 11.

Continued on next page...

SETTING NETWORK OPTIONS

Continued from previous page.

10. To change the default name that the Mac OS Setup Assistant has assigned to your shared folder, type it in the edit box. (The name should be selected as shown in **Figure 29**, so it is not necessary to click in the box first; simply type to overwrite the contents of the box.)

11. Click the right arrow button.

✔ Tips

- You must go through these steps even if your computer is not connected to a network.

- You must provide both a name and password for your computer.

- You can also set network settings in the File Sharing control panel, which I tell you about in **Chapter 10**.

Figure 29 Use this window to set up a shared folder—if you want one.

SETTING NETWORK OPTIONS

Figure 30 Use the Printer Connection window to tell the Mac OS Setup Assistant how your printer is connected.

Figure 31 If you printer is connected to your computer through a network connection, select it in this window.

Figure 32 If your printer is directly connected to your computer, select the type of printer you have in this window.

To set printer options

1. Turn on your printer and if necessary, let it warm up.

2. Read the information in the Printer Connection window of the Mac OS Setup Assistant (**Figure 30**) to learn the difference between a direct connection and a network connection.

3. Select the appropriate connection type by clicking its radio button.

4. Click the right arrow button.

5. If you selected Network connection in step 2, wait while the Mac OS Setup Assistant searches the network for connected printers. Then, in the Printer Selection window that appears (**Figure 31**), select the printer you use most often by clicking its name.

    or

    If you selected Direct connection in step 2, the Printer Type window appears (**Figure 32**). Select the type of printer connected to your computer by clicking its name in the list. Then select the port to which the printer is connected by clicking the Printer Port or Modem Port radio button.

6. Click the right arrow button.

✔ Tips

■ You can also select a printer in the Chooser, which I tell you about in **Chapter 9**.

■ If the type of printer you use does not appear in the Printer Type window (**Figure 32**), you may have to install a printer driver for it. I tell you about that in **Chapter 9**, too.

SETTING PRINTER OPTIONS

To complete the setup process

1. Click the Go Ahead button in the Conclusion window of the Mac OS Setup Assistant (**Figure 33**).

2. Wait while the Mac OS Setup Assistant configures your system. The Conclusion window changes to indicate the configuration progress (**Figure 34**). When the configuration is complete, the Conclusion window tells you that the Mac OS Setup Assistant is done (**Figure 35**).

3. To stop configuring your computer, click the Quit button.

    or

    To go on to the Internet Setup Assistant, click the Continue button.

✔ Tips

- To check your settings one last time before they're written to your computer's configuration files, click the Show Details button (**Figure 33**). The Conclusion window changes to list all configuration options you entered or selected.

- If you have not installed the Internet Access component of Mac OS 9, the Continue button in the Conclusion window (**Figure 35**) will not appear.

- I explain how to use the Internet Setup Assistant in **Chapter 11**.

Figure 33 When the Mac OS Setup Assistant is finished asking for information, it displays this window.

Figure 34 The Conclusion window also indicates the configuration progress.

Figure 35 Finally, the Conclusion window tells you when the configuration is done.

FINDER BASICS

Finder

Figure 1 The Finder is the program that provides a graphic user interface for working with files.

The Finder & Desktop

The *Finder* (**Figure 1**) is a program that is part of Mac OS. It launches automatically when you start your computer.

The Finder provides a graphic user interface called the *Desktop* (**Figure 2**) that you can use to open, copy, delete, list, organize, and perform other operations on computer files.

This chapter provides important instructions for using the Finder and items that appear on the Mac OS Desktop. It's important that you understand how to use these basic Finder techniques, since you'll use them again and again every time you work with your computer.

Menu bar   *Window*   *Desktop*   *Icons*

Figure 2 Basic Desktop elements.   *Control Strip*   *Mouse pointer*

✔ Tips

- Do *not* move or delete the Finder! Doing so will prevent your computer from operating properly.

- You never have to manually launch the Finder; it always starts automatically.

- Under normal circumstances, you cannot Quit the Finder.

- If you're new to Mac OS, don't skip this chapter. It provides the basic information you'll need to use your computer successfully.

The Mouse

Mac OS, like most graphic user interface systems, uses the mouse as an input device. There are several basic mouse techniques you must know to use your computer:

◆ **Point** to a specific item on screen.

◆ **Click** an item to select it.

◆ **Double-click** an item to open it.

◆ **Drag** to move an item or select multiple items.

✔ Tips

■ Some computers use either a trackball or a trackpad instead of a mouse.

■ You can customize the way the mouse works with the Mouse control panel, which I tell you about in **Chapter 14**.

To point

1. Move the mouse on the work surface or mouse pad.

   or

   Use your fingertips to move the ball of the trackball.

   or

   Move the tip of *one* finger (usually your forefinger) on the surface of the trackpad.

   The mouse pointer, which usually looks like an arrow (**Figure 3**), moves on your computer screen.

2. When the tip of the mouse pointer's arrow is on the item to which you want to point (**Figure 4**), stop moving it.

✔ Tip

■ The tip of the mouse pointer is its "business end."

Figure 3 The mouse pointer usually looks like an arrow pointer when you are working in the Finder.

System Folder

Figure 4 Move the mouse pointer so the arrow's tip is on the item to which you want to point.

USING THE MOUSE

Figure 5
Click to select
an icon...

Figure 6 ...or an item in a list.

Figure 7
Drag to move items
such as folders.

To click

1. Point to the item you want to click.

2. Press (and release) the mouse button once. The item you clicked becomes selected (**Figures 5** and **6**).

To double-click

1. Point to the item you want to double-click.

2. Press (and release) the mouse button twice quickly. The item you double-clicked opens.

✔ Tip

■ It is vital that you keep the mouse pointer still while double-clicking. If you move the mouse pointer during the double-click process, you may move the item instead of double-clicking it.

To drag

1. Point to the item you want to drag.

2. Press the mouse button down.

3. While holding the mouse button down, move the mouse pointer. The item you are dragging moves (**Figure 7**).

USING THE MOUSE

Menus

The Finder—and just about every other Mac OS-compatible program—offers menus full of options. There are four types of menus in Mac OS 9:

◆ A **pull-down menu** appears on the menu bar at the top of the screen (**Figure 8**).

◆ A **submenu** appears when a menu option with a right-pointing triangle is selected (**Figure 9**).

◆ A **pop-up menu**, which displays a pair of triangles (or double arrow), appears within a window (**Figures 10** and **11**).

◆ A **contextual menu** appears when you hold down [Control] while clicking an item (**Figure 12**).

✔ Tips

■ A menu option followed by an ellipsis (...) (**Figure 8**) will display a dialog box when chosen. I tell you about dialog boxes in **Chapter 5**.

■ A menu option that is dimmed or gray (**Figure 8**) cannot be chosen. The commands that are available vary depending on what is selected on the Desktop or in a window.

■ A menu option preceded by a check mark (**Figure 9**) is selected, or "turned on."

■ A menu option followed by a series of keyboard characters (**Figure 8**) has a keyboard command. I tell you about keyboard commands later in this chapter.

■ Contextual menus only display options that apply to the item to which you are pointing.

■ Depending on how menu preferences are set, a menu option should blink when chosen. You can set menu blinking preferences in the General Controls control panel, which I discuss in **Chapter 14**.

Figure 8
The menu bar offers pull-down menus.

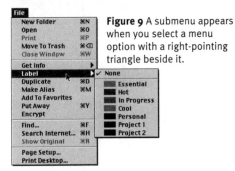

Figure 9 A submenu appears when you select a menu option with a right-pointing triangle beside it.

Figure 10 Pop-up menus can appear within dialog boxes.

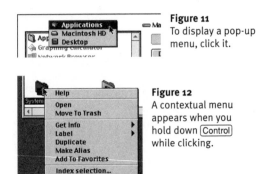

Figure 11
To display a pop-up menu, click it.

Figure 12
A contextual menu appears when you hold down [Control] while clicking.

Figure 13 Point to the menu name.

Figure 14
Hold down the mouse button or just click to display the menu.

Figure 15
Drag to or just click the menu option you want.

To use a menu

1. Point to the name of the menu (**Figure 13**).

2. Press and hold down the mouse button. The menu opens, displaying its options (**Figure 14**).

3. Drag to select the menu option you want (**Figure 15**).

4. Release the mouse button to choose the selected option. The menu disappears.

✔ Tips

- This is the standard way to choose an option from a menu. This method works in all versions of Mac OS.

- Throughout this book, I use the following notation to indicate menu commands: *Menu Name > Submenu Name* (if necessary) > *Command Name*. For example, to instruct you to choose the Essential command from the Label submenu under the File menu (**Figure 9**), I'd say, "choose File > Label > Essential."

To use a sticky menu

1. Point to the name of the menu (**Figure 13**).

2. Click. The menu opens, displaying its options (**Figure 14**).

3. Point to the menu option you want (**Figure 15**).

4. Click to choose the selected option. The menu disappears.

✔ Tips

- This method of choosing a menu option works in Mac OS version 8 and later only.

- To close a sticky menu without choosing an option, click outside the menu.

- A sticky menu will close automatically by itself if no option is chosen after a few seconds.

USING MENUS

To use a contextual menu

1. Point to the item on which you want to act.

2. Press and hold down (Control). A tiny contextual menu icon appears beside the mouse pointer (**Figure 16**).

3. Press and hold down the mouse button.

   or

   Click.

   A contextual menu appears at the item (**Figure 17**).

4. Drag to select the menu option you want (**Figure 18**). Then release the mouse button to choose the option.

   or

   Click the menu option you want (**Figure 18**).

To use a keyboard command

1. Hold down the modifier key(s) in the sequence. This is usually (⌃ ⌘) but can be (Option), (Control), or (Shift).

2. Press the letter, number, or symbol key in the sequence.

For example, to choose the Open command, which can be found under the File menu (**Figure 15**), hold down (⌃ ⌘) and press (O).

✔ Tips

- You can learn keyboard commands by observing the key sequences that appear to the right of some menu commands (**Figure 8**).

- Some commands include more than one modifier key. You must hold all modifier keys down while pressing the letter, number, or symbol key for the keyboard command.

- I provide a list of all Finder keyboard commands in **Appendix A**.

Figure 16
Hold down (Control) while pointing to an item.

System Folder

Figure 17
A contextual menu appears when you click.

Figure 18
Drag or click to select the option you want.

SimpleText   PageMaker   QuickTime Player

Figure 19 Application icons.

Read Me   About Mac OS   Introduction

Figure 20 Document icons, including two different SimpleText documents and a PageMaker document.

My Stuff   Utilities   System Folder

Figure 21 Folder icons.

Apple CD/DVD   Appearance   LaserWriter 8

Figure 22 Icons for System files including an extension, a control panel, and a printer driver (or Chooser extension).

Macintosh HD Installer Disk untitled   Mac OS 9

Figure 23 Four different disk icons: hard disk, Mac OS floppy disk, PC floppy disk, and CD-ROM disc.

HP LaserJet 4MP   Trash   Trash

Figure 24 A Desktop printer icon and the Trash icon when the Trash is empty and full.

Icons

Mac OS uses icons to graphically represent files and other items on the Desktop or within Finder windows:

◆ **Applications** (**Figure 19**) are programs you use to get work done. I tell you more about working with applications in **Chapters 5** through **7**.

◆ **Documents** (**Figure 20**) are the files created by applications. I tell you more about working with documents in **Chapter 5**.

◆ **Folders** (**Figure 21**) are used to organize files. I tell you more about using folders in **Chapters 3** and **4**.

◆ **System files** (**Figure 22**), such as control panels, extensions, and drivers, are used by Mac OS to add capabilities to your computer and operate peripherals. I tell you about various System files in **Chapters 14** and **15** and elsewhere throughout this book.

◆ **Disks** (**Figure 23**) are used to store files. I tell you about working with disks in **Chapter 3**.

◆ **Desktop printers** (**Figure 24**) let you print documents from the Finder and check the status of documents scheduled to be printed. I tell you about printing in **Chapter 9**.

◆ The **Trash** (**Figure 24**) is for discarding items you no longer want. I explain how to use the Trash in **Chapter 3**.

✔ Tip

■ Icons can appear a number of different ways, depending on the view and view options chosen for a window. I tell you about windows later in this chapter and about views in **Chapter 3**.

ICONS

To select an icon

Click the icon that you want to select. The icon darkens and its name becomes highlighted (**Figure 25**).

✔ Tip

■ You can also select an icon in an active window by pressing the keyboard key for the first letter of the icon's name or by pressing Tab, Shift Tab, ←, →, ↑, or ↓ until the icon is selected.

To deselect an icon

Click anywhere in the window or on the Desktop other than on the selected icon.

✔ Tips

■ If you deselect an icon by clicking another icon, the originally selected icon is deselected and the icon you clicked becomes selected instead.

■ I tell you more about windows later in this chapter.

To select multiple icons by clicking

1. Click the first icon that you want to select.

2. Hold down Shift and click another icon that you want to select (**Figure 26**).

3. Repeat step 2 until all icons that you want to select have been selected.

✔ Tip

■ Icons that are part of a multiple selection must be in the same window. I tell you about windows later in this chapter.

Figure 25 To select an icon, click it.

Figure 26 Hold down Shift while clicking other icons to add them to a multiple selection.

Figure 27 Position the mouse pointer above and to the left of the first icon that you want to select.

Figure 28 Drag to draw a selection box around the icons that you want to select.

Figure 29 Release the mouse button to complete the selection.

Figure 30
Choose Select All from the Edit menu.

To select multiple icons by dragging

1. Position the mouse pointer slightly above and to the left of the first icon in the group that you want to select (**Figure 27**).

2. Press the mouse button down, and drag diagonally across the icons you want to select. A gray border appears to indicate the selection area, and the items within it become selected (**Figure 28**).

3. When all the icons that you want to select are included in the selection area, release the mouse button (**Figure 29**).

✔ Tip

■ To select multiple icons by dragging, the icons must be adjacent.

To select all icons in a window

Choose Edit > Select All (**Figure 30**).

or

Press ⌃⌘Ⓐ.

All icons in the active window are selected.

✔ Tip

■ I tell you more about windows, including how to activate them, later in this chapter.

To deselect one icon in a multiple selection

Hold down [Shift] while clicking the icon that you want to deselect. That icon is deselected while the others remain selected.

SELECTING & DESELECTING ICONS

To move an icon

1. Position the mouse pointer on the icon that you want to move (**Figure 31**).

2. Press the mouse button down, and drag the icon to the new location. As you drag, a shadowy image of the icon moves with the mouse pointer (**Figure 32**).

3. Release the mouse button when the icon is in the desired position. The icon moves (**Figure 33**).

✔ Tips

- You cannot drag to reposition icons within windows set to list view. I tell you about views in **Chapter 3**.

- You move icons to rearrange them in a window or on the Desktop, or to copy or move the items they represent to another folder or disk. I discuss copying and moving items in **Chapter 3**.

- You can also move multiple icons at once. Simply select the icons first, then position the mouse pointer on one of the selected icons and follow steps 2 and 3 above. All selected icons move together.

Figure 31 Point to the icon that you want to move.

Figure 32 Drag the icon to the new location.

Figure 33 When you release the mouse button, the icon moves.

Figure 34 Select the icon.

Figure 35 Choose Open from the File menu.

Figure 36 Opening a folder icon opens a window that displays the contents of the folder.

Figure 37 Open folder icons appear shaded.

To open an icon

1. Select the icon you want to open (**Figure 34**).

2. Choose File > Open (**Figure 35**), or press ⌘ O.

or

Double-click the icon that you want to open.

✔ Tips

■ What happens when you open an icon depends on the type of icon you open. For example:

▲ Opening a folder icon opens a new Finder window that displays the contents of that folder (**Figure 36**). I tell you about windows later in this chapter.

▲ Opening an application icon launches the application so that you can work with it. I tell you about working with applications in **Chapters 5** through **7**.

▲ Opening a document icon launches the application that created that document and displays the document so you can view or edit it. I tell you about working with documents in **Chapter 5**.

▲ Opening a Desktop printer icon displays a list of files waiting to be printed so you can reschedule them or remove them from the print queue. I tell you about printing in **Chapter 9**.

▲ Opening the Trash displays items that will be deleted when you empty the Trash. I tell you about using and emptying the Trash in **Chapter 3**.

■ You can identify an open disk, folder, or application icon by its shaded appearance in a Finder window (**Figure 37**).

OPENING ICONS

Windows

Mac OS makes extensive use of windows for displaying icons and other information in the Finder and documents in other applications. **Figures 38** and **39** show examples of Finder windows.

Each window includes a variety of controls you can use to manipulate it:

◆ The **title bar** displays the window's icon and name and can be used to move the window.

◆ The **close box** lets you close the window.

◆ The **zoom box** lets you toggle the window between full size and a custom size.

◆ The **collapse box** lets you toggle the window between collapsed and expanded views.

◆ The **size box** lets you resize the window by dragging.

◆ **Scroll bars** let you scroll the contents of the window into view.

◆ The **header** indicates the number of items in the window and the amount of space available on the disk.

◆ **Column headings** (in list view only) display the names of the columns and let you quickly sort by a column.

◆ **Sort direction button** (in list view only) enables you to change the sort direction to ascending or descending order.

✔ Tip

■ I tell you about views in **Chapter 3**.

Close box   Header   *Title bar*   *Zoom box*   *Collapse box*

Figure 38
A Finder window in Icon view.

Scroll bars   *Size box*

Column headings   *Title bar*   *Zoom box*

Close box   *Header*   *Sort Direction button*   *Collapse box*

Figure 39
A Finder window in list view.

Scroll bars   *Size box*

Figure 40
The active window always has horizontal lines on its title bar.

Figure 41
Position the mouse pointer on the title bar.

Figure 42 As you drag, an outline of the window moves with the mouse pointer.

Figure 43 When you release the mouse button, the window moves.

To activate a window

Click anywhere in or on the window.

✔ Tips

■ It's important to make sure that the window with which you want to work is open and active *before* using commands that work on the active window—like Print Window, Select All, and View menu options.

■ You can distinguish between the active window and inactive windows by the appearance of their title bars; the active window's title bar always has horizontal lines (**Figure 40**).

■ When two or more windows overlap, the active window will always be on top of the stack (**Figure 40**).

To move a window

1. Position the mouse pointer on the window's title bar (**Figure 41**).

   or

   Position the mouse pointer on the border of the window.

2. Press the mouse button down, and drag the window to a new location. As you drag, an outline of the window moves along with your mouse pointer (**Figure 42**).

3. When the outline of the window is in the desired position, release the mouse button. The window moves (**Figure 43**).

✔ Tips

■ If you move a window to the very bottom of the screen, it becomes a pop-up window. I tell you more about pop-up windows in **Chapter 4**.

■ You can also move a window by dragging one of its edges.

ACTIVATING & MOVING WINDOWS

To resize a window

1. Position the mouse pointer on the window's size box (**Figure 44**).

2. Press the mouse button down, and drag. As you drag, dotted lines indicating the right and bottom borders of the window move with the mouse pointer (**Figure 45**).

3. When the dotted lines indicate the desired borders for the window, release the mouse button. The window resizes (**Figure 46**).

✔ Tips

- The larger a window is, the more you can see inside it.

- By resizing and repositioning windows, you can see inside more than one window at a time. This comes in handy when moving or copying the icons for files and folders from one window to another. I tell you about moving and copying files and folders in **Chapter 3**.

Figure 44
Position the mouse pointer on the size box.

Figure 45 As you drag, a dotted border moves with the mouse pointer.

Figure 46 When you release the mouse button, the window resizes.

RESIZING WINDOWS

Figure 47 Click the window's zoom box...

Figure 48 ...to zoom the window to full size.

Figure 49 Click on the collapse box...

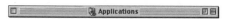

Figure 50 ...to collapse the window so only its title bar shows.

To zoom a window

Click the window's zoom box (**Figure 47**).

✔ Tips

- Each time you click the zoom box, the window's size toggles between full size (**Figure 48**) and the custom size you specified with the size box (**Figure 46**).

- The actual size of a window zoomed to full size varies based on its content. If a window contains only a few icons, zooming the window to full size will make it only as large as it needs to be to display the items it contains (**Figure 49**).

To collapse or expand a window

Click the window's collapse box (**Figure 49**).

✔ Tips

- Each time you click the collapse box, the window either collapses to display just its title bar (**Figure 50**) or expands to display its contents (**Figure 49**).

- A collapsed window can be moved around the screen like any other window.

To collapse or expand all open windows

Hold down Option while clicking the active window's collapse box (**Figure 49**).

ZOOMING & COLLAPSING WINDOWS

To scroll a window's contents

Click one of the scroll bar arrows (**Figure 51**) as follows:

◆ To scroll the window's contents up, click the down arrow on the vertical scroll bar.

◆ To scroll the window's contents down, click the up arrow on the vertical scroll bar.

◆ To scroll the window's contents to the left, click the right arrow on the horizontal scroll bar.

◆ To scroll the window's contents to the right, click the left arrow on the horizontal scroll bar.

Figure 51 Scroll bars, scroll bar arrows, and scroll boxes.

✔ Tips

■ If you have trouble remembering which scroll arrow to click, think of it this way:

▲ Click down to see down.

▲ Click up to see up.

▲ Click right to see right.

▲ Click left to see left.

■ You can also scroll a window's contents by either clicking in the scroll bar between the scroll box and a scroll arrow or by dragging the scroll box to a new position on the scroll bar. Both of these techniques enable you to scroll a window's contents more quickly.

■ If all of a window's contents are displayed, you will not be able to scroll the window. A window that cannot be scrolled will have flat or empty looking scroll bars without scroll boxes (**Figure 49**).

■ You can change the appearance and functionality of scroll bars with the Appearance control panel, which I discuss in **Chapter 15**.

Figure 52 Click the window's close box.

Figure 53
Choose Close
Window from
the File menu.

To close a window

Click the window's close box (**Figure 52**).

or

Choose File > Close Window (**Figure 53**).

or

Press ⌃ ⌘ W.

To close all open windows

Hold down Option while clicking the active window's close box (**Figure 52**).

or

Hold down Option while choosing File > Close Window (**Figure 53**).

or

Press ⌃ ⌘ Option W.

To automatically close the active window when you open an icon within it

1. Select the icon that you want to open.

2. Hold down Option while choosing File > Open (**Figure 35**).

    or

    Press ⌃ ⌘ Option O.

or

Hold down Option while double-clicking the icon that you want to open.

CLOSING WINDOWS

Sleeping, Restarting, & Shutting Down

The Special menu (**Figure 54**) offers several options that change the work state of your computer:

◆ **Sleep** puts the computer into a state where it uses very little power. The screen goes blank and the hard disk may stop spinning.

◆ **Restart** instructs the computer to shut down and immediately start back up.

◆ **Shut Down** closes all open documents and programs, clears memory, and either cuts power to the computer or tells you that it's safe to turn off the power switch.

✔ Tips

■ You can view a dialog box with buttons for Restart, Sleep, and Shut Down commands (**Figure 55**) by pressing the Power key. This feature, however, does not work with all Mac OS-computer models.

■ The Energy Saver control panel, which I tell you about in **Chapter 14**, can automatically put a computer to sleep or shut it down after a specific period of inactivity.

■ Do *not* restart or shut down a computer by simply flicking off the power switch. Doing so prevents the computer from properly closing files, which may result in file corruption and related problems.

Figure 54
Three commands under the Special menu let you change the work state of your computer.

Figure 55 Pressing the Power key on some Mac OS computers displays a dialog box like this one.

To put your computer to sleep

Choose Special > Sleep (**Figure 54**).

or

1. Press the Power key.

2. In the dialog box that appears (**Figure 55**), click Sleep or press $\boxed{S}$.

✔ Tips

■ Not all computers support sleep mode. If your computer does not support sleep mode, the Sleep command will not appear on the Special menu.

■ When you put your computer to sleep, everything in memory is preserved. When you wake the computer, you can quickly continue working where you left off.

■ Sleep mode is an effective way to conserve the battery life of a PowerBook without turning it off.

To wake a sleeping computer

Press any keyboard key. Expect to wait from 10 to 30 seconds for the computer to fully wake.

✔ Tips

■ It's much quicker to wake a sleeping computer than to restart a computer that has been shut down.

■ On some computer models, pressing $\boxed{\text{Caps Lock}}$ or certain other keys may not wake the computer. When in doubt, press a letter key—they always work.

To restart your computer

Choose Special > Restart (**Figure 54**).

or

1. Press the Power key.

2. In the dialog box that appears (**Figure 55**), click Restart or press R.

✔ Tips

- Restarting the computer clears memory and reloads the System, Finder, and all system files.

- It's a good idea to restart your computer after a program unexpectedly quits so your computer's memory can start fresh.

To shut down your computer

Choose Special > Shut Down (**Figure 54**).

or

1. Press the Power key.

2. In the dialog box that appears (**Figure 55**), click Shut Down or press S.

   or

   Press Return or Enter.

✔ Tip

- On most computers, the Shut Down command will cut power to the computer as part of the shut down process. If it doesn't, a dialog box will appear on screen, telling you it's safe to turn off your computer. You can then use the power switch to cut power to the computer.

FILE MANAGEMENT

File Management

In Mac OS, you use the Finder to organize and manage your files.

- ◆ View the contents of your disks in windows in a variety of ways.

- ◆ Automatically sort items by name, kind, creation date, or other criteria in ascending or descending order.

- ◆ Assign colored labels to items.

- ◆ Rename items.

- ◆ Create folders to store related items.

- ◆ Move items stored on disk to organize them so they're easy to find and back up.

- ◆ Copy items to other disks to back them up or share them with others.

- ◆ Delete items you no longer need.

- ◆ Mount and eject disks.

- ◆ Format and erase floppy disks.

✔ Tip

- ■ If you're brand new to Mac OS, be sure to read the information in **Chapter 2** before working with this chapter. That chapter contains information and instructions about techniques that are used throughout this chapter.

Views

Every Finder window's contents can be viewed a variety of ways:

◆ **As Icons** displays the window's contents as small or large icons (**Figure 1**).

◆ **As Buttons** displays the window's contents as clickable buttons (**Figure 2**).

◆ **As List** displays the window's contents as a sorted list (**Figure 3**).

In addition to setting a specific view for a Finder window, you can use the View Options dialog box (**Figures 6**, **7**, and **9**) to specify view options that fine tune the view.

✔ Tip

■ Button view works a little differently than icon and list views. I tell you about working with button view a little later in this chapter.

To change a window's view

1. Activate the window whose view you want to change.

2. Choose the view option you want from the View menu (**Figure 4**). The view of the active window changes.

✔ Tips

■ Commands on the View menu (**Figure 4**) work on the active window only.

■ A check mark appears on the View menu beside the name of the view currently applied to the active window (**Figure 4**).

■ You can set the view for each window individually.

Figure 1
You can display a window's contents as icons...

Figure 2
...as clickable buttons...

Figure 3
...or as a list.

Figure 4
Choose one of the three window content view options from the View menu.

SETTING VIEWS

Figure 5
Choose View Options from the View menu.

Figure 6
The View Options dialog box for an icon view window.

Figure 7
The View Options dialog box for a button view window.

Figure 8
Use the Keep arranged pop-up menu to choose an automatic arrangement option.

To set View Options for icon or button view

1. Activate a window displayed in icon view (**Figure 1**) or button view (**Figure 2**).

2. Choose View > View Options (**Figure 5**). The View Options dialog box for icon view (**Figure 6**) or button view (**Figure 7**) appears.

3. Select an Icon Arrangement or Button Arrangement option:

    ▲ To remove any automatic icon or button arrangement, click the None radio button.

    ▲ To force icons or buttons to snap to an invisible grid within the window, click the Always snap to grid radio button.

    ▲ To automatically keep icons or buttons arranged in a certain order, turn on the Keep arranged radio button. Then choose an option from the pop-up menu beside it (**Figure 8**).

4. Select an Icon Size or Button Size option by clicking the radio button beneath the size you want.

5. Click OK to accept your changes.

✔ Tips

■ You can restore the window's settings to the standard settings for all windows by clicking the Set to Standard Views button. I explain how to set standard view options when I tell you about the Preferences window in **Chapter 4**.

■ You can set grid spacing options in the Preferences window, which I tell you about in **Chapter 4**.

■ I provide more details about working with dialog boxes in **Chapter 5**.

To set View Options for list view

1. Activate a window displayed in list view (**Figure 3**).

2. Choose View > View Options (**Figure 5**). The View Options dialog box for list view appears (**Figure 9**).

3. To display the date in relative terms (that is, using the words "today" and "yesterday"), make sure the Use relative date check box is turned on.

4. To display the total disk space occupied by the contents of folders in the list, make sure the Calculate folder sizes check box is turned on.

5. Select the columns you want to appear in list view by turning Show Columns check boxes on or off:

   ▲ **Date Modified** is the date and time an item was last changed.

   ▲ **Date Created** is the date and time an item was first created.

   ▲ **Size** is the amount of disk space the item occupies.

   ▲ **Kind** is the type of item. I tell you about types of icons in **Chapter 2**.

   ▲ **Label** is the label assigned to the item. I tell you about labels later in this chapter.

   ▲ **Comments** is the information you entered in the comments field of the Info window. I tell you about the Info window in **Chapter 4**.

   ▲ **Version** is the item's version number.

6. Select an Icon Size option by clicking the radio button beneath the size you want.

7. Click OK to accept your changes.

Figure 9
The View Options dialog box for a list view window.

✔ Tips

■ Turning on the Calculate folder sizes check box in step 4 could slow down the opening of list view windows.

■ You can restore the window's settings to the standard settings for all windows by clicking the Set to Standard Views button. I explain how to set standard view options when I tell you about the Preferences window in **Chapter 4**.

■ I provide more details about working with dialog boxes in **Chapter 5**.

Figures 10 & 11
Point to the *name* of the button (left). When you click, the button is selected (right).

Apple E:tras   Apple Extras

Figure 12 Drag a button's name to move the button.

Figure 13 When you release the mouse button, the button moves to its new position.

Figure 14
Choose Open from the File menu.

Button View

Designed for novices and to give the Finder a more user-friendly look, button view works a bit differently from icon and list views. Here's a summary of the differences.

To select a button

Click the name of the button (**Figure 10**). The button becomes selected (**Figure 11**).

To move a button

1. Position the mouse pointer on the button name (**Figure 10**)—*not* the button itself.

2. Press the mouse button down and drag the button to a new position. As you drag, the shadow of the button moves with the mouse pointer (**Figure 12**).

3. Release the mouse button to complete the move (**Figure 13**).

To open a button

Click the button once.

or

1. Select the button that you want to open (**Figure 11**).

2. Choose File > Open (**Figure 14**).

   or

   Press ⌘O.

WORKING WITH BUTTON VIEW

Cleaning Up & Arranging Icons & Buttons

Even if you're not a neat freak, you'll like the automatic clean-up and arrangement features that are part of the Finder.

◆ **Clean Up** neatly arranges icons or buttons in the window's invisible grid.

◆ **Arrange** lets you specify the order in which icons or buttons should appear in the window.

To clean up a window

1. Activate the window that you want to clean up (**Figure 15**).

2. Choose View > Clean Up (**Figure 16**). The icons move into empty slots in the window's invisible grid (**Figure 17**).

✔ Tips

■ To have an icon you are moving automatically move into an empty grid slot, hold down ⌃ ⌘ as you drag it. When you release the mouse button, the icon's position adjusts automatically.

■ You can set the grid spacing in the Preferences window, which I tell you about in **Chapter 4**.

To arrange a window's contents

1. Activate the window whose contents you want to arrange (**Figure 17**).

2. Choose an option from the Arrange submenu under the View menu (**Figure 18**). The icons are sorted by the option you selected (**Figure 19**).

✔ Tip

■ You can specify a default arrangement order for the window in the View Options dialog box, which I tell you about earlier in this chapter.

Figure 15
Start with a messy window like this one...

Figure 16
...then choose Clean Up from the View menu.

Figure 17
The icons are moved into empty slots of the window's invisible grid.

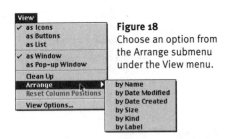

Figure 18
Choose an option from the Arrange submenu under the View menu.

Figure 19
These icons are arranged by name.

Figure 20 Point to the heading for the column by which you want to sort.

Figure 21 The list view is sorted by the column you clicked.

Figure 22 Clicking the sort direction button reverses the sort order.

List Views

A list view window can be modified in the following ways:

◆ Sort by any column in ascending or descending order.

◆ Change the width of columns.

◆ Change the order in which columns appear.

To sort a window's contents

Click the column heading for the column by which you want to sort (**Figure 20**). The list is sorted by that column (**Figure 21**).

✔ Tips

■ You can always identify the column by which a list is sorted because its column heading is dark and its column is shaded (**Figures 20** and **21**).

■ To properly sort folders in a window sorted by size, you should turn on the Calculate folder sizes check box in the View Options dialog box (**Figure 9**) for that window. Otherwise, a folder has no size and is sorted to the top or bottom of the list.

To reverse the sort order of a window's contents

Click the sort direction button at the top of the window's vertical scroll bar (**Figure 21**). The sort order reverses (**Figure 22**).

✔ Tip

■ When the sort direction button points up, the items are sorted in descending order. When it points down, the items are sorted in ascending order. You can see this in **Figures 21** and **22**.

To change a column's width

1. Position the mouse pointer on the line between the heading for the column whose width you want to change and the column to its right. The mouse pointer turns into a vertical bar with two arrows (**Figure 23**).

2. Press the mouse button down and drag as follows:

   ▲ To make the column narrower, drag to the left (**Figure 24**).

   ▲ To make the column wider, drag to the right.

3. When the column is displayed at the desired width, release the mouse button.

✔ Tip

■ If you make a column too narrow to display all of its contents, information may be truncated or condensed.

To change a column's position

1. Position the mouse pointer on the heading for the column you want to move.

2. Press the mouse button down and drag as follows:

   ▲ To move the column to the left, drag to the left (**Figure 25**).

   ▲ To move the column to the right, drag to the right.

   As you drag, the mouse pointer turns into a grabbing hand. Vertical lines indicate the column's position (**Figure 25**).

3. When the mouse pointer is on the column where you want to move the column you are dragging, release the mouse button. The column changes its position (**Figure 26**).

✔ Tip

■ You cannot change the position of the Name column.

Figure 23 Position the mouse pointer between two column headings.

Figure 24 As you drag, the column's width changes.

Figure 25 Drag a column on top of the column where you want to move it.

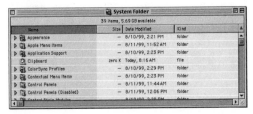

Figure 26 When you release the mouse button, the column moves.

Figure 27
Choose Reset
Column Positions
from the View
menu.

Figure 28 Use this dialog box to confirm that you really do want to reset column width and positions.

To reset the column widths & positions

1. Activate the window for which you want to reset column widths and positions.

2. Choose View > Reset Column Positions (**Figure 27**).

3. A dialog box like the one in **Figure 28** appears. Click the Reset button. The column widths and positions return to the default settings.

✔ Tips

■ Here are three things to keep in mind about the Reset Column Positions command:

   ▲ It works only on the active window.

   ▲ It resets both column widths and positions.

   ▲ It is only available if the active window's column widths, positions, or both have been changed.

RESETTING COLUMN WIDTHS & POSITIONS

Labels

The label feature lets you assign a colored label to each icon. This makes it possible to:

◆ Visually identify items based on the color assigned.

◆ Arrange or sort items based on the label assigned.

Figure 29 Select the icon(s) to which you want to apply a color or label.

✔ Tips

■ You can use labels to organize icons by project or importance.

■ I tell you how to arrange icon and button view windows and how to sort list view windows earlier in this chapter.

To assign a label to an icon

1. Select the icon to which you want to assign a label (**Figure 29**).

2. Choose the desired label from the Label submenu under the File menu (**Figure 30**).

Figure 30 Choose a label from the Label submenu.

✔ Tips

■ To see the color assigned to the selected icon, deselect the icon (**Figure 31**).

■ As shown in **Figures 29** and **31**, you can assign a label to more than one icon at a time.

■ You can also assign a label to an icon in the Info window, which I tell you about in **Chapter 4**.

■ You can use the Preferences window to change the labels and colors that are associated with each command in the Label submenu. I tell you how in **Chapter 4**.

Figure 31 The color of the selected icon(s) changes.

To remove a label from an icon

1. Select the icon from which you want to remove a label.

2. Choose File > Label > None (**Figure 32**).

Figure 32 Choose None from the Label submenu.

Figure 33
Point to the name of
the icon.

Figure 34
When you click, an edit box
appears around the name.

Figure 35
Type a new name
for the icon.

Figure 36
When you press Return,
the name changes.

Icon Names

Mac OS is very flexible when it comes to
names for files, folders, and disks.

◆ A file or folder name can be up to 31
characters long. A disk name can be up
to 27 characters long.

◆ A name can contain any character except
a colon (:).

This makes it easy to give your files, folders,
and disks names that make sense to you.

✔ Tips

■ Normally, you name documents when you
save them. I tell you how to save documents
in **Chapter 5**.

■ No two documents in the same window
can have the same name.

■ I tell you about disks later in this chapter.

To rename an icon

1. Point to the name of the icon (**Figure 33**),
and click. After a brief pause, an edit box
appears around the name and the name
becomes highlighted (**Figure 34**).

2. Type the new name. The text you type
automatically overwrites the highlighted
text (**Figure 35**).

3. Press Return or Enter, or click anywhere
else in the window or on the Desktop. The
icon is renamed (**Figure 36**).

✔ Tips

■ Not all icons can be renamed. If the edit
box does not appear around an icon name
(**Figure 34**), that icon cannot be renamed.

■ Renaming some folders may remove their
special icons (**Figures 33** and **36**).

■ You can also rename an icon in the Info
window, which I tell you about in **Chapter 4**.

Folders

Mac OS uses folders to organize files and other folders on disk. You can create a folder, give it a name that makes sense to you, and move files and other folders into it. It's a lot like organizing paper files and folders in a file cabinet.

✔ Tips

- ■ A folder can contain any number of files and other folders.

- ■ It's a very good idea to use folders to organize the files on your hard disk. Imagine a file cabinet without file folders—that's how your hard disk would appear if you never used folders to keep your files tidy.

To create a folder

1. Choose File > New Folder (**Figure 37**).

   or

   Press ⌘N.

   A new untitled folder (**Figure 38**) appears in the active window.

2. While the edit box appears around the new folder's name (**Figure 38**), type a name for it (**Figure 39**) and press Return.

✔ Tips

- ■ You can rename a folder the same way you rename any other icon. I tell you how on the previous page.

- ■ I tell you more about windows, including how to activate them, in **Chapter 2**.

Figure 37
Choose New Folder from the File menu.

Figure 38
A new folder appears.

Figure 39
Enter a name for the folder while the edit box appears around it.

Moving & Copying Items

In addition to moving icons around within a window or on the Desktop, which I discuss in **Chapter 2**, you can move or copy items to other locations on the same disk or to other disks by dragging them:

◆ When you drag an item to a location on the same disk, the item is moved to that location.

◆ When you drag an item to a location on another disk, the item is copied to that location.

◆ When you hold down (Option) while dragging an item to a location on the same disk, the item is copied to that location.

I provide instructions for of all these techniques, as well as instructions for duplicating items, on the next few pages.

✔ Tips

■ You can move or copy more than one item at a time. Begin by selecting all the items that you want to move or copy, then drag any one of them to the destination. All items will be moved or copied.

■ You can continue working with the Finder—even start more copy jobs—while a copy job is in progress.

MOVING & COPYING ITEMS

To move an item to another location on the same disk

1. Drag the icon for the item that you want to move as follows:

   ▲ To move the item into a specific folder on the disk, drag the icon to the icon for the folder. The icon becomes high-lighted when the mouse pointer moves over it (**Figure 40**).

   ▲ To move the item into a specific window on the disk, drag the icon into the window (**Figure 41**).

2. Release the mouse button. The item moves.

✔ Tips

- If the destination location is on another disk, the item you drag will be copied rather than moved. You can always delete the original after the copy is made. I tell you how to delete items later in this chapter.

- You can also move a disk or folder whose window is open by dragging the icon in the title bar of the open window (**Figure 42**). This feature works with Mac OS 8.5 and later only.

Figure 40 Drag the icon onto the icon for the folder to which you want to move it...

Figure 41 ...or drag the icon into the window in which you want to move it.

Figure 42 You can drag a window's title bar icon to move a disk or folder whose window is open.

Figure 43 Drag the icon to the destination disk's icon...

Figure 44 ...or to an open window on the destination disk...

Figure 45 ...or to a folder icon in a window on the destination disk.

Figure 46
A window like this indicates copy progress.

Figure 47
You can expand the Copy window to show more information.

To copy an item to another disk

1. Drag the icon for the item that you want to copy as follows:

   ▲ To copy the item to the top (or *root*) level of a disk, drag the icon to the icon for the destination disk (**Figure 43**).

   ▲ To copy the item into a specific window on the disk, drag the icon into the window (**Figure 44**).

   ▲ To copy the item into a folder on the disk, drag the icon to the icon for the folder on the destination disk (**Figure 45**).

   When the item you are dragging moves on top of the destination location, a plus sign appears beside the mouse pointer. If the destination is an icon, the icon becomes highlighted.

2. Release the mouse button. A Copy status window like the one in **Figure 46** appears. When it disappears, the copy operation is complete.

✔ Tips

- You can also copy a disk or folder whose window is open by dragging the icon in the title bar of the open window.

- You can expand the Copy status window (**Figure 46**) to show more information (**Figure 47**). Simply click the right-pointing triangle near the bottom of the window. You can collapse the window by clicking the triangle again.

- You cannot copy items to a disk that is write protected. I tell you about write-protecting disks later in this chapter.

COPYING ITEMS TO ANOTHER DISK

To copy an item to another location on the same disk

1. Hold down (Option) while dragging the icon for the item that you want to copy onto a folder icon (**Figure 48**) or into a window (**Figure 49**).

   When the mouse pointer on the item you are dragging moves on top of the destination location a plus sign appears beside it. If the destination is an icon, the icon becomes highlighted.

2. Release the mouse button. A Copy status window like the one in **Figure 46** appears. When it disappears, the copy operation is complete.

✔ Tips

- When copying an item to a new location on the same disk, you *must* hold down (Option). If you don't, the item will be moved rather than copied.

- You can expand the Copy status window (**Figure 46**) to show more information (**Figure 47**). Simply click the right-pointing triangle near the bottom of the window. You can collapse the window by clicking the triangle again.

To duplicate an item

1. Select the item that you want to duplicate.

2. Choose File > Duplicate (**Figure 50**).

   or

   Press (⌘ D).

or

Hold down (Option) while dragging the item that you want to duplicate to a different location in the same window.

A copy of the item you duplicated appears beside the original. The word *copy* appears at the end of the file name (**Figure 51**).

Figure 48 Hold down (Option) while dragging the item onto a folder...

Figure 49 ...or into a window on the same disk.

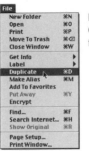

Figure 50
Choose Duplicate from the File menu.

Figure 51
A duplicate appears beneath the original.

Figure 52 To move an item to the Trash, drag it there...

Figure 53
...or select the item and choose Move To Trash from the File menu.

Figure 54 When an item has been moved to the Trash, the Trash icon looks full.

The Trash & Deleting Items

The Trash is a special place on your hard disk where you place items you want to delete. Items in the Trash remain there until you empty the Trash, which permanently deletes them.

To move an item to the Trash

1. Drag the icon for the item you want to delete to the Trash icon on the Desktop.

2. When the mouse pointer moves over the Trash icon, the Trash icon becomes selected (**Figure 52**). Release the mouse button.

or

1. Select the item that you want to delete.

2. Choose File > Move To Trash (**Figure 53**).

   or

   Press ⌃ ⌘ Delete.

✔ Tips

- The Trash icon's appearance indicates its status:

   ▲ If the Trash is empty, the Trash icon looks like a covered trash can.

   ▲ If the Trash is not empty, the Trash icon looks like an open trash can filled with papers (**Figure 54**).

- You can delete more than one item at a time. Begin by selecting all the items you want to delete, then drag any one of them to the Trash. All items will be moved to the Trash.

- Moving a disk icon to the Trash does not delete or erase it. Instead, it ejects, or *unmounts*, it. I tell you more about working with disks later in this chapter.

To move an item out of the Trash

1. Open the Trash using one of these techniques:

   ▲ Double-click the Trash icon.

   ▲ Select the Trash icon, and choose File > Open (**Figure 14**) or press ⌘O.

   A Trash window opens (**Figure 55**).

2. Drag the item from the Trash window to the Desktop or to another window on your hard disk.

   or

   Select the item, and choose File > Put Away (**Figure 56**) or press ⌘Y.

✔ Tip

■ The Put Away command automatically moves a selected icon from the Desktop or Trash to the folder in which it was located before being moved to the Desktop or Trash.

To empty the Trash

1. Choose Empty Trash from the Special menu (**Figure 57**).

2. A Trash warning dialog box like the one in **Figure 58** appears. Click OK to permanently remove all items that are in the Trash.

✔ Tips

■ You can disable the Trash warning dialog box by turning off the Warn before emptying check box in the Trash Info window (**Figure 59**). I tell you about the Info window in **Chapter 4**.

■ Technically speaking, it may be possible to recover accidently deleted items using utility software such as Norton Utilities for Macintosh. File recovery software is not included with Mac OS.

Figure 55 Opening the Trash displays the Trash window.

Figure 56
Choose Put Away
from the File menu.

Figure 57
Choose Empty
Trash from the
Special menu.

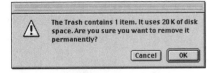

Figure 58 The Trash warning dialog box asks you to confirm that you really do want to delete the items in the Trash.

Figure 59
You can
disable the
Trash warning
dialog box by
turning off the
Warn before
emptying
check box in
the Trash Info
window.

Table 1

Terminology for Storage Media Capacity		
TERM	**ABBREVIATION**	**SIZE**
byte	byte	1 character
kilobyte	KB	1,024 bytes
megabyte	MB	1,024 KB
gigabyte	GB	1,024 MB

Figure 60 The header in a disk window indicates how much space is available on the disk and whether the disk is write-protected or locked.

Disks & Other Storage Media

A Mac OS-compatible computer can read data from or write data to a wide range of storage media, including:

◆ **Hard disks**—high capacity magnetic media.

◆ **Floppy disks or diskettes**—low capacity, removable magnetic media.

◆ **CD-ROM, CD-R, and DVD discs**—high capacity, removable optical media.

◆ **Zip, Jaz, or other disks or cartridges**—high capacity, removable magnetic media.

To use storage media, it must be:

◆ **Mounted**—inserted, attached, or otherwise accessible to your computer.

◆ **Formatted** or **initialized**—specially prepared for use with your computer.

I tell you about all of these things on the following pages.

✔ Tips

■ Don't confuse storage media with memory. The term *memory* usually refers to the amount of RAM in your computer, not disk space. I tell you about RAM in **Chapter 5**.

■ At a minimum, all new Mac OS computers come with a hard disk and CD-ROM disc drives.

■ Disk and other storage media drives can be internal (inside your computer) or external (attached to your computer by a cable).

■ External storage devices must be properly connected and turned on *before* you start your computer or your computer may not recognize the device.

■ Disk storage media capacity is specified in terms of bytes, kilobytes, megabytes, and gigabytes (**Table 1**).

■ You can tell how much space is available on a disk by checking the header in any of the disk's windows (**Figure 60**).

■ If a disk is *write-protected* or *locked*, files cannot be saved or copied to it. To write protect a floppy disk, move the plastic tab on the back of the disk so it exposes the square hole beneath it. To unlock a disk, move the plastic tab on the back of the disk so it covers the square hole.

■ All windows for a write-protected or locked disk display a padlock icon in the upper left corner (**Figure 60**).

■ Unless you have a special CD-Recordable drive and recording software, you cannot write data to a CD-ROM disc.

Mounting Disks

You *mount* a disk by inserting it in the disk drive so it appears on the Mac OS Desktop.

✔ Tips

- You must mount a disk to use it.

- I tell you more about mounting PC disks in **Chapter 8**.

- To learn how to mount disks that are not specifically covered in this book, consult the documentation that came with the disk drive.

- If you cannot successfully mount a CD-ROM disc or Zip disk by following these instructions, check to be sure the appropriate driver software has been installed and loaded. I tell you about driver software in **Chapter 14**.

Figure 61 Here's a Desktop with a hard disk, floppy disk, Zip disk, and CD-ROM disc mounted.

To mount a floppy disk

Insert the disk in the floppy disk drive, label side up, metal side in. The disk's icon appears on the Desktop (**Figure 61**).

To mount a CD-ROM disc

1. Follow the manufacturer's instructions to open the CD-ROM disc tray or eject the CD-ROM caddy.

2. Place the CD-ROM disc in the tray or caddy, label side up.

3. Gently push the tray or caddy into the CD-ROM drive. After a moment, the CD-ROM disc icon appears on the Desktop (**Figure 61**).

To mount a Zip disk

Insert the disk in the Zip drive, label side up, metal side in. After a moment, the Zip disk icon appears on the Desktop (**Figure 61**).

MOUNTING DISKS

Figure 62
Select the disk, and then choose Eject from the Special menu...

Figure 63
...or drag the disk icon to the Trash.

Figure 64 A dialog box like this appears if you try to eject a disk that contains open files.

Ejecting Disks

When you eject a disk, the disk is physically removed from the disk drive and its icon disappears from the Desktop.

✔ Tip

■ When the disk's icon disappears from the Desktop, it is said to be *unmounted*.

To eject a disk

1. Click the disk's icon once to select it.

2. Choose Special > Eject (**Figure 62**), or press ⌘ E.

   or

   Choose File > Put Away (**Figure 56**), or press ⌘ Y.

or

1. Drag the disk's icon to the Trash.

2. When the mouse pointer moves over the Trash icon, it becomes highlighted (**Figure 63**). Release the mouse button.

✔ Tip

■ If you try to eject a disk that contains one or more files that are in use by your computer, a dialog box like the one in **Figure 64** appears. Click OK or press Return or Enter to dismiss the dialog box, then quit the open application. You should then be able to eject the disk. I tell you more about working with applications in **Chapter 5**.

EJECTING DISKS

Formatting Disks

To use a floppy disk or other magnetic media, it must be *formatted* or *initialized* for the computer on which it will be used. A Mac OS computer can format disks for three different computer platforms:

◆ **Mac OS**—for Macintosh and Macintosh-compatible computers.

◆ **MS-DOS**—for Intel-based computer systems, including systems running Microsoft Windows and OS/2.

◆ **ProDOS**—for old Apple II computers.

✔ Tips

■ The terms *formatting* and *initializing* are sometimes used interchangeably. Although these two words don't mean exactly the same thing, they're close enough for our purposes.

■ Nowadays, most removable magnetic media come preformatted. If you buy preformatted disks, make sure they are formatted for Macintosh computers. Otherwise, you'll have to reformat them for use with your Mac OS system.

■ Formatting or initializing a disk erases all the information on the disk. If the disk is brand new, however, it probably doesn't have any information on it anyway.

■ High capacity magnetic media such as hard disks and Zip and Jaz disks must be formatted using special software that comes with the device drive. For example, you format an Apple hard disk with Drive Setup. For more information, consult the documentation that came with the drive. I tell you about Drive Setup in **Chapter 6**.

■ You cannot format a write-protected or locked disk.

Figure 65 When you insert a brand new unformatted disk, a dialog box like this appears.

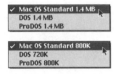

Figure 66 Enter a name for the disk in the Name edit box.

Figure 67a & 67b
The options under the Format pop-up menu depend on the type of disk inserted: high density (top) or double-sided (bottom).

Figure 68 A warning dialog box like this appears when you format a disk.

Figure 69
Choose Erase Disk from the Special menu.

Figure 70 This dialog box appears when you use the Erase Disk command to erase a selected disk.

To format a disk for the first time

1. Insert the disk into the disk drive. A dialog box like the one in **Figure 65** appears.

2. Type a name for the disk in the Name edit box (**Figure 66**).

3. If desired, choose an option from the Format pop-up menu. As you can see in **Figures 67a** and **67b**, the options vary depending on the type of disk you inserted.

4. Click Initialize.

5. A warning dialog box like the one in **Figure 68** appears. If you're sure you want to initialize the disk, click Continue.

6. A status window appears while the disk is initialized and verified. Wait until it disappears. The icon for the formatted disk appears on the Desktop with the name you gave it.

To erase a disk

1. Insert the disk into the disk drive. If the disk is readable, its icon appears on the Desktop.

2. If necessary, click the disk icon once to select it.

3. Choose Special > Erase Disk (**Figure 69**). A dialog box like the one in **Figure 70** appears.

4. If desired, type a new name for the disk in the Name edit box (**Figure 66**).

5. If desired, choose an option from the Format pop-up menu (**Figures 67a** and **67b**).

6. Click Erase.

7. A status window appears while the disk is erased and verified. Wait until it disappears. The icon for the disk appears on the Desktop with the name you gave it.

FORMATTING & ERASING DISKS

61

ADVANCED FINDER TECHNIQUES

Advanced Finder Techniques

In addition to the basic Finder and file management techniques covered in **Chapters 1** and **2**, Mac OS 9 offers more advanced techniques you can use to customize the Finder, work with windows, and manage files:

◆ Use the Preferences window to change the way the Finder looks and works.

◆ Use hierarchical outlines in list view windows.

◆ Use pop-up windows to keep frequently used windows handy but out of sight.

◆ Use spring-loaded folders to automatically open and then close multiple levels of folders while copying or moving items.

◆ Use aliases to make frequently used files easier to access without actually moving them.

◆ Use the Info window to learn more about an item or set options for it.

✔ Tips

■ If you're brand new to Mac OS, be sure to read the information in **Chapters 2** and **3** before working with this chapter. Those chapters contain information and instructions about techniques that are used throughout this chapter.

■ This chapter is especially useful for experienced Mac OS users since it goes beyond the basics with new or advanced Mac OS features.

Finder Preferences

The Finder's Preferences window lets you customize many aspects of Finder appearance and operation. There are three categories of options:

◆ **General** (**Figure 3**) lets you set Simple Finder, Spring-loaded folder, and Grid Spacing options.

◆ **Views** (**Figure 7**) lets you set the standard view options for Icon, Button, and List view windows.

◆ **Labels** (**Figure 9**) lets you set the name and color of options on the Label submenu under the File menu.

✔ Tip

■ I tell you about more Mac OS 9 customization features in **Chapters 14** and **15**.

To open the Preferences window

Choose Edit > Preferences (**Figure 1**). The Preferences window appears (**Figure 3**, **7**, or **9**).

To close the Preferences window

Click the Preferences window's close box.

or

1. Activate the Preferences window.

2. Choose File > Close Window (**Figure 2**), or press ⌃ ⌘ W.

✔ Tip

■ Closing the Preferences window automatically saves all the settings within it.

Figure 1
Choose Preferences from the Edit menu.

Figure 2
Choose Close Window from the File menu.

Figure 3 The default settings in the General tab of the Preferences window.

Figure 4 Use the slider control to set the spring-loaded folder delay.

To enable or disable Simple Finder

1. In the Preferences window, click the General tab to display its options (**Figure 3**).

2. To enable Simple Finder, turn on the Simple Finder check box.

   or

   To disable Simple Finder, turn off the Simple Finder check box.

✔ Tips

- Simple Finder simplifies Finder menus by reducing the number of options.

- The illustrations throughout this book were created with Simple Finder disabled.

- **Appendix A** illustrates both standard Finder and Simple Finder menus.

To set spring-loaded folder options

1. In the Preferences window, click the General tab to display its options (**Figure 3**).

2. To enable the spring-loaded folders feature, turn on the Spring-loaded folders check box. Then use the slider bar beside it (**Figure 4**) to set the delay from the time an item is dragged onto a folder to the time the folder opens.

   or

   To disable the spring-loaded folders feature, turn off the Spring-loaded folders check box.

✔ Tip

- I tell you how to use spring-loaded folders later in this chapter.

SETTING GENERAL PREFERENCES

To set grid spacing

1. In the Preferences window, click the General tab to display its options (**Figure 3**).

2. For less space between icons or buttons in icon or button view windows (**Figure 5**), select the Tight radio button.

   or

   For more space between icons or buttons in icon or button view windows (**Figure 6**), select the Wide radio button.

✔ Tip

■ Wide grid spacing yields a neater arrangement because file names are less likely to overlap (**Figure 6**).

To set standard view options

1. In the Preferences window, click the Views tab to display its options (**Figure 7**).

2. Select the type of view for which you want to set standard options from the pop-up menu (**Figure 8**).

3. Turn on check boxes for view options and select an Icon Size radio button as desired.

4. Repeat steps 2 and 3 for each type of view that you want to set.

✔ Tips

■ I tell you about the options for icon, button, and list views in **Chapter 3**.

■ The options you set in the Preferences window affect only those windows for which you did not set options in the View Options dialog box. I discuss the View Options dialog box in **Chapter 3**.

Figure 5
Tight spacing enables you to view more icons in less space.

Figure 6 Wide spacing offers a neater arrangement because names don't overlap.

Figure 7 The default settings in the Views tab of the Preferences window.

Figure 8 Use this pop-up menu to select the type of view for which you want to set standard options.

Figure 9 The default settings in the Labels tab of the Preferences window.

Figure 10 Type in a new label.

Figure 11 The new label appears in the Label submenu under the File menu.

Figure 12 The Color Picker dialog box lets you select a new color.

To change the text of labels

1. In the Preferences window, click the Labels tab to display its options (**Figure 9**).

2. Drag the mouse pointer over the text in the edit box containing the label you want to change. This selects the text (**Figure 9**).

3. Type the text you want to use as a label (**Figure 10**).

4. Repeat steps 2 and 3 for each label that you want to change.

✔ Tip

■ The changes you make are reflected in the Labels submenu under the File menu (**Figure 11**).

To change the color of labels

1. In the Preferences window, click the Labels tab to display its options (**Figure 9**).

2. Click the color you want to change. The Color Picker dialog box appears (**Figure 12**).

3. Click in the color wheel to select a new color. The color appears in the New sample area.

4. If desired, use the slider near the bottom of the dialog box to change the brightness of the color.

5. Click OK. The color you clicked in the Preferences window changes.

6. Repeat steps 2 though 5 for each color that you want to change.

✔ Tip

■ The changes you make are reflected in the Label submenu under the File menu and in the color of the icons which have labels applied.

Outlines in List View

Windows displayed in list view have a feature not found in icon or button views: They can display the contents of folders within the window as an outline (**Figure 13**).

✔ Tip

- I tell you more about views in **Chapter 2**.

To display a folder's contents

Click the right-pointing triangle beside the folder (**Figure 14**).

or

Click the folder once to select it, and press ⌘→.

The items within that folder are listed below it, slightly indented (**Figure 15**).

✔ Tip

- As shown in **Figure 13**, you can use this technique to display multiple levels of folders in the same window.

To hide a folder's contents

Click the down-pointing triangle beside the folder (**Figure 15**).

or

Click the folder once to select it, and press ⌘←.

The outline collapses to hide the items in the folder (**Figure 14**).

Figure 13
The outline feature lets you display the contents of folders within the same list view window.

Click here to expand the outline

Figure 14
The contents of a folder can be hidden...

Click here to collapse the outline

Figure 15
...or displayed.

Figure 16 A pop-up window has a tab that you can click...

Figure 17 ...to hide the window at the bottom of the screen.

Figure 18
Choose as Pop-up Window from the View menu.

Pop-up Windows

The pop-up windows feature changes the appearance and functionality of a window by adding a tab and hiding the window at the very bottom of the screen. Click the tab to display the window (**Figure 16**). Click either outside the window or on the tab to hide the window again (**Figure 17**).

✔ Tip

■ This feature makes it easy to keep frequently used windows handy without letting them clutter up the screen.

To turn a window into a pop-up window

1. Activate the window that you want to turn into a pop-up window.

2. Choose View > as Pop-up Window (**Figure 18**). The window changes to a pop-up window (**Figure 16**).

   or

   Drag the window's title bar to the bottom of the screen. When a tab shape appears at the top of its gray outline (**Figure 19**), release the mouse button. The window changes into a pop-up window tab (**Figure 17**).

Figure 19 Drag the window's title bar until a tab appears on its outline.

WORKING WITH POP-UP WINDOWS

To activate or deactivate a pop-up window

Click the tab at the top of the window.

If the window is active (fully visible) when you click its tab, it disappears, displaying only a tab at the bottom of the screen (**Figure 17**).

If the window is inactive (displayed as a tab) when you click its tab, it appears (**Figure 16**).

✔ Tip

■ You can also deactivate a pop-up window by clicking anywhere outside the window frame.

To resize a pop-up window

1. Position the mouse pointer on one of the top corners of the active pop-up window (**Figure 20**).

2. Drag to make the window larger or smaller. As you drag, a dotted line border indicates the new edges of the window (**Figure 21**).

3. Release the mouse button. The window resizes (**Figure 22**).

To turn a pop-up window into a standard window

1. Activate the pop-up window that you want to turn into a standard window.

2. Choose View > as Window (**Figure 23**). The window changes to a standard window.

   or

   Position the mouse pointer on the tab of the pop-up window and drag up until the tab disappears from the gray outline of the window (**Figure 24**). Release the mouse button. The window changes to a standard window.

Figure 20 A pop-up window has size boxes on the two upper corners of the active window.

Figure 21 As you drag a size box, a dotted-line border indicates the window's new borders.

Figure 22 When you release the mouse button, the window resizes.

Figure 23 Choose as Window from the View menu.

Figure 24 Drag a pop-up window's tab up until the tab disappears from the gray outline.

WORKING WITH POP-UP WINDOWS

Figure 25 Drag an icon onto a folder icon and wait...

Figure 26 ...until the folder opens.

Spring-Loaded Folders

The spring-loaded folders feature lets you move or copy items into folders deep within the file structure of your disk—without manually opening a single folder. Instead, you simply drag icons onto folders (**Figures 25** and **27**) and wait as they're automatically opened (**Figures 26** and **28**). When you drop the icon into the final window, all windows except the source and destination windows automatically close (**Figure 29**).

✔ Tips

- The spring-loaded folders feature is sometimes referred to as *spring-open folders*.

- Using the spring-loaded folders feature requires a steady hand, good mouse skills, and knowledge of the location of folders on your disk.

- To use the spring-loaded folders feature, the Spring-loaded folders check box must be turned on in the General tab of the Preferences window (**Figure 3**). You can also set the spring-loaded folder delay length in the Preferences window (**Figure 4**). I tell you about Preferences at the beginning of this chapter.

- To use the spring-loaded folders feature to move or copy more than one item at a time, select the items first, then drag any one of them.

To move an item using spring-loaded folders

1. Drag the item you want to move onto the folder in which you want to move it (**Figure 25**), but do not release the mouse button. After a moment, the folder blinks and opens (**Figure 26**).

2. Without releasing the mouse button, repeat step 1. The destination folder becomes selected (**Figure 27**), then blinks and opens (**Figure 28**). Do this until you reach the final destination.

3. Release the mouse button to place the item into the destination window (**Figure 29**).

✔ Tips

- In steps 1 and 2, to open a folder immediately, press Spacebar while dragging an item onto it.

- To close a folder's window so you can open a different folder in the same window, drag the item away from the open window. The window closes so you can drag the item onto a different folder and open it.

To copy an item using spring-loaded folders

Hold down Option while following the above steps.

✔ Tip

- If the destination folder is on another disk, it is not necessary to hold down Option to copy items; they're automatically copied.

Figure 27 Continue to drag the icon onto a folder in that window and wait...

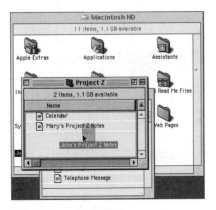

Figure 28 ...until that folder opens.

Figure 29 The icon appears in the final destination window.

USING SPRING-LOADED FOLDERS

Figure 30 Point to the folder you want to browse.

Figure 31 When you click one and a half times on the folder, the mouse pointer turns into a magnifying glass...

Figure 32 ...and the folder opens.

To browse folder or disk contents with "click and a half"

1. Position the mouse pointer on the folder or disk you want to browse (**Figure 30**).

2. Double-click the mouse button but do not release the mouse button during the second click. After a moment, the mouse pointer turns into a magnifying glass (**Figure 31**) and the folder or disk blinks and opens (**Figure 32**).

3. Without releasing the mouse button, drag the magnifying glass pointer over a folder you want to open within the open window. The folder becomes selected, then blinks and opens. Repeat as necessary to open other folders.

4. Release the mouse button to close all windows except the last one that was opened (and any others that were already open when you began step 1).

✔ Tips

- In steps 2 and 3, to open a folder immediately, press Spacebar while pointing to it.

- To close a folder's window so you can open a different folder in the same window, move the mouse pointer out of the open window. The window closes so you can move the mouse pointer onto a different folder and open it.

BROWSING FOLDERS WITH "CLICK AND A HALF"

Aliases

An *alias* is a pointer to an item. You can make an alias of an item and place it anywhere on your computer. Then, when you need to open the item, just open its alias.

✔ Tips

■ It's important to remember that an alias is not a copy of the item—it's a pointer. If you delete the original item, the alias will not open.

■ You can use the Fix Alias dialog box (**Figure 58**) to reassign an original to an alias. I explain how later in this chapter.

■ By putting aliases of frequently used items together where you can quickly access them—like on the Desktop or in a pop-up window—you make the items more accessible without actually moving them. I tell you about pop-up windows earlier in this chapter.

■ The Favorites and Recent Items features work with aliases. I tell you about both of these features a little later in this chapter.

■ You can make an alias for any item on your computer—including items accessible over a network. I tell you more about networking in **Chapter 10**.

■ You can name an alias anything you like, as long as you follow the file naming guidelines I discuss in **Chapter 3**. An alias's name does not need to include the word *alias*.

■ The icon for an alias looks very much like the icon for the original item but includes a tiny arrow (**Figure 33**). An alias's name appears in italic letters.

■ You can move, copy, rename, open, and delete an alias just like any other file.

SimpleText   *SimpleText alias*

Figure 33 The icon for an alias looks like the original item's icon but includes an arrow. An alias's name always appears in italic letters.

Figure 34 To create an alias, begin by selecting the item for which you want to make an alias.

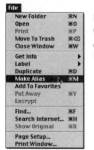

Figure 35
Choose Make Alias from the File menu.

Figure 36
The alias appears right beneath the original.

Figure 37
Select the alias's icon.

Figure 38
Choose Show Original from the File menu.

Figure 39 The original item appears selected in its window.

To create an alias

1. Select the item for which you want to make an alias (**Figure 34**).

2. Choose File > Make Alias (**Figure 35**), or press ⌘M.

   The alias appears right beneath the original item (**Figure 36**).

or

Hold down ⌘Option and drag the item for which you want to make an alias to a new location. The alias appears in the destination location.

✔ Tip

■ An alias's name is selected right after it is created (**Figure 36**). If desired, you can immediately type in a new name to replace the default name.

To find an alias's original file

1. Select the alias's icon (**Figure 37**).

2. Choose File > Show Original (**Figure 38**), or press ⌘R.

   The original item appears selected in the window in which it resides on disk (**Figure 39**).

WORKING WITH ALIASES

Favorites

Favorites enables you to add frequently used documents, applications, network servers and volumes, and Internet locations to a submenu on the Apple menu. This makes them quick and easy to access.

✔ Tips

- Favorites also appear in the Network Browser and the new Open and Save As dialog boxes. I discuss the Network Browser in **Chapter 10** and the new Open and Save As dialog boxes in **Chapter 5**.

- The favorites feature works with aliases, which I discuss on the previous two pages.

- The Mac OS 9 installer puts two items on the Favorites submenu:
  - ▲ **apple.com** uses the Network Browser to connect to Apple Computer's network.
  - ▲ **www.apple.com** uses your Web browser to connect to Apple Computer's home page.

- I tell you more about network servers and volumes in **Chapter 10** and Internet locations in **Chapter 11**.

To add a favorite item

1. In the Finder, select the icon for the item that you want to add as a favorite item (**Figure 40**).

2. Choose File > Add To Favorites (**Figure 41**).

   The item is added to the Favorites submenu under the Apple menu (**Figure 42**).

✔ Tip

- You can also add an item to the Favorites folder by making an alias of the item and dragging the alias into the Favorites folder inside the System Folder.

Figure 40
Select the item that you want to add as a favorite item.

Figure 41
Choose Add To Favorites from the File menu.

Figure 42
The item is added to the Favorites submenu under the Apple menu.

Figure 43 As you add Favorites, the Favorites folder can get cluttered with items.

Figure 44 You can use folders to organize the contents of the Favorites folder.

Figure 45
Folders within the Favorites folder appear as submenus on the Favorites submenu.

To organize favorites

1. Choose Apple menu > Favorites (**Figure 42**) to open the Favorites folder window (**Figure 43**).

2. Create and name folders for different groups of items. Store the appropriate items in each folder (**Figure 44**).

3. Close the Favorites folder window.

   The Favorites submenu displays each folder within it as a submenu (**Figure 45**).

To use a favorite item

From the Favorites submenu under the Apple menu (**Figures 42** and **45**), choose the item you want to open.

To remove a favorite

1. Choose Apple menu > Favorites (**Figure 42**) to open the Favorites folder window (**Figures 43** or **44**).

2. Drag the item that you want to remove out of the window.

3. Close the Favorites folder window.

   The item is removed from the Favorites submenu.

ORGANIZING, USING, & REMOVING FAVORITES

Recent Items

Recent items are recently opened applications, documents, and servers. Mac OS automatically tracks the things you open and creates submenus of the ten most recently opened items in each category, making it quick and easy to open them again.

Figure 46
Mac OS tracks the most recently used applications...

To open recent items

To open a recently used application, choose its name from the Recent Applications submenu under the Apple menu (**Figure 46**).

or

To open a recently used document, choose its name from the Recent Document submenu under the Apple menu (**Figure 47**).

or

To open a recently used server, choose its name from the Recent Servers submenu under the Apple menu (**Figure 48**).

Figure 47
...the most recently used documents...

✔ Tips

- The favorites feature works with aliases, which I discuss earlier in this chapter.

- You can change the number of tracked items in the Apple Menu Options control panel, which I tell you about in **Chapter 14**.

- If your computer is not connected to a network, or you have never connected to a network server, there will be no Recent Servers submenu.

- When you select a server from the Recent Servers submenu, you may be prompted to log on to the server machine by providing a User Name and Password.

- I tell you about applications and documents in **Chapter 5** and about servers in **Chapter 10**.

Figure 48
...and the most recently used server volumes.

Figure 49
The Info window for a hard disk.

Figure 50
The Info window for a folder.

Figure 51
The Info window for an application.

Figure 52
The Info window for a document.

The Info Window

You can learn more about an item by opening its Info window (**Figures 49** through **52**). Depending on the type of icon (disk, folder, application, document, alias, Trash, etc.), the General Information in the Info window will provide some or all of the following information:

◆ **Icon** that appears in the Finder.

◆ **Name** of the item.

◆ **Kind** or type of item.

◆ **Format** of item (disks only).

◆ **Capacity** of item (disks only).

◆ **Available** space (disks only).

◆ **Used** space (disks only).

◆ **Size** of item or contents (folders and files only).

◆ **Where** item is on disk.

◆ **Contents** (Trash only).

◆ **Created** date and time.

◆ **Modified** date and time.

◆ **Version** number or copyright date (files only).

◆ **Original** location on disk (aliases only).

◆ **Label** assigned to item.

◆ **Comments** entered by users (like you).

◆ **Locked** check box to prevent the file from being deleted or overwritten (files only).

◆ **Stationery** check box to convert the file into a stationery format file (documents only).

◆ **Warn before emptying** check box to toggle the Trash warning dialog box (Trash only).

✔ Tips

■ I tell you about stationery pads in **Chapter 5**.

■ I tell you about File Sharing and Memory information in the Info window in **Chapters 10** and **5** respectively.

THE INFO WINDOW

To open the Info window

1. Select the item for which you want to open the Info window (**Figure 53**).

2. Choose File > Get Info > General Information (**Figure 54**), or press ⌥ ⌘ I.

   The Info window for that item appears (**Figure 50**).

To close the Info window

Click the Info window's close box.

or

1. Activate the Info window.

2. Choose File > Close Window (**Figure 2**), or press ⌥ ⌘ W.

✔ Tip

- Closing the Info window saves all changes you made to its options.

To change an item's name

1. In the Info window, drag the mouse pointer over the item's name to select it.

2. Type in the new name. What you type replaces the selected text.

✔ Tip

- You can change the name of an item only if its name appears within an edit box (**Figures 49** through **52**). If there is no edit box around the item's name, you cannot rename it.

To change an item's label

In the Info window, choose a label from the Label pop-up menu (**Figure 55**). The label is applied to the item.

✔ Tip

- I tell you more about labels in **Chapter 3**.

Figure 53
Select the item for which you want to open the Info window.

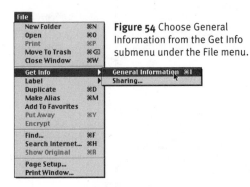

Figure 54 Choose General Information from the Get Info submenu under the File menu.

Figure 55
Choose a label from the Label pop-up menu.

Figure 56
You can enter information about the item in the Comments box.

Figure 57
You can click the Select New Original button in the Info window for an alias to assign a new original to the alias.

Figure 58 Use the Fix Alias dialog box to locate and choose a new original for an alias.

To enter comments in the Info window

1. Open the Info window for the item for which you want to enter comments.

2. Click in the Comments box to position the blinking insertion point there.

3. Type your comments (**Figure 56**).

To lock an application or document

1. Open the Info window for the item you want to lock (**Figure 51** or **52**).

2. Turn on the Locked check box.

✔ Tip

- Locked items cannot be deleted or over-written. They can, however, be moved.

To select a new original item for an alias

1. In the Info window for the alias (**Figure 57**), click the Select New Original button.

2. Use the Fix Alias dialog box that appears (**Figure 58**) to locate and select the item that you want to use as the original for the alias.

3. Click Choose. The item you selected is assigned to the alias.

✔ Tip

- The Fix Alias dialog box takes advantage of the Navigation Services feature that first appeared in Mac OS 8.5. I explain how to use dialog boxes like this one in **Chapter 5**.

APPLICATION BASICS

Applications

Applications, which are also known as *programs*, are software packages you use to get work done. Here are some examples:

- ◆ **Word processors**, such as SimpleText and Microsoft Word, are used to write letters, reports, and other text-based documents.

- ◆ **Spreadsheets**, such as Microsoft Excel, have built-in calculation features that are useful for creating number-based documents like worksheets and charts.

- ◆ **Databases**, such as FileMaker Pro, are used to organize related information, like the names and addresses of customers or the artists and titles in a record collection.

- ◆ **Graphics** and **presentation** programs, such as Adobe Photoshop, Macromedia FreeHand, and Microsoft PowerPoint, are used to create illustrations, presentations, and animations.

- ◆ **Communications** programs, such as Remote Access, Microsoft Internet Explorer, and America Online, are used to connect to other computers, including online services and the Internet.

- ◆ **Integrated** software, such as AppleWorks and Microsoft Works, combines "lite" versions of most other types of software into one cost-effective package.

- ◆ **Utility** software, such as Disk First Aid, Drive Setup, and Norton Utilities, performs tasks to help manage computer files or keep your computer in good working order.

✔ Tips

- ■ Your Mac OS-compatible computer comes with some application software, most of which is discussed throughout this book.

- ■ Unless you have a DOS compatibility card, Virtual PC, or SoftWindows installed in your computer, you should make sure the software you buy is Mac OS-compatible. I tell you more about working with PCs in **Chapter 8**.

Using Applications & Creating Documents

You use an application by opening, or *launching*, it. It loads into the computer's memory, or *RAM*. Its menu bar replaces the Finder's menu bar and offers commands that can be used only with that application. It may also display a document window and tools specific to that program.

Most applications create *documents*—files written in a format understood by the application. When you save documents, they remain on disk so you can open, edit, print, or just view them at a later date.

For example, you may use Microsoft Word to write a letter. When you save the letter, it becomes a Word document file that includes all the text and formatting you put into the letter, written in a format that Microsoft Word can understand.

Your computer keeps track of applications and documents. It automatically associates documents with the applications that created them. That's how your computer is able to open a document with the correct application when you open the document from the Finder.

✔ Tips

- You can launch an application by opening a document that it created.

- You can often tell which documents were created by a specific application just by looking at their icons. **Figure 1** shows some examples.

- A document created by an application that is not installed on your computer is sometimes referred to as an *orphan* document since no *parent* application is available. An orphan document usually has a generic document icon (**Figure 2**).

Microsoft Word   Document

FrameMaker5   Document

Claris Home Page   Document

Acrobat™ Reader   Document

Figure 1 Application and document icons often share elements that make them appear as part of a matched set.

Ducati.jpg

Figure 2
An orphan document often has a generic document icon like this one.

Figure 3
Select the icon for the application that you want to open.

Figure 4
Choose Open from the File menu.

Figure 5 When you launch SimpleText by opening its application icon, it displays an empty document window.

Figure 6 Select the icon for the document that you want to open.

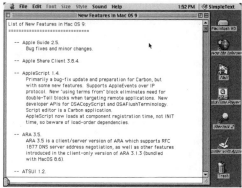

Figure 7 When you launch SimpleText by opening one of its documents, it displays the document.

To launch an application

Double-click the application's icon.

or

1. Select the application's icon (**Figure 3**).

2. Choose File > Open (**Figure 4**), or press ⌘O.

The application opens (**Figure 5**).

To launch an application & open a document at the same time

Double-click the icon for the document that you want to open.

or

1. Select the icon for the document that you want to open (**Figure 6**).

2. Choose File > Open (**Figure 4**), or press ⌘O.

The application that created the document launches. The document appears in a window (**Figure 7**).

✔ Tips

■ If the application that created the document is already open, it does not launch again. Instead, it becomes active and displays the document in a window.

■ If you try to open an orphan document, a dialog box will either tell you it can't open the document (**Figure 10**) or offer to open it with an installed application (**Figure 9**). I tell you more about opening orphan documents on the next page.

LAUNCHING APPLICATIONS

To open a document with drag & drop

1. Drag the icon for the document that you want to open onto the icon for the application with which you want to open it.

2. When the application icon becomes selected (**Figure 8**), release the mouse button. The application launches and displays the document (**Figure 7**).

✔ Tips

- This is a good way to open a document with an application other than the one that created it.

- Not all applications can read all documents. Dragging a document icon onto the icon for an application that can't open it either won't launch the application or will display an error message.

To open an orphan document

Double-click the icon for the document that you want to open.

or

1. Select the icon for the document that you want to open.

2. Choose File > Open (**Figure 4**), or press ⌘O.

3. If a dialog box like the one in **Figure 9** appears, click to select the name of the application with which you want to try to open the document. Then click Open. The application you selected launches and attempts to open the document.

   or

   If a dialog box like the one in **Figure 10** appears, you don't have an application that will open the file. Click OK.

Figure 8 Drag the document icon onto the application icon.

Figure 9 A dialog box like this appears if you try to open an orphan document and have at least one program that can open it.

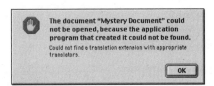

Figure 10 If you don't have any programs that can open an orphan document, a dialog box like this appears.

✔ Tip

- If you don't have a program that will open an orphan file, find someone who does, open it on his machine, and save it in a format you can open.

Figure 11
The Application menu lists all open applications, identifies the active application, and lets you activate the application of your choice.

Figure 12 Clicking the vertical bar to the left of the application menu collapses it to display only the application's icon.

Multitasking & the Application Menu

Mac OS uses a form of *multitasking* that makes it possible for more than one application to be open at the same time. Only one application, however, can be *active*. The active application is the one whose menu bar appears at the top of the screen and whose windows are at the top of the stack of windows on your screen.

The Application menu at the far right end of the menu bar (**Figure 11**) lets you do a number of things:

◆ Identify the active application. The name and icon for the active application appears at the top of the application menu. When you display the menu, the active application has a check mark to the left of its name (**Figure 11**).

◆ Activate a different open application.

◆ Hide the active application.

◆ Hide all applications except the active application.

◆ Show all open applications.

✔ Tips

■ One application that is always open is the Finder, which I cover in detail in **Chapters 2** through **4**.

■ The number of applications that can be opened at the same time depends on the amount of RAM in your computer. I tell you more about RAM later in this chapter.

■ Hiding an application removes all of its windows from the screen, thus reducing screen clutter.

■ If you click the vertical bar to the left of the application menu, it collapses to display only the icon for the active application (**Figure 12**). (This is how the application menu appeared prior to Mac OS 8.5.)

To switch from one open application to another

From the Application menu, choose the application you want (**Figure 13**).

or

Click on a window of the application that you want (**Figure 14**). You may have to move windows that are blocking your view.

To hide an application

1. If necessary, activate the application.

2. From the Application menu, choose Hide *Application* (**Figure 15**). Although the exact wording of this command changes depending on the name of the application, it's always the first option on the Application menu.

✔ Tips

■ You cannot hide the active application if it is the only application that is open or if all the other open applications are already hidden.

■ The icon for a hidden application appears faded on the Application menu (**Figure 17**).

To hide all applications except the active one

1. If necessary, activate the application that you don't want to hide.

2. From the Application menu, choose Hide Others (**Figure 16**).

To unhide all applications

From the Application menu, choose Show All (**Figure 17**).

✔ Tip

■ The Show All command is gray if all applications are already showing (**Figure 15**).

Figure 13
Choose the application that you want from the Application menu.

Click here to activate this program.

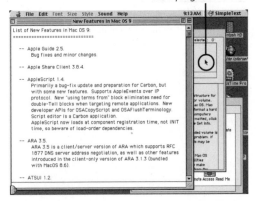

Figure 14 In this example, SimpleText is the active application. Clicking on the Disk First Aid window sticking out behind it will activate Disk First Aid.

Figure 15
The first command under the Application menu hides the active application.

Figure 16
The Hide Others command hides all applications except the active one.

Figure 17
The Show All command shows all applications, including those that were hidden.

Figure 18
To display the Application Switcher, drag the Application menu down to "tear it off" the menu bar.

Close box   *Zoom box*   *Collapse box*

Figure 19
When you release the mouse button, the Application Switcher's window appears.

Figure 20
Clicking the Application Switcher's zoom box displays it as a column of icons without application names.

Figure 21 You can move the Application Switcher like any other window—by dragging its title bar.

Using the Application Switcher

The Application Switcher offers another way to switch from one open application to another. It displays a floating palette with a button for each open application. Simply click a button to activate its application.

To display the Application Switcher

1. In the menu bar, position the mouse pointer on the name of the application that appears at the top of the Application menu.

2. Press the mouse button down and drag down. As you drag, the application menu appears. Then a gray rectangle appears to indicate that the menu is being "torn off" the menu bar (**Figure 18**).

3. Release the mouse button. The Application Switcher window appears (**Figure 19**).

✔ Tips

- To display the Application Switcher as a column of icons (**Figure 20**), click its zoom box.

- To display the Application Switcher with larger icons, hold down (Option) while clicking its zoom box. This works for the Application Switcher's standard icon and application name view as well as its icon only view.

To move the Application Switcher

1. Position the mouse pointer on the Application Switcher's title bar.

2. Press the mouse button down and drag. As you drag, a gray border indicates where the Application Switcher will appear when you release the mouse button (**Figure 21**).

3. When the Application Switcher's border is in the desired position, release the mouse button. It moves.

To switch from one open application to another

Click the Application Switcher button for the application you want.

Figure 22
The icon for a hidden application appears faded in the Application Switcher window.

✔ Tip

■ The active application's button always appears "pushed in," or selected (**Figures 19** and **20**).

To hide the active application while switching to another application

Hold down (Option) while clicking the Application Switcher button for the application you want.

✔ Tips

■ The icon for a hidden application appears faded in the Application Switcher window (**Figure 22**).

■ This technique also works when activating an application by clicking its window or choosing its name from the Application menu as discussed earlier in this chapter.

To hide the Application Switcher

Click the Application Switcher's close box (**Figure 19**). It disappears.

Figures 23a, 23b, & 23c The Quit command is always under the File menu. Here are three examples: SimpleText (top-left), Disk First Aid (bottom-left), and Microsoft Word (right).

Figure 24 If there are unsaved documents, a dialog box like this one appears for each one, giving you a last chance to save them.

Quitting an Application

When you're finished using an application, you should properly quit it. This completely clears the application out of RAM, freeing up RAM for other applications you may want to launch.

✔ Tip

■ Closing all of an application's open windows is not the same as quitting. An application is still running—and still taking up RAM—until you quit it.

To quit an application

1. If necessary, activate the application that you want to quit.

2. Choose File > Quit (**Figures 23a**, **23b**, and **23c**), or press ⌃ ⌘ Q.

3. If unsaved documents are open, a dialog box like the one in **Figure 24** appears for each unsaved document.

   ▲ Click Save or press Return or Enter to save the document.

   ▲ Click Don't Save to quit without saving the document.

   ▲ Click Cancel or press Esc to return to the application without quitting.

   The application closes all windows, saves preference files (if applicable), and quits.

✔ Tip

■ I tell you more about saving documents later in this chapter.

Dialog Boxes

Mac OS-compatible applications use *dialog boxes* to tell you things (**Figure 25**) and get information from you (**Figures 26** through **29**). Think of it as the way your computer has a conversation—or dialog—with you.

Every application has its own set of dialog boxes, but there are some dialog boxes that are basically the same from one application to another:

◆ **Open** dialog box (**Figure 26**) lets you open a document from within an application (as opposed to opening it from the Finder).

◆ **Save As** dialog box (**Figure 27**) lets you save a document with the name and in the disk location you specify.

◆ **Page Setup** dialog box (**Figure 28**) lets you specify page and PostScript settings.

◆ **Print** dialog box (**Figure 29**) lets you specify print settings and print.

This part of the chapter explains how to use the standard parts of a dialog box—edit boxes, radio buttons, check boxes, scrolling lists, and push buttons—as well as how to use the Open and Save As dialog boxes.

✔ Tips

■ I tell you how to use the Page Setup and Print dialog boxes in **Chapter 9**.

■ It is often difficult to distinguish between windows and dialog boxes since Mac OS uses both to communicate with you. Throughout this book, a dialog box will refer to a window-like box that appears on screen and requires you to click a button to dismiss it. A window, on the other hand, can always be closed by clicking a close box or using the Close or Close Window command under the File menu.

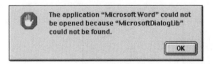

Figure 25 This dialog box just gives you a message.

Figure 26 Four SimpleText dialog boxes: the Open dialog box,...

Figure 27 ...the Save As dialog box,...

Figure 28 ...the Page Setup dialog box,...

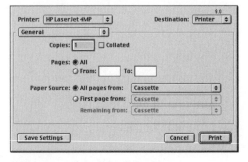

Figure 29 ...and the Print dialog box.

Edit   Scrolling   Check   Pop-up   Push
box   list   box   Tab   menu   buttons

Figure 30 One Microsoft Word dialog box illustrates most standard dialog box parts...

Scrolling   Radio   Edit   Push
list   button   box   button

Figure 31 ...and another illustrates the rest.

To use dialog box parts

◆ Enter text or numbers into edit boxes (**Figures 30** and **31**).

◆ Use scroll bars to view the contents of scrolling lists (**Figures 30** and **31**). Click a list item once to select it.

◆ Click a check box (**Figure 30**) to turn it on or off.

◆ Click a tab (**Figure 30**) to view its options.

◆ Click a pop-up menu (**Figure 30**) to display its options. Drag through the menu to choose an option.

◆ Click a push button (**Figures 30** and **31**) to select it.

◆ Click a radio button (**Figure 31**) to select it.

✔ Tips

■ If an edit box has a pair of arrows or triangles beside it (**Figure 31**) you can click the triangles to increase or decrease a value already in the edit box.

■ The default push button is the one with the dark border around it (**Figures 30** and **31**). You can always select a default button by pressing [Enter] and often by pressing [Return].

■ You can usually select a Cancel button (**Figures 30** and **31**) by pressing [Esc] or [⌃ ⌘ .].

■ One and only one radio button in a group must be selected (**Figure 31**). If you try to select a second button, the first button becomes deselected.

■ If you click the Cancel button in a dialog box (**Figures 30** and **31**), any options you set are lost.

To use the Open dialog box

1. Choose File > Open (**Figure 32**), or press
   ⌃ ⌘ O .

   A dialog box similar to the one in **Figure 26** appears.

2. Use these two techniques to navigate to the file you want to open:

   ▲ To open an item in a scrolling list, click to select it and then click Open or double-click it.

   ▲ To back up out of the current folder to a previous folder in the file hierarchy, choose a folder from the pop-up menu above the scrolling list (**Figures 33** and **34**) or press ⌃ ⌘ ↑ to back up one folder level at a time.

3. Click to select the name of the file that you want to open, and then click Open (**Figure 35**) or press Return or Enter .

   or

   Double-click the name of the file that you want to open.

✔ Tips

- To use this dialog box successfully, you must understand the file hierarchy. Remember that files reside in folders that are sometimes inside other folders.

- To quickly view the items on the Desktop, click the Desktop button (**Figures 26** and **35**) or press ⌃ ⌘ D. This enables you to open folders, files, and other disks on your Desktop.

- Some Open dialog boxes offer pop-up menus that let you narrow down a file list by document or file type.

Figure 32
Choose Open from the application's—in this case SimpleText's—File menu.

Figure 33 Use the pop-up menu above the scrolling list to choose a different folder in the hierarchy...

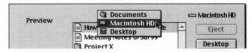

Figure 34
...and the contents of that folder appear in the scrolling list.

Figure 35 Select the file's name and click Open to open it within the application.

Figure 36
Choose Save As from the application's—in this case, SimpleText's—File menu.

Save this document as:

Letter to Dianna|

Figure 37 Enter a name for the document in the edit box.

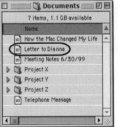

Figure 38
An icon for the document you saved appears in the folder in which you saved it.

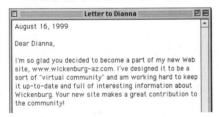

Figure 39 The name of the document appears in the title bar of the document window.

To use the Save As dialog box

1. Choose File > Save As (**Figure 36**). A dialog box similar to the one in **Figure 27** appears.

2. Use these two techniques to navigate to the folder in which you want to save the document:

   ▲ To open an item in a scrolling list, click to select it and then click Open or double-click it.

   ▲ To back up out of the current folder to a previous folder in the file hierarchy, choose a folder from the pop-up menu above the scrolling list (**Figure 33**) or press ⌃ ⌘ ↑ to back up one folder level at a time.

3. In the edit box beneath the scrolling list, enter the name that you want to give the document (**Figure 37**).

4. Click Save, or press Return or Enter.

The file is saved to disk in the destination you specified (**Figure 38**). The name you gave it appears in the title bar of the document window (**Figure 39**).

✔ Tips

■ If you have never saved the document, you can also choose Save from the application's file menu or press ⌃ ⌘ S to display the Save As dialog box.

■ The folder navigation techniques in the Save As dialog box work just like those in the Open dialog box discussed on the previous page.

■ To quickly view the items on the Desktop, click the Desktop button (**Figure 27**) or press ⌃ ⌘ D. This enables you to open folders and other disks on your Desktop.

■ Some Save As dialog boxes offer a pop-up menu you can use to save a file in a specific file format.

USING THE SAVE AS DIALOG BOX

Navigation Services

Navigation Services, which was added to Mac OS in version 8.5, changes the appearance and functionality of the Open (**Figure 40**) and Save As (**Figure 41**) dialog boxes, making them more flexible and convenient to use.

✔ Tips

- Throughout this book, I refer to the dialog boxes introduced with Navigation Services as the "new" Open and Save As dialog boxes.

- This feature must be implemented within a program for the dialog boxes on this page to appear.

- Within Mac OS 9, you can see this new feature at work in:

  - ▲ The Fix Alias dialog box, which I discuss in **Chapter 4**.

  - ▲ Network Browser, which I discuss in **Chapter 10**.

  - ▲ The Appearance control panel, which I discuss in **Chapter 15**.

- As more software developers adopt the Navigation Services technology, the dialog boxes depicted on these pages will become more and more common.

Figure 40 The new Open dialog box...

Figure 41 ...and the new Save As dialog box.

NAVIGATION SERVICES

Figure 42 Click a triangle to display the items within its folder or disk.

Figure 43
The Shortcuts button displays the desktop, network connections, and other mounted disks.

Figure 44
The Favorites button displays your Favorites.

Figure 45 The Recent button displays items recently opened with that application.

To use the new Open & Save As dialog boxes

All of the instructions in the section titled "To use the Open dialog box" apply to the new Open dialog box (**Figure 40**).

and

All of the instructions in the section titled "To use the Save As dialog box" apply to the new Save As dialog box (**Figure 41**).

The following procedures also work with these dialog boxes:

◆ Click the triangle to the left of the name of a disk or folder that you want to open to display its contents along with the contents of other disks or folders (**Figure 42**). (This works with the Open dialog box only.)

◆ Open several files at once by holding down (Shift) while clicking the names of the files you want to open. (This works with the Open dialog box only.)

◆ Choose an option from the Shortcuts button menu (**Figure 43**) to quickly access the desktop, mounted disks, or disks available over the network or Internet.

◆ Choose an item from the Favorites button menu (**Figure 44**) to open a Favorite item.

◆ Choose an item from the Recent button's menu (**Figure 45**) to open an item you recently opened with that application.

✔ Tip

■ I cover networking in **Chapter 10**, the Internet in **Chapter 11**, and favorites in **Chapter 4**.

USING THE NEW OPEN & SAVE AS DIALOGS

Stationery Pads

A *stationery pad is* a document used as a form for creating similar documents. It's like a template—you open and modify it to suit your specific needs. When you save it, it automatically prompts you to give it a different name, making it very difficult to accidentally overwrite the original file.

To turn an existing document into stationery

1. Select the icon for the document that you want to turn into stationery (**Figure 46**).

2. Choose File > Get Info > General Information (**Figure 47**), or press ⌃ ⌘ I. The Info window for the file appears.

3. Turn on the Stationery Pad check box (**Figure 48**).

4. Close the Info window.

✔ Tip

■ I tell you more about General Information options in the Info window in **Chapter 4**.

To create stationery from scratch

1. In the application of your choice, create the document that you want to turn into stationery.

2. Choose File > Save As.

3. In the Save As dialog box, enter a name for the file, select a disk location, and choose a file type of Stationery or Stationery Pad (**Figures 49** and **50**).

✔ Tip

■ Not all applications let you save files as stationery. If the application you want to use doesn't, save the file as a regular document and turn it into a stationery pad in the Finder as instructed above.

Figure 46
Select the icon for the file that you want to turn into a stationery pad.

Figure 47 Choose General Information from the Get Info submenu under the File menu.

Figure 48
Turn on the Stationery Pad check box in the Info window.

Figure 49
SimpleText offers a radio button to choose stationery pad format.

Figure 50 Word offers a pop-up menu for file types, including stationery pad format.

untitled clipping

Figure 51 Dragging a selection from a document window to the Finder creates a clipping file.

Figure 52 Opening a clipping file displays its contents in a window.

Figure 53 Drag the selection to a new destination.

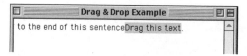

Figure 54 When you release the mouse button, the selection moves.

Macintosh Drag & Drop

Macintosh drag and drop enables you to copy or move information by dragging selections from one location to another:

◆ Dragging a selection from one location in a document window to another moves the selection.

◆ Dragging a selection from one document window to another in the same application copies the selection.

◆ Dragging a selection from one application's document window to another application's document window copies the selection.

◆ Holding down Option while dragging a selection copies the selection.

◆ Dragging a selection from a document window to the Finder creates a clipping file (**Figure 51**) containing the selection (**Figure 52**).

◆ Dragging a Finder icon into a document window copies the contents of that icon into the document.

✔ Tips

■ Not all applications support Macintosh drag and drop. Try it in your favorite applications to see if they do.

■ A selection can include text or graphics or sometimes a combination of the two.

To use Macintosh drag & drop

1. Select the text or graphics that you want to move or copy.

2. Drag the selection to the new destination. Depending on what you drag, an insertion point might appear to indicate where the selection will be inserted (**Figure 53**).

3. When the selection is in the desired position, release the mouse button. The selection moves (**Figure 54**) or is copied.

RAM

RAM (random access memory) is your computer's working memory. All the applications and documents you open are loaded into RAM so your computer's *CPU* (central processing unit) can access them quickly.

The amount of RAM an application needs to run is called its *RAM allocation*, or *application heap*. Although every application's RAM allocation is preset by the programmer, you can raise it to make the application run more smoothly or lower it so the application requires less RAM to run.

✔ Tips

- Don't confuse memory or RAM with hard disk space. I tell you about hard disks in **Chapter 3**.

- The more RAM your computer has, the more applications it can open at once.

- Programs that work with large graphics files, like Photoshop and Director, need lots of RAM to work efficiently.

- Lowering an application's RAM allocation isn't recommended because it can cause the application to behave erratically and unexpectedly crash.

To change an application's RAM allocation

1. Select the icon for the application whose RAM allocation you want to change (**Figure 55**).

2. Choose File > Get Info > Memory (**Figure 56**). The Memory information of the Info window for the application appears (**Figure 57**).

3. Enter a value for the desired RAM allocation in the Preferred Size edit box (**Figure 58**).

4. Close the Info window.

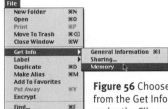

Figure 55 Select the icon for the application whose RAM allocation you want to change.

Figure 56 Choose Memory from the Get Info submenu under the File menu.

Figure 57 Use the Info window to change an application's RAM allocation.

Figure 58 Enter the desired RAM allocation value in the Preferred Size edit box.

Figure 59 The About This Computer window provides information about your computer's System software and memory.

Figure 60 Most About windows display version and programmer information, like this one from SimpleText...

Figure 61 ...and this one from AppleCD Audio Player.

Figure 62 This About The Finder window is an example of an Easter egg.

The About Window

The very first option on the Apple menu opens the About window. Its name varies based on the current application:

◆ When the Finder is active, choose About This Computer to display a window like the one in **Figure 59**. This window provides information about the version of System software running on your computer as well as the installed and available RAM and open applications.

◆ When an application is active, choose About *Application Name* to display a window like the ones in **Figures 60** and **61**.

✔ Tip

■ An *Easter egg* is an undocumented program feature included in a program by its programmers. Mac OS is known for its Easter eggs. Here's one for you to try: With the Finder active, hold down (Option) while choosing Apple menu > About The Finder. A photograph of the courtyard between the buildings at Infinite Loop in Cupertino, CA appears. (Want more Easter eggs? Visit the companion Web site for this book: *http://www.gilesrd.com/macosvqs/*.)

THE ABOUT WINDOW

USING MAC OS SOFTWARE

Mac OS 9 Software

Mac OS 9 includes a number of applications and utilities that are installed when you complete a standard installation:

◆ **Calculator** and **Graphing Calculator**, which enable you to perform quick calculations and graph formulas.

◆ **Key Caps**, which displays the characters in any installed font.

◆ **Scrapbook**, which stores frequently used text, graphics, and sounds.

◆ **Stickies**, which enables you to place colorful notes on your computer screen.

◆ **AppleCD Audio Player**, which enables you to play music CDs in your CD-ROM drive.

◆ **SimpleSound**, which enables you to record sounds using your computer's microphone.

◆ **QuickTime**, **QuickTime Player**, and **PictureViewer**, which enable you to work with QuickTime and other graphic files.

◆ **Apple System Profiler**, which provides information about your computer and its installed software.

◆ **Disk First Aid**, which enables you to diagnose and repair disk problems.

◆ **Drive Setup**, which enables you to initialize and update hard disks.

◆ **DiskCopy**, which enables you copy floppy disks and create and mount disk images.

✔ Tips

■ I tell you about Mac OS 9 components in the **Introduction** and about installing Mac OS in **Chapter 1**.

■ Mac OS 9 includes a number of other applications and utilities that are discussed elsewhere in this book:

▲ SimpleText is covered in **Chapter 7**.

▲ Network Browser is covered in **Chapter 10**.

▲ Apple Remote Access is covered in **Chapters 10** and **11**.

▲ Apple File Security and Apple Verifier are covered in **Chapter 12**.

▲ Sherlock 2 is covered in **Chapter 13**.

Calculators

Mac OS 9 includes two calculators:

◆ **Calculator** (**Figure 2**) is a simple calculator that can perform addition, subtraction, multiplication, and division.

◆ **Graphing Calculator** (**Figure 4**) is a charting tool that can create static and dynamic 2-D and 3-D graphs based on formulas.

To use the Calculator

1. Choose Apple menu > Calculator (**Figure 1**). The Calculator window appears (**Figure 2**).

2. Use your mouse to click buttons for numbers and operators.

   or

   Press keyboard keys corresponding to numbers and operators.

   The numbers you enter and the results of your calculations appear at the top of the Calculator window.

✔ Tip

■ You can use the Cut, Copy, and Paste commands to copy the results of calculations into documents. I tell you about cutting and copying in **Chapter 7**.

Figure 1
Many of Mac OS 9's programs appear on the Apple menu.

Figure 2
The Calculator has the same functionality as a $5 pocket calculator.

Figure 3 You can find more Mac OS 9 programs in the Applications folder on your hard disk.

Figure 4 The Graphing Calculator window before you enter a formula.

Figure 5 The Graphing Calculator can even create animated, three-dimensional graphs.

Figure 6
Use the Demo menu to view a variety of Graphing Calculator demos.

Figure 7
Graphing Calculator's keypad makes it easy to enter complex functions.

To use the Graphing Calculator

1. Double-click the Graphing Calculator icon inside the Applications folder on your hard disk (**Figure 3**). The Graphing Calculator window appears (**Figure 4**).

2. In the window, enter the formula that you want to graph.

3. Click Graph to create the graph (**Figure 5**).

✔ Tips

- If a formula is already in the Graphing Calculator when you open it, it appears as a split window (**Figure 5**). You can enter a new formula in the top half of the window to create a different graph.

- If the graph you create is three-dimensional (**Figure 5**), it rotates.

- You can use commands under the Demo menu (**Figure 6**) to view Graphing Calculator demonstrations.

- To display a clickable keypad of functions that you can include in your formulas (**Figure 7**), choose Equation > Show Keypad.

- You can use the Copy Graph command under the Edit menu to copy the graph for inclusion in other documents.

USING THE GRAPHING CALCULATOR

105

Key Caps

Key Caps enables you to see what the characters in your fonts are and where they are located on your keyboard.

To use Key Caps

1. Choose Apple menu > Key Caps (**Figure 1**). The Key Caps window appears (**Figure 8**).

2. To see what characters look like with various modifier keys pressed (such as Shift, Option, or Ctrl), press the modifier key. The Key Caps characters change (**Figure 9**).

3. To see what the characters of a different font look like, choose the font name from the Fonts menu (**Figure 10**). The Key Caps characters change (**Figure 11**).

✔ Tips

- You can type in the Key Caps window to see what a string of text looks like.

- Key Caps offers a great way to learn where special characters are hidden away in a font. For example, hold down Option while looking at the Key Caps window (**Figure 9**) to see a bullet (•), trademark symbol (™), registered trademark symbol (®), and copyright symbol (©). To type one of these characters in a document, hold down Option while pressing the appropriate keyboard key: Option 8 for •, Option 2 for ™, Option R for ®, Option G for ©.

- Some special characters, such as accented characters (for example, é, á, and ü), require two keystrokes to type. First type the keystroke for the accent that you want, then type the character that you want the accent to appear over. For example, to type á, press Option E and then A. The two-stroke characters appear in Key Caps with a gray box around them (**Figure 9**).

Figure 8 The Key Caps window displaying some characters of the Charcoal font.

Figure 9 In this example, holding down Option displays additional characters in the Charcoal font.

Figure 10 Choose the font whose characters you want to view from the Fonts menu...

Figure 11 ...and they appear in the Key Caps window.

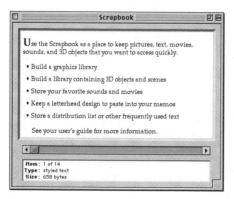

Figure 12 The Scrapbook window.

Figure 13
Use the Edit menu's commands to add, use, or remove Scrapbook items.

Figure 14 Choosing the Paste command pastes the contents of the Clipboard into the Scrapbook.

Scrapbook

The Scrapbook offers an unlimited number of entries for storing formatted text, sounds, graphics, and movies. The Scrapbook is best used to store things that you use over and over in documents, such as a company logo, formatted text, or your signature.

To use the Scrapbook

1. Choose Apple menu > Scrapbook (**Figure 1**). The Scrapbook window appears (**Figure 12**).

2. Click the scroll bar arrows to view the entries in the Scrapbook file.

3. Use Edit menu commands (**Figure 13**) to work with Scrapbook items:

   ▲ To add an item to the Scrapbook, open and select it in the application in which it was created, choose Edit > Copy to copy it to the Clipboard, switch to the Scrapbook, and choose Edit > Paste (**Figure 13**) to paste it into the Scrapbook (**Figure 14**).

   ▲ To use a Scrapbook item in another document, display the item you want to use, choose Edit > Copy (**Figure 13**) to copy it to the Clipboard, switch to the document in which you want to paste the item, and choose Edit > Paste to paste it into the document.

   ▲ To remove an item from the Scrapbook, display the item you want to remove and choose Edit > Cut (**Figure 13**).

✔ Tips

■ You can use the Scrapbook to store frequently used formatted text, graphics, movies, and sounds.

■ I tell you about the Copy, Cut, and Paste commands in **Chapter 7**.

■ The contents of the Scrapbook are automatically saved when you close it.

Stickies

Stickies are computerized sticky notes that you can use to place reminders on your screen.

To use Stickies

1. Choose Apple menu > Stickies (**Figure 1**). A Stickies note window should appear (**Figure 15**); if one doesn't appear, choose File > New Note (**Figure 20**) or press ⌘ ⌘N.

2. Type the text that you want to include in the note (**Figure 16**).

3. To change the style of note text, choose Note > Text Style (**Figure 17**) or press ⌘ ⌘T. Select font, size, and style options in the Text Style dialog box that appears (**Figure 18**). Then click OK. All the text in the note changes.

4. To change the color of the note, choose a color from the Color menu (**Figure 19**).

✔ Tips

- You can use options under the File menu (**Figure 20**) to create a new note, save all notes, or print notes.

- If you close a Stickies note, a dialog box like the one in **Figure 21** tells you it will be deleted from the Desktop and offers to save its contents to a text file. If you click Save, use the Save As dialog box that appears to save the note as text.

- Stickies notes remain on the Desktop until you quit Stickies.

- When you quit Stickies, all notes are automatically saved to disk.

- The first time you quit Stickies, a dialog box like the one in **Figure 22** lets you specify whether you want Stickies to automatically appear on your Desktop when you restart your computer.

Close box   Zoom box

Figure 15
An empty
Stickies note.

— Size box

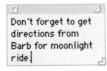

Figure 16
Stickies notes
are perfect for
reminders.

Don't forget to get directions from Barb for moonlight ride

Figure 17 Choose Text Style from the Note menu.

Figure 18
Use the Text Style
dialog box to
format the text in
a note.

Figure 19
Use the Color
menu to change
the color of a note.

Figure 20
Use the File
menu to
create, save,
and print
notes.

Figure 21 This dialog box appears when you click a note's close box.

Figure 22 This dialog box appears the first time you quit Stickies.

Figure 23 The AppleCD Audio Player's icon can be found in the AppleCD Audio Player ƒ folder.

Figure 24 The controls on AppleCD Audio Player look a lot like the ones you'd find on a regular CD player.

Figure 25 AppleCD Audio Player's window expanded to show the play list.

Figure 26 If you enter CD and track information, it will automatically appear the next time you play the CD.

AppleCD Audio Player

AppleCD Audio Player enables you to play audio compact discs on your CD-ROM drive.

✔ Tip

- You insert an audio CD disc just like you insert a CD-ROM disc. I tell you how in **Chapter 3**.

To open AppleCD Audio Player

1. Open the AppleCD Audio Player ƒ folder (**Figure 23**) inside the Applications folder (**Figure 3**) on your hard disk.

2. Double-click the AppleCD Audio Player icon (**Figure 23**).

   The AppleCD Audio Player window appears (**Figure 24**).

✔ Tip

- The AppleCD Audio Player window's status area is blank when no audio CD is in the CD-ROM drive.

To show the play list

Click the Show/Hide Track List control button (**Figure 24**). The window expands to show the play list (**Figure 25**).

✔ Tip

- If desired, you can enter the name of the CD and each CD track in the edit boxes of AppleCD Audio Player. Click a box to select it, then type in the appropriate information. **Figure 26** shows an example. The information you enter is saved to a preferences file so it appears automatically when you play the CD.

APPLECD AUDIO PLAYER

To control audio CD play

Click the control buttons (**Figure 24**) to control the play of an audio CD:

◆ **Normal** plays CD tracks in order.

◆ **Shuffle** plays CD tracks in random order.

◆ **Program** plays CD tracks in the order you specify in the Playlist (see below).

◆ **Repeat** plays the CD until you stop it.

◆ **Stop** stops play.

◆ **Play/Pause** starts play or, if the CD is already playing, pauses play.

◆ **Previous** plays the previous track.

◆ **Next** plays the next track.

◆ **Scan Backward** quickly reverses the CD.

◆ **Scan Forward** fast forwards the CD.

◆ **Eject** ejects the CD.

◆ **Volume** control changes play volume; drag the slider up or down.

To program CD play

1. If necessary, display the play list (**Figures 25** and **26**).

2. Click the Program button (**Figure 24**). The Playlist area changes to display Tracks and Playlist (**Figure 27**).

3. Drag a track from the Tracks side to the Playlist side (**Figure 28**). When you release the mouse button, the track appears on the Playlist side (**Figure 29**).

4. Repeat step 3 for each track that you want to include in the program.

To customize AppleCD Audio Player appearance & sound

Under the Options menu, choose customization commands from the Window Color (**Figure 30**), Indicator Color (**Figure 31**), and Sound (**Figure 32**) submenus.

Figure 27 Click the Program button to program CD play.

Figure 28 Drag a track from the list on the left to the list on the right.

Figure 29 When you release the mouse button, the track appears in the list on the right side.

Figure 30 The Window Color submenu lets you change the color of the window.

Figure 31 The Indicator Color submenu lets you change the color of the numbers and track names.

Figure 32 The Sound submenu lets you change the way stereo sound is played.

Figure 33
The Alert Sounds window lists all installed alert sounds.

Figure 34 Use the Recording dialog box to record, play, and save a sound.

Figure 35
You'll see this dialog box when you save an alert sound.

Figure 36
The Alert Sounds window also lists the sounds you add.

SimpleSound

SimpleSound is an application you can use to select an alert sound or add sounds to your System.

✔ Tip

■ To record sounds with your Macintosh, you must have a microphone.

To select an alert sound

1. Double-click the SimpleSound icon inside the Applications folder (**Figure 3**) on your hard disk. The Alert Sounds window appears (**Figure 33**).

2. Click to select the name of the sound that you want. It plays back so you can hear it.

3. Close the Alert Sounds window to save your selection.

To add an alert sound

1. Double-click the SimpleSound icon inside the Applications folder (**Figure 3**) on your hard disk. The Alert Sounds window appears (**Figure 33**).

2. Click Add to display the Recording dialog box (**Figure 34**).

3. Click Record, and record a sound with your microphone.

4. When you are finished recording the sound, click Stop.

5. To play back the sound, click Play.

6. To save the sound, click Save.

7. A dialog box like the one in **Figure 35** appears. Enter a name for the sound, and click OK.

   The sound you recorded appears in the Alert Sounds window (**Figure 36**).

To create a sound file

1. Double-click the SimpleSound icon inside the Applications folder (**Figure 3**) on your hard disk. The Alert Sounds window appears (**Figure 33**).

2. Choose File > New (**Figure 37**) or press ⌘ ⌘ N to display the Recording dialog box (**Figure 34**).

3. Click Record, and record a sound with your microphone.

4. When you are finished recording the sound, click Stop.

5. To play back the sound, click Play.

6. To save the sound, click Save.

7. A sound document window (**Figure 38**) and a Save As dialog box (**Figure 39**) appear. Use the Save As dialog box to save the file to disk.

   A sound document icon (**Figure 40**) appears in the Finder in the location in which you saved the sound file.

✔ Tips

- I tell you how to use the Save As dialog box in **Chapter 5**.

- You can play a sound file by double-clicking its icon.

To delete an alert sound

1. Double-click the SimpleSound icon inside the Applications folder (**Figure 3**) on your hard disk. The Alert Sounds window appears (**Figure 33**).

2. Select the sound that you want to delete, and click Remove.

3. A confirmation dialog box appears (**Figure 41**). Click OK.

   The alert sound is removed from the list.

Figure 37
Choose New from the File menu.

Figure 38
A sound document window...

Figure 39 ...and a Save As dialog box appear when you save a sound file.

Sound of Silence

Figure 40
A sound document icon.

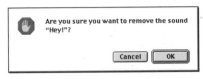

Figure 41 This confirmation dialog box appears when you try to delete a sound.

USING SIMPLESOUND

Figure 42 You can find the QuickTime files in the QuickTime folder inside the Applications folder on your hard disk.

Figure 43
Select the icon for the QuickTime movie that you want to open.

Figure 44 The first frame of the movie appears in a QuickTime Player window.

Figure 45
QuickTime Player's File menu.

QuickTime, QuickTime Player, & PictureViewer

QuickTime is a video and audio technology developed by Apple Computer, Inc. Mac OS uses the QuickTime System extension to understand files in QuickTime format.

QuickTime Player and PictureViewer are applications you can use to work with QuickTime and graphics files. You can find these programs in the QuickTime folder (**Figure 42**) inside the Applications folder (**Figure 3**) on your hard disk. Mac OS 9 also includes the QuickTime Plugin file for your Web browser so you can view QuickTime files on the Web.

On the next few pages, I tell you what you need to know to get started using QuickTime.

✔ Tips

■ QuickTime version 4, which is included with Mac OS 9, has fewer features than the Pro version, which also enables you to edit and save QuickTime files.

■ I tell you more about System extensions in **Chapter 14** and about the Web in **Chapter 11**.

To open a QuickTime movie

Double-click the QuickTime movie's icon.

or

1. Select the icon for the movie that you want to open (**Figure 43**).

2. Choose File > Open, or press ⌘O.

QuickTime Player launches. The movie's first frame appears in a window (**Figure 44**).

✔ Tip

■ You can also open a QuickTime movie by using the Open command on QuickTime Player's File menu (**Figure 45**). I explain how to use the Open dialog box in **Chapter 5**.

To control movie play

You can click buttons in the QuickTime Player window (**Figure 44**) to control movie play:

◆ **Play** starts playing the movie.

◆ **Pause** pauses the movie.

◆ **Time line** tracks movie progress. By dragging the slider, you can scroll through the movie without sound.

◆ **Volume** changes movie volume; drag the control up or down.

If you click the Controls button in the QuickTime Player window (**Figure 44**), the window expands to display the Controls Tray (**Figure 46**). You can then use the following buttons to control movie play:

◆ **Fast Rewind** plays the movie backward quickly, with sound.

◆ **Fast Forward** plays the movie forward quickly, with sound.

◆ **Step Back** moves backward through the movie, one frame at a time, without sound.

◆ **Step Forward** moves forward through the movie, one frame at a time, without sound.

◆ **Go To Start** displays the first movie frame.

◆ **Go To End** displays the last movie frame.

◆ **Balance**, **Bass**, and **Treble** enable you to adjust the sound balance and quality. Click the buttons on either side of a control to make an adjustment.

✔ Tip

■ Clicking the Info button in the QuickTime Player window displays information about the movie (**Figure 47**).

To specify movie size

Select a size option from the Movie menu (**Figure 48**). The size of the movie's window changes accordingly.

Figure 46 Clicking the Controls button displays additional controls for playing a movie.

Fast Rewind — *Step Back* — *Go To Start* — *Controls Tray* — *Sound balance and quality controls*

Fast Forward — *Step Forward* — *Go To End*

Figure 47 When you click the Info button in the QuickTime Player window, the window expands to display the copyright and other information.

Figure 48 Options under the Movie menu let you change the viewing size of a QuickTime movie.

Figure 49
The Favorites menu offers commands for working with your favorite QuickTime files.

Figure 50 The Favorites Drawer displays icons for all of your favorite QuickTime files. Here's what the QuickTime Player looks like with a streaming video channel playing.

To add a QuickTime file as a favorite

1. Open the QuickTime file you want to add as a favorite (**Figure 44**).

2. Choose Favorites > Add Favorite (**Figure 49**), or press ⌃⌘D.

   The file is added as a favorite at the bottom of the Favorites menu.

✔ Tip

- QuickTime Player's favorites feature makes it quick and easy to play your favorite QuickTime files.

To play a favorite QuickTime file

Choose the file you want to play from the Favorites menu (**Figure 49**).

or

1. Choose Favorites > Open Favorites Drawer (**Figure 49**), press ⌃⌘], or drag the Favorites Drawer tab (**Figure 44**) down. The Favorites Drawer slides out of the bottom of the QuickTime Player window (**Figure 50**).

2. Click the icon for the file you want to play.

✔ Tips

- QuickTime is preconfigured with a number of Favorites for *streaming* (or live) audio or video on the Web (**Figure 50**). If you have an Internet connection, you may want to explore these "QuickTime Channels" on your own. I tell you about the Internet in **Chapter 11**.

- To close the Favorites Drawer, choose Favorites > Close Favorites Drawer, press ⌃⌘], or drag the Favorites Drawer tab (**Figure 50**) up.

To open a graphic file

Drag the icon for the graphic file onto the icon for the PictureViewer application (**Figure 51**). PictureViewer launches and displays the graphic file (**Figure 52**).

✔ Tip

■ You can also open a graphic file by using the Open command on PictureViewer's File menu (**Figure 53**). I explain how to use the Open dialog box in **Chapter 5**.

To specify picture size

Select a size option from PictureViewer's Image menu (**Figure 54**). The size of the graphic's window changes accordingly.

To update QuickTime

1. Double-click the QuickTime Updater icon in the QuickTime window (**Figure 42**).

2. The QuickTime Updater window appears (**Figure 55**). Read the information in the window and click Continue.

3. Wait while the QuickTime Updater connects to the Internet and searches for updates. When it's finished, it displays a window like the one in **Figure 56**. Follow the instructions in that window to install new software or quit the QuickTime Updater.

✔ Tip

■ You must have Internet access to update QuickTime with the QuickTime Updater.

Figure 51 Drag a graphic file's icon onto the Picture-Viewer icon to open the file with PictureViewer.

Figure 52
The graphic file opens in a window like this. (This is a picture of yours truly with my favorite horse, Misty.)

Figure 53
PictureViewer's
File menu...

Figure 54 ...and
Image menu.

Figure 55 Use the QuickTime Updater window to check Apple's Web site for QuickTime updates.

OPENING GRAPHICS, UPDATING QUICKTIME

Figure 56 Follow the instructions in this window to either update your QuickTime files or if no update is available (as in this case) quit the installer.

Figure 57
The Registration options in the QuickTime Settings control panel window.

Figure 58 Follow the instructions in this window to purchase a QuickTime Pro registration number or key.

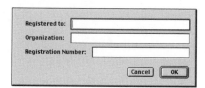

Figure 59 Enter your Name, Organization, and the Registration Number provided by Apple.

To upgrade to QuickTime Pro

1. If you have Internet access, launch QuickTime Player and choose Edit > Preferences > Registration. In the QuickTime Settings window that appears (**Figure 57**), click the Register On-line button. Then wait while your computer connects to the Internet. Follow the instructions that appear in your Web browser window (**Figure 58**) to obtain a QuickTime Pro registration number. You can then disconnect from the Internet and quit your Web browser software.

   or

   If you do not have Internet access, call *1-888-295-0648* to obtain an access key.

2. From within QuickTime Player, choose Edit > Preferences > Registration to display the QuickTime Settings window (**Figure 57**).

3. Click the Enter Registration button to display the Registration window (**Figure 59**).

4. Enter your Name, Organization, and the Registration Number provided by Apple in the appropriate edit boxes.

5. Click OK. The information you entered appears in the QuickTime Settings window, along with the words *QuickTime: Pro Player Edition*.

6. Close the window.

✔ Tips

- To learn more about QuickTime Pro, use your Web browser to visit *http://www.apple.com/quicktime/upgrade/*.

- QuickTime Pro costs $29.99. You must provide credit card information when requesting a registration number.

Apple System Profiler

Apple System Profiler (**Figure 60**) is an application that can provide information about your computer, its software, and its network and Internet connections. Each tab on its window displays different information:

◆ **System Profile** (**Figure 60**) provides information about your computer's hardware, Mac OS version, printer, and network connections.

◆ **Devices and Volumes** provides information about devices attached to your computer and lists all accessible storage media.

◆ **Control Panels** provides information about all installed control panels.

◆ **Extensions** provides information about all installed extensions.

◆ **Applications** provides information about all installed applications on the startup disk.

◆ **System Folders** provides information about all System Folders on your startup disk (there should be only one).

✔ Tips

■ The information available from Apple System Profiler is especially useful when you need technical support to solve a problem.

■ I cover networking in **Chapter 10**, connecting to the Internet in **Chapter 11**, control panels and extensions in **Chapters 14** and **15**, and applications in **Chapter 5**.

Figure 60 The Apple System Profiler's System Profile tab provides information about your computer's hardware, Mac OS version, printer, and network connections.

Figure 61 When you click a right-pointing triangle, you expand the item to see its details.

Figure 62 Click an item in a list to learn more about it.

Figure 63 Use this dialog box to select the items that you want to include in a report.

Figure 64 Here's a report for the newest member of my Macintosh family.

To get system information with Apple System Profiler

1. Choose Apple menu > Apple System Profiler (**Figure 1**). The Apple System Profiler window appears (**Figure 60**).

2. Click the tab for the type of information you want to view.

✔ Tips

- You can click the triangle to the left of an item to expand (**Figure 61**) or collapse the item.

- You can click an item in a list to learn more about it (**Figure 62**).

To create a report of system information

1. Choose File > New Report, or press ⌘ N.

2. In the New Report dialog box that appears (**Figure 63**), turn on the check boxes for the information you want to include in the report.

3. Click OK.

A system report window appears on screen (**Figure 64**).

✔ Tip

- You can use the File menu's Save and Print commands to save and print reports you create. I tell you about saving documents in **Chapter 5** and about printing in **Chapter 9**.

USING APPLE SYSTEM PROFILER

Disk First Aid

Disk First Aid is a utility that enables you to check for and repair minor directory damage on your hard disk caused by bad media, crashes, improper shutdowns, and other problems.

✔ Tip

■ It's a good idea to use Disk First Aid to verify all your important disks on a regular basis—at least once a month.

To verify or repair a disk

1. Open the Disk First Aid icon, which can be found in the Utilities folder (**Figure 65**) on your hard disk. The Disk First Aid window appears (**Figure 66**). It displays all mounted disks and provides information about what it does.

2. Select the disks you want to verify or repair.

3. If you select a disk with open files or a write-protected disk, a dialog box appears, telling you that certain disks cannot be repaired. Click OK to dismiss it.

4. To verify the selected disks, click Verify or press [Return] or [Enter].

   or

   To repair the selected disks, click Repair.

5. Wait while Disk First Aid checks or checks and repairs the selected disks. You can monitor its progress in the bottom half of the Disk First Aid window (**Figure 67**). When it is finished, the condition of the disk appears in bold in the window (**Figure 68**).

✔ Tips

■ I tell you about mounting disks in **Chapter 3**.

■ To select more than one disk, hold down [Shift] while clicking each disk.

■ The Repair button will be gray if you selected a disk that cannot be repaired.

Figure 65
You can find Mac OS utilities in the Utilities folder.

Figure 66 The Disk First Aid window.

Figure 67 You can monitor Disk First Aid's progress in the bottom of its window.

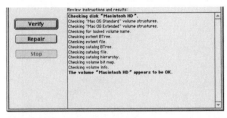

Figure 68 Disk First Aid's diagnosis appears in bold in the Disk First Aid window.

■ You can choose File > Save Results to save a report of Disk First Aid's results.

■ You can choose Option > Erase Disk to erase a selected disk. Just be sure to select the correct disk!

Figure 69
Open the Drive
Drive Setup Setup icon.

Figure 70 In this example, Drive Setup has found my internal hard disk, CD-ROM drive, and Zip drive (which is set up as the startup disk).

Figure 71 When you select a disk, a window at the bottom of the Drive Setup window tells you whether you can initialize it.

Figure 72 Click Initialize in the Initialize dialog box only if you're sure you want to erase the disk.

Drive Setup

Drive Setup is a utility that enables you to initialize a hard disk, install or update a disk driver, and test a disk.

✔ Tips

- ■ Drive Setup is not compatible with all hard disks. It should, however, work with the hard disk inside your Macintosh.

- ■ You should use the disk utility software that came with your external hard disk, Zip or Jaz disk, or other storage device to prepare that device's media for use.

To launch Drive Setup

Open the Drive Setup icon (**Figure 69**) in the Drive Setup ƒ folder inside the Utilities folder (**Figure 65**) on your hard disk. The Drive Setup window appears. It displays all storage devices connected to your computer (**Figure 70**).

To initialize a disk

1. Select the disk that you want to initialize by clicking its name in the Drive Setup window (**Figure 71**).

2. Click Initialize. The Initialize dialog box appears (**Figure 72**).

3. If you are absolutely sure you want to erase the disk, click Initialize.

4. Wait while Drive Setup initializes the disk. This can take a while, depending on the size of the disk.

✔ Tips

- ■ Initializing a disk completely erases it. If a disk contains important files, back them up *before* initializing the disk!

- ■ You cannot initialize a disk if file sharing is turned on. I tell you about file sharing in **Chapter 10**.

- ■ You cannot initialize the startup disk.

To update a disk's driver

1. In the Drive Setup window (**Figure 71**), select the disk whose driver you want to update by clicking its name.

2. Choose Functions > Update Driver (**Figure 73**).

3. Wait a moment while Drive Setup updates the driver on the disk. When it is finished, a dialog box like the one in **Figure 74** appears. Click OK.

4. Restart your computer to automatically load the updated driver.

✔ Tips

■ Every hard disk or other high-capacity magnetic storage media has a driver written to the disk. The driver tells the computer how to read the disk.

■ You should update the driver on your hard disk whenever you install a new version of Mac OS.

To test a disk

1. Select the disk that you want to test by clicking its name in the Drive Setup window (**Figure 71**).

2. Choose Functions > Test Disk (**Figure 73**).

3. A dialog box like the one in **Figure 75** appears. It explains what the test does. Click Start to dismiss the dialog box and begin the test.

4. Wait while the test is conducted. You can monitor its progress in the Drive Setup window (**Figure 76**). When the test is finished, its results appear in the bottom of the Drive Setup window (**Figure 77**).

✔ Tip

■ A bad block is a portion of the disk that is badly corrupted and can no longer be used.

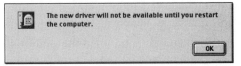

Figure 73
Drive Setup's
Functions menu.

Figure 74 This dialog box appears after the driver has been updated.

Figure 75 The Test Disk dialog box explains what the test is for.

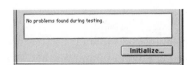

Figure 76 You can monitor the test progress in the Drive Setup window.

Figure 77 Test results appear in the bottom of the Drive Setup window.

UPDATING DISK DRIVERS, TESTING DISKS

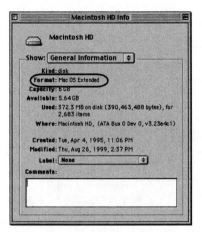

Figure 78 The Info window for a disk displays the disk's format.

Mac OS Extended Format (or HFS Plus)

With Mac OS 8.1, Apple introduced *Mac OS Extended Format*, or *HFS Plus*. Designed for high-capacity hard disks, HFS Plus decreases the minimum size of an allocation block, thus decreasing the amount of disk space that small files require. The net effect: You can store more information on disk.

✔ Tips

- To use HFS Plus, the computer to which the hard disk is directly connected must have Mac OS 8.1 or later installed.

- Do not use HFS Plus to format removable media (Zip, Jaz, etc.) that is shared with computers running Mac OS versions prior to 8.1. Those computers will not be able to read individual files on HFS Plus disks.

- HFS Plus works best with hard disks that are 1 GB or larger in capacity.

- The "old" format for hard disks that works with all versions of the System software is now called *Mac OS Standard Format* (or just plain *HFS*).

- You can identify a disk's format by checking its Info window (**Figure 78**). I tell you about the Info window in **Chapter 5**.

- In case you're wondering, HFS stands for *Hierarchical File System*.

MAC OS EXTENDED FORMAT (OR HFS PLUS)

To format a disk with HFS Plus

1. Back up all data on the hard disk you plan to format as HFS Plus. *Do not skip this step!*

2. In the Finder, select the icon for the disk you plan to format as HFS Plus.

3. Choose Special > Erase Disk (**Figure 79**).

4. The Erase Disk dialog box appears (**Figure 80**). Choose Mac OS Extended from the Format pop-up menu (**Figure 81**).

5. **Stop!** Did you complete step 1? If not, click Cancel and start over again. If your data is backed up, click the Erase button. The selected disk is erased and formatted as HFS Plus.

6. Restore the backed up files to the erased hard disk.

✔ Tips

- If you fail to back up the data on a disk you format as HFS Plus, all the data on the disk will be lost forever.

- To format a startup disk as HFS Plus, you must start your computer with another disk, preferably the Mac OS 9 CD-ROM disc. I tell you how to select a startup disk in **Chapter 14**.

- You may also be able to use Drive Setup to format a hard disk with HFS Plus formatting. Follow the instructions on page 119 to initialize the disk, but click Custom Setup in the Initialize dialog box (**Figure 72**) to display the Custom Setup dialog box (**Figure 82**). Choose Mac OS Extended from the Type pop-up menu (**Figure 83**), and click OK. Then complete the initialization process.

Figure 79 Choose Erase Disk from the Special menu.

Figure 80 The Erase Disk dialog box.

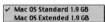

Figure 81 The two options on the Format pop-up menu.

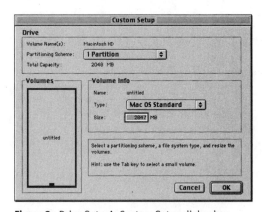

Figure 82 Drive Setup's Custom Setup dialog box.

Figure 83 Choose Mac OS Extended from the Type pop-up menu.

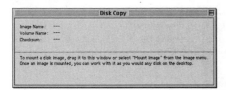

Figure 84 Disk Copy's window.

Figure 85 Drag the disk icon into the Disk Copy window.

Figure 86 Use this dialog box to save the disk image.

Figure 87 Disk Copy displays this dialog box while it works.

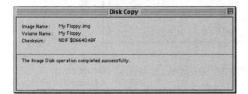

Figure 88 Disk Copy's window provides status information.

Disk Copy

Disk Copy is a utility that you can use to create and mount disk images. A *disk image* is a single file that contains everything on a disk. Once you have a disk image file, you can mount it on your desktop just like any other disk—even if you don't have a floppy disk drive!—or create a floppy disk from the image.

✔ Tips

- Disk images are commonly used by computer companies to distribute software updates and drivers on the Web.

- I tell you about mounting disks in **Chapter 3**.

To launch Disk Copy

Open the Disk Copy icon, which can be found in the Utilities folder (**Figure 65**) on your hard disk. The Disk Copy window appears (**Figure 84**).

To make a disk image

1. Drag the icon for the disk you want to make an image of into the Disk Image window (**Figure 85**).

2. Use the Save Disk Image As dialog box that appears (**Figure 86**) to name and save the disk image file.

3. Wait while Disk Copy reads and saves the disk image file. While it works, it displays the Imaging Disk dialog box (**Figure 87**). When it's finished, the Disk Copy window displays information about the task (**Figure 88**).

✔ Tips

- You can also create a disk image by dragging a disk's icon onto the Disk Copy icon. Disk Copy launches, creates the disk image, and quits.

- If you leave the Mount Image check box turned on, Disk Copy will mount the disk image after it creates it.

To mount a disk image

Double-click the disk image file's icon (**Figure 89**). A dialog box like the one in **Figure 90** appears to display the progress. When it disappears, the disk image mounts on the desktop as a disk (**Figure 91**).

To create a floppy from a disk image

1. Hold down Option while double-clicking a disk image icon (**Figure 89**).

2. A dialog box like the one in **Figure 92** appears briefly. Then the Making Floppy dialog box shown in **Figure 93** appears. Insert a floppy disk in your disk drive.

3. If the floppy you insert is not blank, a dialog box like the one in **Figure 94** appears. To overwrite the floppy with the contents of the disk image file, click Yes.

4. Wait while Disk Copy formats and copies to the disk. While it is working, it displays a dialog box like the one in **Figure 95**. When it is finished, it ejects the newly copied disk.

MOUNTING DISK IMAGES, MAKING FLOPPIES

Figure 89
A disk image file, saved to the desktop.

Figure 90 A progress dialog box like this one appears while the image is being mounted.

Figure 91
The disk image's disk appears on the desktop. It can be opened like any other disk.

Figure 92
Disk Copy displays this dialog box while it reads the disk image file.

Figure 93
Then it tells you what kind of disk to insert.

Figure 94
You may need to confirm that you want to replace the disk's contents.

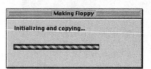

Figure 95
A dialog box like this appears while Disk Copy makes the floppy.

USING SIMPLETEXT

Figure 1
The SimpleText
application icon.

SimpleText

Figure 2
A SimpleText read-only
document's icon.

About Mac OS 9

Figure 3
A standard SimpleText
document's icon.

Letter to Janet

SimpleText

SimpleText (**Figure 1**) is a basic text editing application that comes with Mac OS. Simple-Text lets you:

◆ Create, open, edit, and print text documents, including the "Read Me" files that come with many applications.

◆ Open and print PICT, GIF, and other graphic format documents and QuickTime movies.

In this chapter, I tell you how to use Simple-Text to create, edit, format, open, and save documents.

✔ Tips

■ QuickTime Player, which also comes with Mac OS, offers more features than Simple-Text for working with QuickTime movies. I tell you about QuickTime and QuickTime Player in **Chapter 6**.

■ SimpleText read-only documents cannot be edited. You can identify a SimpleText read only document by its icon, which looks like a newspaper (**Figure 2**). A regular SimpleText document icon looks like a piece of paper with its corner folded down (**Figure 3**).

■ Although SimpleText offers many of the basic features found in a word processing application, it falls far short of the feature list of word processors such as Microsoft Word and the word processing components of integrated software such as AppleWorks.

■ If you're new to Mac OS, don't skip this chapter. Not only does it explain how to use SimpleText but it provides instructions for basic text editing skills—like text entry and the Copy, Cut, and Paste commands—that you'll use in all Mac OS-compatible applications.

Launching & Quitting SimpleText

Like any other application, you must launch SimpleText before you can use it. This loads it into RAM so your computer can work with it. Likewise, when you're finished using Simple-Text, its important to quit it to clear it from RAM.

To launch SimpleText

Double-click the SimpleText application icon.

or

1. Select the SimpleText application icon (**Figure 1**).

2. Choose File > Open (**Figure 4**), or press ⌘⌘O.

SimpleText launches. An untitled document window appears (**Figure 5**).

✔ Tip

■ As illustrated in **Figure 5**, the SimpleText document window has the same standard window parts found in Finder windows. I tell you how to use Finder windows in **Chapter 2**; SimpleText and other application windows work the same way.

To quit SimpleText

1. Choose File > Quit (**Figure 6**), or press ⌘⌘Q.

2. If unsaved documents are open, a dialog box like the one in **Figure 7** appears for each unsaved document.

   ▲ Click Save or press Return or Enter to save the document.

   ▲ Click Don't Save to quit without saving the document.

   ▲ Click Cancel or press Esc to return to the application without quitting.

SimpleText closes all windows and quits.

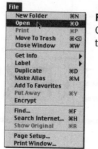

Figure 4
Choose Open from the File menu.

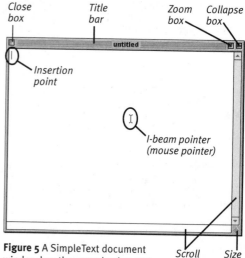

Close box · Title bar · Zoom box · Collapse box · Insertion point · I-beam pointer (mouse pointer) · Scroll bars · Size box

Figure 5 A SimpleText document window has the same basic parts as a Finder window.

Figure 6
Choose Quit from the File menu.

Figure 7 A dialog box like this appears when you quit SimpleText and unsaved documents are open.

✔ Tip

■ I tell you more about saving SimpleText documents later in this chapter.

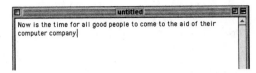

Figure 8 The text you type appears at the blinking insertion point.

Entering & Editing Text

You enter text into a SimpleText document by typing it in. Don't worry about making mistakes; you can fix them as you type or when you're finished. This section tells you how.

✔ Tip

■ The text entry and editing techniques covered in this section work exactly the same in most word processors, as well as many other Mac OS applications.

To enter text

Type the text you want to enter. It appears at the blinking insertion point (**Figure 8**).

✔ Tips

■ It is not necessary to press Return at the end of a line. When the text you type reaches the end of the line, it automatically begins a new line. This is called *word wrap* and is a feature of all word processors.

■ The insertion point moves as you type.

■ To correct an error as you type, press Delete. This key deletes the character to the left of the insertion point.

ENTERING TEXT

To move the insertion point

Press ←, →, ↑, or ↓ to move the insertion point left, right, up, or down one character or line at a time.

or

1. Position the mouse pointer, which looks like an I-beam pointer, where you want the insertion point to appear (**Figure 9**).

2. Click the mouse button once. The insertion point appears at the mouse pointer (**Figure 10**).

✔ Tips

- Since the text you type appears at the insertion point, it's a good idea to know where the insertion point is *before* you start typing.

- When moving the insertion point with the mouse, you must click to complete the move. If you simply point with the I-beam pointer, the insertion point will stay right where it is (**Figure 9**).

To insert text

1. Position the insertion point where you want the text to appear (**Figure 11**).

2. Type the text that you want to insert. The text is inserted at the insertion point (**Figure 12**).

✔ Tip

- Word wrap changes automatically to accommodate inserted text.

Figure 9 Position the mouse pointer...

Figure 10 ...and click to move the insertion point.

Figure 11 Position the insertion point...

Figure 12 ...and type in the text that you want to appear.

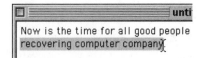

Figure 13 Drag the mouse pointer over the text that you want to select.

Figure 14 Double-click the word that you want to select.

Figure 15
Choose Select
All from the
Edit menu.

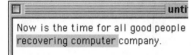

Figure 16 Select the text that you want to delete.

Figure 17 When you press (Delete), the selected text disappears.

Figure 18 Select the text that you want to replace.

Figure 19 The text you type replaces the selected text.

To select text

To select any amount of text, drag the I-beam pointer over the text (**Figure 13**).

or

To select a single word, double-click the word (**Figure 14**).

or

To select the entire document, choose Edit > Select All (**Figure 15**) or press ⌃⌘A.

The text you select becomes highlighted (**Figures 13** and **14**).

✔ Tips

- There are other selection techniques in SimpleText and other applications. These are the basic techniques and they work in every application.

- In some applications, double-clicking a word also selects the space after the word.

To delete text

1. Select the text that you want to delete (**Figure 16**).

2. Press (Delete) or (Del). The selected text disappears (**Figure 17**).

✔ Tip

- You can delete a character to the left of the insertion point by pressing (Delete). You can delete a character to the right of the insertion point by pressing (Del).

To replace text

1. Select the text that you want to replace (**Figure 18**).

2. Type the new text. The selected text is replaced by what you type (**Figure 19**).

Formatting Text

SimpleText also offers some basic formatting features that you can use to change the appearance of text.

To apply a different font to text

1. Select the text to which you want to apply a different font (**Figure 20**).

2. Choose a font from the Font menu (**Figure 21**). The font you chose is applied to the selected text (**Figure 22**).

✔ Tips

■ Generally speaking, a *font* is a style of typeface.

■ The Font menu displays all fonts that are properly installed in your System. Your Font menu may differ from the one illustrated in **Figure 21**.

■ A check mark appears on the Font menu beside the font currently applied to the selected text (**Figure 21**).

■ I tell you more about fonts in **Chapter 14**.

To change the size of text characters

1. Select the text that you want to resize (**Figure 22**).

2. Choose a size from the Size menu (**Figure 23**). The size you chose is applied to the selected text (**Figure 24**).

✔ Tips

■ The larger the text size, the less text appears on screen or on a printed page.

■ A check mark appears on the Size menu beside the size currently applied to the selected text (**Figure 23**).

Figure 20 Select the text to which you want to apply a different font.

Figure 21 Choose the font that you want to apply.

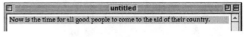

Figure 22 The font you chose is applied.

Figure 23 Choose the size that you want to apply.

Figure 24 The size you chose is applied.

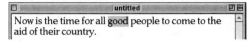

Now is the time for all good people to come to the aid of their country.

Figure 25 Select the text to which you want to apply a style.

Figure 26 Choose the style that you want to apply.

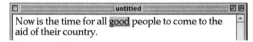

Now is the time for all good people to come to the aid of their country.

Figure 27 The style you chose is applied.

Figure 28 A check mark appears beside the name of each style applied to selected text.

Figure 29 Choose Undo from the Edit menu.

To apply a different style to text

1. Select the text to which you want to apply a different style (**Figure 25**).

2. Choose a style from the Style menu (**Figure 26**). The style you chose is applied to the selected text (**Figure 27**).

✔ Tips

- You can apply more than one style to text (**Figure 28**). Simply select each style you want to apply.

- A check mark appears on the Style menu beside each style applied to a selection (**Figure 28**).

- The Plain Text style removes all other styles from text.

- To remove an applied style (except Plain Text), choose it from the Style menu again.

- Some text styles can be applied with keyboard commands: $⌘T$ for Plain Text, $⌘B$ for Bold, $⌘I$ for Italic, and $⌘U$ for Underline.

Undoing Actions

The Undo command enables you to reverse your last action, thus offering an easy way to fix errors immediately after you make them.

To undo the last action

Choose Undo from the Edit menu (**Figure 29**), or press $⌘Z$. The last thing you did is undone.

✔ Tips

- The Undo command is available in most applications and can always be found at the top of the Edit menu.

- Although some programs, like Microsoft Word 98 and Adobe Photoshop 5, offer multiple levels of undo, most programs let you undo only the very last thing you did.

Copy, Cut, & Paste

The Copy, Cut, and Paste commands enable you to duplicate or move document contents. Text that is copied or cut is placed on the Clipboard, where it can be viewed if desired.

✔ Tip

- Almost all Mac OS applications include the Copy, Cut, and Paste commands on the Edit menu. These commands work very much the same in all applications that support them.

To copy text

1. Select the text that you want to copy (**Figure 30**).

2. Choose Edit > Copy (**Figure 31**), or press ⌘ C.

   The text is copied to the Clipboard so it can be pasted elsewhere. The original remains in the document.

To cut text

1. Select the text that you want to cut (**Figure 30**).

2. Choose Edit > Cut (**Figure 31**), or press ⌘ X.

   The text is copied to the Clipboard so it can be pasted elsewhere. The original is removed from the document.

To paste Clipboard contents

1. Position the insertion point where you want the Clipboard contents to appear (**Figure 32**).

2. Choose Edit > Paste (**Figure 31**), or press ⌘ V.

   The Clipboard's contents are pasted into the document (**Figure 33**).

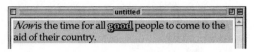
Figure 30 Select the text you want to copy or cut.

Figure 31
The Copy, Cut, and Paste commands are all on the Edit menu.

Figure 32 Position the insertion point where you want the contents of the Clipboard to appear.

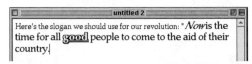
Figure 33 The contents of the Clipboard are pasted into the document.

Figure 34
Choose Show
Clipboard from
the Edit menu.

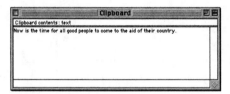

Figure 35 The Clipboard window displays the contents of the Clipboard.

Figure 36
Choose Hide
Clipboard
from the Edit
menu...

Figure 37
...or choose
Close from the
File menu.

To view the Clipboard

Choose Edit > Show Clipboard (**Figure 34**).

✔ Tips

■ The Clipboard window (**Figure 35**) displays the last thing you copied or cut.

■ The Clipboard is shared by all applications. This makes it possible to copy something created in one document or application and paste it in another.

■ Items remain on the Clipboard until you use the Cut or Copy commands again or shut off your computer.

To close the Clipboard

Click the Clipboard window's close box (**Figure 35**).

or

Choose Edit > Hide Clipboard (**Figure 36**).

or

1. If necessary, activate the Clipboard window.

2. Choose File > Close (**Figure 37**), or press ⌃ ⌘ W.

VIEWING THE CLIPBOARD

Find & Replace

SimpleText's Find and Replace commands enable you to quickly locate or replace occurrences of text strings in your document.

Figure 38 You'll find the Find and Replace commands on the Edit menu.

✔ Tip

- Most word processing and page layout applications include find and replace features. Although these features are somewhat limited in SimpleText, full-featured applications such as Microsoft Word and PageMaker enable you to search for text, formatting, and other document elements as well as plain text.

To find text

1. Choose Edit > Find (**Figure 38**), or press ⌘ F. The Find dialog box appears (**Figure 39**).

2. Enter the text that you want to find in the Find what edit box.

3. Click Find. The Find what text is highlighted in the document.

To replace text

1. Choose Edit > Replace (**Figure 38**), or press ⌘ R. The Replace dialog box appears (**Figure 40**).

2. Enter the text that you want to find in the top edit box.

3. Enter the text that you want to replace it with in the bottom edit box.

4. To replace just the next occurrence of the text, click Replace. The text is replaced.

    or

    To replace all occurrences of the text, click Replace All. Every occurrence of the text from the insertion point to the end of the document is replaced.

Figure 39 Use the Find dialog box to enter the text that you want to find.

Figure 40 Use the Replace dialog box to enter the text that you want to find and the text that you want to replace it with.

Figure 41
Once you've entered information in the Find or Replace dialog box, you can use the Find Again or Replace Again commands.

✔ Find & Replace Tips

■ Once you've conducted a search, you can use the Find Again (⌘ G) or Replace Again (⌘ D) commands under the Edit menu (**Figure 41**) to repeat the Find or Replace procedure with the same settings.

■ To find only text that matches the capitalization of the Find what text, turn on the Case Sensitive check box (**Figures 39** and **40**).

■ To continue the search at the beginning of the document, turn on the Wrap-Around Search check box (**Figures 39** and **40**). Otherwise, the search begins at the insertion point and ends at the end of the document.

FINDING & REPLACING TEXT

Speech & Sound

Mac OS includes Text-to-Speech software that makes it possible for your Mac to read the contents of text documents. In addition, if your Mac has a microphone (either built-in or external), you can record sounds. SimpleText supports both of these features.

✔ Tip

■ I explain how to set speech and sound options in **Chapter 14**.

To speak text

1. Select the text you want to hear.

2. Choose Sound > Speak Selection (**Figure 42**), or press ⌃ ⌘ J.

or

1. Make sure no text is selected.

2. Choose Sound > Speak All (**Figure 43**), or press ⌃ ⌘ J.

✔ Tips

■ You can stop text from being spoken by choosing Sound > Stop Speaking (**Figure 44**) or pressing ⌃ ⌘ . .

■ You can change the voice with which text is spoken by choosing a voice from the Voices submenu under the Sound menu (**Figure 45**).

■ I tell you more about speaking text and alerts in **Chapter 14**.

Figure 42
Choose the Speak Selection command to have your computer read selected text...

Figure 43
...or choose the Speak All command to have your computer read all the text in the document.

Figure 44
Choose Stop Speaking to shut your computer up.

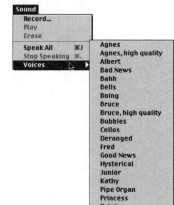

Figure 45
The Voices submenu offers a variety of male and female voices.

Figure 46
Choose Record from the Sound menu.

Figure 47 Use the Recording dialog box to record and save a sound.

Figure 48
Once you've recorded a sound, you can use the Play and Erase commands.

To record & play a sounds

1. Choose Sound > Record (**Figure 46**).

2. Use the Recording dialog box that appears (**Figure 47**) to record a sound.

3. Click the Save button to save the sound in the SimpleText file.

4. Choose Sound > Play (**Figure 48**) to play back the sound.

✔ Tips

■ Your computer must have a microphone (either built-in or external) to record sounds.

■ I explain how to use the Recording dialog box in **Chapter 6**.

■ You can only record one sound per Simple-Text document.

■ To erase the sound, choose Sound > Erase (**Figure 87**).

Saving & Opening Files

When you're finished working with a Simple-Text document, you may want to save it. You can then open it another time to review, edit, or print it.

To save a document for the first time

1. Choose File > Save (**Figure 49**), or press ⌘ ⌘ S .

   or

   Choose File > Save As (**Figure 49**).

2. Use the Save As dialog box that appears (**Figure 50**) to enter a name and select a location for the file.

3. Click Save, or press Return or Enter .

The document is saved with the name you entered in the location you specified. The name of the document appears on the document's title bar.

✔ Tips

- I explain how to use the Save As dialog box in **Chapter 5**.

- There's only one difference between the Save and Save As commands:

  ▲ The Save command opens the Save As dialog box only if the document has never been saved.

  ▲ The Save As command always opens the Save As dialog box.

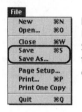

Figure 49
Use the Save and Save As commands to save the active document.

Figure 50 Use the Save As dialog box to set options for saving a file.

To save changes to an existing document

Choose File > Save (**Figure 49**), or press ⌘ ⌘ S.

The document is saved. No dialog box appears.

✔ Tip

■ It's a good idea to save changes to a document frequently as you work with it. This helps prevent loss of data in the event of a system crash or power outage.

To save an existing document with a new name or in a new location

1. Choose File > Save As (**Figure 49**).

2. Use the Save As dialog box that appears (**Figure 50**) to enter a different name or select a different location (or both) for the file.

3. Click Save, or press Return or Enter.

A copy of the document is saved with the name you entered in the location you specified. The new document name appears in the document's title bar. The original document remains untouched.

✔ Tip

■ You can use the Save As command to create a new document based on an existing document—without overwriting the original document with your changes.

SAVING DOCUMENTS

To open a document

1. Choose File > Open (**Figure 51**).

   or

   Press ⌘ O.

2. Use the Open dialog box that appears
   (**Figure 52**) to locate and select the document that you want to open.

3. Click Open, or press Return or Enter.

✔ Tip

■ I explain how to use the Open dialog box in
   Chapter 5.

Figure 51
Choose Open from
the File menu.

Figure 52 Use the Open dialog box to locate and open
a file.

WORKING WITH PC FILES

Working with PC Files

Documents created on a DOS- or Windows-compatible computer aren't the same as those created on a Mac OS-compatible computer. Some differences include:

◆ Disk formats vary based on the operating system that formatted the disk.

◆ Document formats vary based on characters and special codes recognized or required by each operating system.

◆ Document formats also vary based on application codes and formats.

Mac OS 9 comes with File Exchange, a software tool that helps you work with PC files by performing three functions:

◆ Reads PC-formatted disks on your Mac OS computer.

◆ Maps DOS and Windows extensions to Mac OS applications.

◆ Displays a list of the applications that can open a document you double-click if the creator application is not installed on your computer.

I tell you about all these things in this chapter.

✔ Tip

■ If you're interested in running DOS or Windows software on your computer, here are two options:

▲ A DOS compatibility card puts PC chips and circuitry inside your Mac. Orange Micro offers these cards.

▲ Software emulation "fools" PC software into thinking it's running on a PC. Connectix's Virtual PC and Insignia Solutions' SoftWindows are two examples.

Reading PC Disks

File Exchange makes it possible for your Mac OS computer to read PC-formatted disks. It does this automatically without any additional effort on your part. File Exchange, which is automatically installed as part of a standard Mac OS 9 installation, is preconfigured to do this job so there's nothing to set up.

Figure 1
When you insert a PC-formatted disk, its icon appears on the Desktop like any other disk.

✔ Tip

- File Exchange works with all kinds of PC disks, including floppy disks, Zip and Jaz disks, and hard disks connected directly to your computer with a SCSI, USB, or FireWire cable.

To read a PC-formatted disk

1. Insert the PC disk into your disk drive. After a moment, the disk's icon appears on your Desktop (**Figure 1**).

2. Double-click the disk icon to open a window displaying its contents (**Figure 2**).

Figure 2 When you double-click the disk, its files appear as icons in the disk window just like any Mac disk.

✔ Tips

- If you look carefully, you can see the letters *PC* on a PC disk icon (**Figure 1**).

- You can work with a PC-formatted disk just like any other disk. I tell you about working with files and disks in **Chapter 3**.

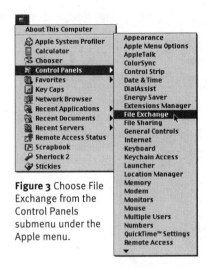

Figure 3 Choose File Exchange from the Control Panels submenu under the Apple menu.

Figure 4 The default settings in the PC Exchange exchange tab of the File Exchange control panel.

PC Exchange

PC Exchange is the part of File Exchange that enables you to *map*, or match, PC file extensions, or suffixes, to Mac OS applications. This does two things:

◆ It enables your Mac to display the correct icons for PC files (**Figure 2**).

◆ It enables you to open a PC file with a specific application by simply double-clicking it.

PC Exchange is preconfigured with many common extension mappings, but you can add, remove, or modify mappings as desired.

✔ Tip

■ Mapping an extension to an application doesn't guarantee that the application can successfully open the document.

To set file mapping options

1. Choose Apple menu > Control Panels > File Exchange (**Figure 3**).

2. If necessary, click the PC Exchange tab in the File Exchange window to display its options (**Figure 4**).

3. Toggle the check boxes near the top of the window as desired:

   ▲ **Map PC extensions for Mac OS file types on PC disks** enables extension mapping. With this option turned off, PC files are treated as text files.

   ▲ **Open unmapped files on any disk using mappings below** uses the PC Exchange extension mappings to open files types that are not mapped in the File Translation tab of the File Exchange control panel.

4. Close File Exchange to save your settings.

To change an extension mapping

1. Choose Apple menu > Control Panels > File Exchange (**Figure 3**).

2. If necessary, click the PC Exchange tab in the File Exchange window to display its options (**Figure 4**).

3. In the scrolling list of mappings, click to select the Extension for which you want to change the mapping (**Figure 5**).

4. Click Change to display the Change Mapping dialog box (**Figure 6**).

5. In the Application list, select the program you want to associate with the extension (**Figure 7**).

6. If necessary, choose a document type from the File Type pop-up menu (**Figure 8**).

7. Click Change. The revised mapping appears in the PC Exchange tab of the File Exchange window (**Figure 9**).

8. Close File Exchange to save your change.

✔ Tips

- The File Type pop-up menu (**Figure 8**) displays only the file types supported by the currently selected application.

- When you change a mapping, the icon for files using that mapping may also change (**Figure 10**).

- Clicking the Show Advanced Options button expands the dialog box to display options of interest to advanced users (**Figure 11**). Coverage of these options are beyond the scope of this book.

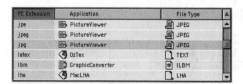
Figure 5 Select the mapping you want to change.

Figure 6 The Change Mapping dialog box.

Figure 7 Select the application you want to associate with the extension.

Figure 8 If necessary, select the type of file from the File Type pop-up list.

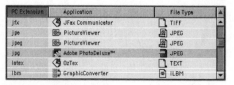
Figure 9 The mapping change appears in the PC Exchange tab of the File Exchange window.

Figure 10 Changing a mapping can change a file's icon.

Figure 11 When you click the Show Advanced Options button, the Change Mapping dialog box expands to show additional options for advanced users.

Figure 12
The Add Mapping dialog box.

To add an extension mapping

1. Choose Apple menu > Control Panels > File Exchange (**Figure 3**).

2. If necessary, click the PC Exchange tab in the File Exchange window to display its options (**Figure 4**).

3. Click Add to display the Add Mapping dialog box (**Figure 12**).

4. In the Extension edit box, enter the three-character extension for a type of DOS file. Do not include the period (or "dot") before the extension.

5. In the Application list, select the progam you want to associate with the extension.

6. If necessary, choose a document type from the File Type pop-up menu.

7. Click Add. The new mapping appears.

8. Close File Exchange to save your change.

✔ Tip

■ PC Exchange's mapping list is extensive. Before adding an extension, scroll through the list to make sure a mapping does not already exist for the extension you want to add.

ADDING EXTENSION MAPPINGS

To remove an extension mapping

1. Choose Apple menu > Control Panels > File Exchange (**Figure 3**).

2. If necessary, click the PC Exchange tab in the File Exchange window to display its options (**Figure 4**).

3. In the scrolling list of mappings, select the Extension you want to remove.

4. Click Remove.

5. In the confirmation dialog box that appears (**Figure 13**), click OK. The mapping is removed.

6. Close File Exchange to save your change.

✔ Tip

- If you remove a mapping, Mac OS will no longer associate the extension with an application.

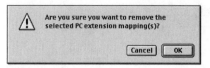

Figure 13 Click OK in this dialog box to remove the mapping.

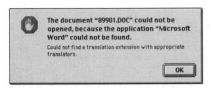

Figure 14 A dialog box like this appears when you double-click the icon for a document that cannot be opened by any of your installed applications.

Figure 15 This file translation window enables you to select an application to open a document—but only if the application that created the document is not installed on your computer.

Figure 16 In this example, Internet Explorer is displaying a JPEG file created with Adobe PhotoDeluxe. (Now you know where Wickenburg is.)

File Translation

File Translation is the part of File Exchange that enables you to open documents that were created by applications that are not installed on your computer. This feature works with PC and Mac OS files, using mappings in the PC Exchange tab and translation preferences in the File Translation tab of the File Exchange window.

To use file translation

1. Double-click an icon for a file created by an application not installed on your computer.

2. One of two things happens:

   ▲ If the file cannot be opened by any program on your computer, a dialog box like the one in **Figure 14** appears. Click OK and skip the rest of these steps—you'll have to install a program that can open the file or take the file to someone else's computer and open it there.

   ▲ If the file can be opened by a program on your computer, a dialog box like the one in **Figure 15** appears. Continue to step 3.

3. Select an application to open the file.

4. Click OK. The file opens (**Figure 16**).

✔ Tips

■ Not every program listed in the translation window (**Figure 15**) will always be able to successfully open the file.

■ The choices you make in the translation dialog box (**Figure 15**) are automatically saved as preferences in the File Translation tab of the File Exchange control panel (**Figure 17**).

To set file translation options

1. Choose Apple menu > Control Panels > File Exchange (**Figure 3**).

2. If necessary, click the File Translation tab in the File Exchange window to display its options (**Figure 17**).

3. Toggle the check boxes near the top of the window as desired:

   ▲ **Translate documents automatically** enables file translation. This option must be turned on to select either of the first two options beneath it.

   ▲ **Always show choices when translating files** displays the translation dialog box (**Figure 15**) each time your computer needs to translate a file. If this option is turned off, the dialog box only appears if a translation preference does not already exist for the file you want to open. This option must be turned on to select the first option beneath it.

   ▲ **Don't show choices if there's only one** does not display the translation dialog box (**Figure 15**) if there's only one translation option. Instead, it automatically opens the file using the only option.

   ▲ **Include applications on servers in translation choices** checks all mounted hard disks, including server volumes, for possible translation applications and includes them in the translation dialog box (**Figure 15**).

4. Close the File Exchange window to save your settings.

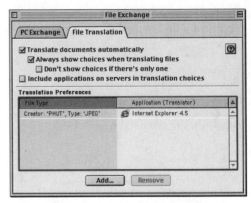

Figure 17 The File Translation tab of the File Exchange control panel.

SETTING FILE TRANSLATION OPTIONS

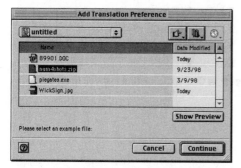

Figure 18 Use an Open dialog box like this one to locate and select a document like the one for which you want to set a translation preference.

To add a translation preference

1. Choose Apple menu > Control Panels > File Exchange (**Figure 3**).

2. If necessary, click the File Translation tab in the File Exchange window to display its options (**Figure 17**).

3. Click the Add button.

4. Use the Add Translation Preference dialog box that appears (**Figure 18**) to locate and select a document file like the one for which you want to set a translation preference.

5. Click Continue.

6. In the translation dialog box that appears (**Figure 15**), select the application with which you want to open the document.

7. Click OK. The preference is added to the File Translation tab of the File Exchange control panel window.

8. Close the File Exchange window to save your changes.

✔ Tips

- Translation preferences are automatically added or updated each time you use the translation dialog box (**Figure 15**).

- You cannot add a preference for a type of file for which a preference already exists. You must first remove the existing preference, as instructed on the next page.

ADDING TRANSLATION PREFERENCES

To remove a translation preference

1. Choose Apple menu > Control Panels > File Exchange (**Figure 3**).

2. If necessary, click the File Translation tab in the File Exchange window to display its options (**Figure 17**).

3. Click to select the translation preference you want to remove.

4. Click the Remove button.

5. In the confirmation dialog box that appears (**Figure 19**), Click OK. The preference is removed from the File Translation tab of the File Exchange control panel window.

6. Close the File Exchange window to save your changes.

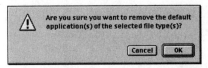

Figure 19 Click OK to confirm that you really do want to remove the translation preference.

PRINTING

Printing

On a Mac OS system, printing is handled by the operating system rather than the individual applications. You choose the Print command in the application that created the document you want to print. Mac OS steps in, displaying the Print dialog box and telling the application how to send information to the printer. There are two main benefits to this:

◆ If you can print documents created with one application, you can probably print documents created with any application on your computer.

◆ The Page Setup and Print dialog boxes, which are generated by Mac OS, look very much the same in every application.

This chapter covers most aspects of printing on a computer running Mac OS 9.

To print (an overview)

1. If necessary, select a printer.
2. Open the window or document that you want to print.
3. If desired, set options in the Page Setup dialog box, and click OK.
4. Set options in the Print dialog box, and click Print.

or

1. Drag the icon for the document you want to print onto a desktop printer icon.
2. Set options in the Print dialog box, and click Print.

To print the Finder Desktop

1. If necessary, activate the Finder by choosing Finder from the Application menu.

2. Click on the Desktop to activate it rather than any open windows.

3. Choose File > Print Desktop (**Figure 1**).

4. Use the Print dialog box that appears to set print options.

5. Click Print.

Figure 1
To print the Finder Desktop, choose Print Desktop from the File menu.

✔ Tip

■ I explain how to set options in the Print dialog box later in this chapter.

Figure 2
To print a Finder window, choose Print Window from the File menu.

To print a Finder window

1. If necessary, activate the Finder by choosing Finder from the Application menu.

2. Activate the window that you want to print by clicking it.

3. Choose File > Print Window (**Figure 2**).

4. Use the Print dialog box that appears to set print options.

5. Click Print.

✔ Tip

■ I explain how to set options in the Print dialog box later in this chapter.

Figure 3 The printer drivers installed as part of a Mac OS 9 standard installation.

Printer Drivers

A *printer driver*, which is a type of *Chooser extension*, is a software file that Mac OS uses to communicate with a specific kind of printer. It contains information about the printer and instructions for using it. You can't open and read a printer driver, but your computer can.

There are basically two kinds of printers:

◆ A **PostScript** printer uses PostScript technology developed by Adobe Systems. Inside the printer is a *PostScript interpreter*, which can process PostScript language commands to print high-quality text and graphics. Examples of PostScript printers include most Apple LaserWriter printers and Hewlett-Packard LaserJet printers.

◆ A **QuickDraw** printer relies on the computer to send it all of the instructions it needs for printing text and graphics. It cannot process PostScript commands. Examples of Quick-Draw printers include Apple ImageWriters and StyleWriters, Hewlett-Packard DeskJet printers, and most Epson Stylus printers.

Mac OS comes with printer drivers for a variety of Apple-branded PostScript and QuickDraw printers, including LaserWriters, StyleWriters, and ImageWriters. Mac OS-compatible printers by other manufacturers, such as Hewlett-Packard and Epson, come with the printer drivers you need to use them with your computer.

✔ Tips

■ If you do not have an appropriate printer driver for your printer, you may not be able to print.

■ Printer drivers are stored in the Extensions folder. **Figure 3** shows the printer drivers automatically installed as part of a basic installation of Mac OS 9.

PRINTER DRIVERS

To install a printer driver

1. Insert the disk containing the printer driver that you want to install.

2. If necessary, double-click the disk to open it and view its contents (**Figures 4** and **5**).

3. If the disk includes an installer (**Figure 4**), double-click the installer to open it. Then follow the on-screen instructions to install the printer software. You may have to restart your computer when the installation is complete.

   or

   If the disk does not include an installer (**Figure 5**), drag the printer driver file icon onto the closed System Folder icon on your hard disk (**Figure 6**). When you release the mouse button, a dialog box like the one in **Figure 7** appears. Click OK, and wait while the printer driver is properly installed in the Extensions folder.

✔ Tip

- If you need to, you can use the Mac OS 9 installer to reinstall just the printer drivers. Do a custom installation of Mac OS 9 and select just the printing software. I tell you about installing Mac OS 9 and doing custom installations in **Chapter 1**.

To uninstall a printer driver

1. Open the Extensions folder inside the System Folder on your hard disk.

2. Locate the icon for the printer driver that you want to uninstall.

3. Drag the printer driver out of the Extensions folder (**Figure 8**). You can leave it on the Desktop or in another window if you want to keep it, or you can drag it to the Trash if you want to delete it.

Figure 4
This disk contains printer driver software and an installer...

Figure 5
...and this disk contains printer driver software without an installer.

Figure 6 Drag the printer driver icon onto the System Folder icon.

Figure 7 When you drag a Chooser extension to the System Folder, a dialog box like this appears.

Figure 8
To uninstall a printer driver, simply drag it out of the Extensions folder.

Figure 9
Choose Chooser from the Apple menu.

The Chooser

The Chooser is a desk accessory that lets you select printers, file servers, and some other devices connected to your computer.

✔ Tips

- The Mac OS Setup Assistant, which I discuss in **Chapter 1**, sets the printer in the Chooser for you.

- I tell you about file servers in **Chapter 10**.

To open the Chooser

Choose Apple menu > Chooser (**Figure 9**).

The Chooser window appears (**Figure 10**). It displays icons for printer drivers and other Chooser files, such as AppleShare, in the left side of the window.

Figure 10 The Chooser window. If you're on a network with multiple zones, the Chooser window will look a little different on your computer.

To select a network printer

1. Make sure the printer that you want to use is turned on and warmed up.

2. In the Chooser window, select the icon for the printer driver that you want to use (**Figure 11**).

3. If your computer is on a network with multiple zones, select the name of the zone in which the printer you want to use resides.

4. In the list of printers, select the name of the printer that you want to use (**Figure 11**).

✔ Tips

- The LaserWriter 8 printer driver works for most PostScript laser printers.

- If you're not sure which zone to select in a multiple-zone network, ask your system administrator.

- When selecting a network printer, make sure the Active radio button beside Apple-Talk is selected (**Figure 11**).

Figure 11 Select the printer driver, the zone (if applicable; not shown here), and the printer.

OPENING THE CHOOSER, SELECTING A PRINTER

To select a directly connected printer

1. Make sure the printer that you want to use is turned on and warmed up.

2. In the Chooser window, select the icon for the printer driver that you want to use (**Figure 12**).

3. In the Connect to list, select the name or icon for the port to which the printer is connected (**Figure 12**).

✔ Tips

- If you're not sure which port the printer is connected to, check to see where the printer cable is connected to the back of your computer.

- You cannot directly connect a printer to the printer port if your computer is on a LocalTalk network. Instead, connect the printer to the modem port or, if possible, to the network.

To set background printing options

After selecting a printer in the Chooser window, select the Background Printing area's On or Off radio button (**Figure 12**) to set your preference.

✔ Tips

- Background printing, when turned on, enables your computer to print while you continue working on other things.

- The Background Printing option is not available for all printer drivers or printers. Consult the documentation that came with your printer for more information about this option.

Figure 12 Select the printer driver and the appropriate port for a directly connected printer.

Figure 13 Click the Auto Setup button in this dialog box to have Mac OS automatically set up your printer.

Figure 14 When this dialog box appears, wait while Mac OS gets setup information from your printer.

Figure 15 Select a PPD file for your printer, or click the Generic button.

To create or set up a PostScript printer

1. After selecting a printer in the Chooser window, click Create (**Figure 11**) or Setup.

2. If you clicked a Setup button in step 1, a Setup dialog box like the one in **Figure 13** appears. Click Auto Setup.

3. A dialog box like the one in **Figure 14** appears. After a moment, a dialog box like the one in **Figure 15** may appear. Use it to locate and select a PPD file for your printer. If there's no PPD file listed for your specific printer, click Generic.

4. Wait while your computer creates a desktop printer.

5. If you clicked a Setup button in step 1, the Setup dialog box (**Figure 13**) reappears. Click OK to dismiss it.

✔ Tips

■ The name of the button in step 1 depends on which printer driver is selected and whether the printer has been used before.

■ PPD (or *PostScript Printer Description*) files, which usually come with printer drivers, should be installed in the Printer Descriptions folder inside the Extensions folder in the System Folder on your hard disk.

■ I tell you about desktop printers later in this chapter.

CREATING/SETTING UP POSTSCRIPT PRINTERS

To set sharing setup options for a directly connected printer

1. After selecting a printer in the Chooser window, click Setup (**Figure 12**). A Sharing Setup dialog box appears (**Figure 16**).

2. To share the printer with other network users, turn on the Share this Printer check box. Then enter a printer name and, if desired, password (**Figure 17**).

3. To automatically create a log of printer use, turn on the Keep Log of Printer Usage check box.

4. Click OK to save your settings.

✔ Tips

- Not all directly connected printers can be shared.

- When you name a directly connected printer, its name appears in the Chooser window (**Figure 18**).

To close the Chooser

1. Click the Chooser's close box (**Figure 18**).

   or

   Choose File > Close (**Figure 19**), or press ⌘ ⌘ W.

2. If you selected a different printer than what was originally selected, a dialog box like the one in **Figure 20** appears, telling you to check the options in the Page Setup dialog box of open applications. Click OK to dismiss it.

✔ Tips

- I tell you about the Page Setup dialog box next.

- If a desktop printer does not already exist for the printer you selected, one is created. I tell you about desktop printers later in this chapter.

Figure 16 The Sharing Setup dialog box lets you share a directly connected printer with other users on your network.

Figure 17 Once you turn on the Share this Printer check box, you can enter a name and password for the printer.

Figure 18 The name of a shared printer appears in the Chooser window.

Figure 19 Choose Close from the Chooser's File menu.

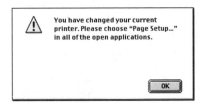

Figure 20 When you change your printer, a dialog box like this appears.

Figure 21 A Color StyleWriter 1500 offers only a few Page Setup options.

Figure 22 A LaserWriter offers two categories of Page Setup options: Page Attributes...

Figure 23 ...and PostScript™ Options.

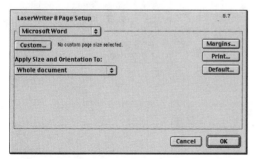

Figure 24 Some applications offer more Page Setup options. These are options for Microsoft Word ...

The Page Setup dialog box

The Page Setup dialog box lets you set page options prior to printing. Although it is a standard dialog box, two things can cause its appearance and options to vary:

◆ Page Setup options vary depending on the selected printer driver (**Figures 21**, **22**, and **23**).

◆ Additional options may be offered by specific applications (**Figures 24** and **25**).

In this section, I tell you how to set the basic options—those options available for most printers and most applications—in the Page Setup dialog box.

✔ Tips

■ For information about using Page Setup options specific to an application, consult the documentation that came with the application.

■ Because Page Setup options can change when you change printers, it's a good idea to check Page Setup options after changing your printer. That's what the dialog box in **Figure 20** is all about.

Figure 25 ...and these are options for Microsoft Excel.

THE PAGE SETUP DIALOG BOX

To open the Page Setup dialog box

Choose File > Page Setup (**Figures 26a, 26b,** and **26c**).

To set Page Attributes

1. Open the Page Setup dialog box (**Figures 21** and **22**).

2. In the Page Setup dialog box for a PostScript printer, select Page Attributes from the top pop-up menu (**Figure 27**).

3. If necessary, select the correct printer from the Format for pop-up menu (**Figure 22**).

4. Select the correct paper size from the Paper or Page Size pop-up menu (**Figures 21** and **22**).

5. To print more than one document page on each sheet of paper, choose a Layout option (**Figure 21**). If you select an option other than 1 Up, you can also turn on the Borders check box to put a border around each document page (**Figure 28**).

6. Enter a scaling percentage in the Scaling (%) or Scale edit box (**Figures 21** and **22**). You may also be able to select a percentage from a pop-up menu beside the Scaling (%) edit box (**Figure 29**).

7. Select an Orientation option by clicking it (**Figures 21** and **22**).

8. Click OK to save your settings and dismiss the Page Setup dialog box.

✔ Tip

■ Options in each of the above steps vary depending on the printer driver selected for the printer.

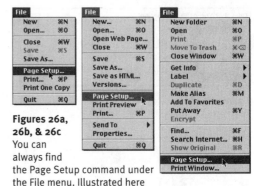

Figures 26a, 26b, & 26c
You can always find the Page Setup command under the File menu. Illustrated here are the File menus for SimpleText (left), Microsoft Word (middle), and the Finder (right).

Figure 27 In the Page Setup dialog box for a PostScript printer, select Page Attributes.

Figure 28 Layout options enable you to print more than one document page on each sheet of paper.

Figure 29
Some Page Setup dialog boxes let you select a scaling percentage from a pop-up menu like this one.

SETTING PAGE ATTRIBUTES

Figure 30 Choose PostScript™ Options from the pop-up menu at the top of the Page Setup dialog box for a PostScript printer.

Figure 31 Changing check box settings changes the dogcow in the sample image.

To set PostScript options

1. Open the Page Setup dialog box for your PostScript printer (**Figure 22**).

2. Select PostScript™ Options from the top pop-up menu (**Figure 30**).

3. Click check boxes (**Figure 23**) to turn the following PostScript features on or off:

   ▲ **Flip Horizontal** makes a mirror image of the page.

   ▲ **Flip Vertical** turns the page upside down.

   ▲ **Invert Image** turns black to white and white to black.

   ▲ **Substitute Fonts** uses Times, Helvetica, and Courier PostScript fonts instead of New York, Geneva, and Monaco True-Type fonts.

   ▲ **Smooth Text** prints bitmapped fonts more clearly.

   ▲ **Smooth Graphics** prints graphics more clearly by smoothing jagged edges.

   ▲ **Precision Bitmap Alignment** reduces the document to correct for possible distortions in bitmap graphic images.

   ▲ **Unlimited Downloadable Fonts** lets you use as many fonts as you like in a document. This could, however, slow printing.

4. Click OK to save your settings and dismiss the Page Setup dialog box.

✔ Tips

■ Many of the changes you make in the check boxes are reflected in the sample image to the left of the check boxes in the Page Setup dialog box (**Figure 31**).

■ Another piece of Mac OS trivia: the animal that appears in the Page Setup dialog box is called a *dogcow*. Its name is Clarus (*not* Claris), and it says "Moof!"

SETTING POSTSCRIPT OPTIONS

To set application-specific options

1. Open the Page Setup dialog box (**Figures 22** and **32**).

2. In the Page Setup dialog box for a Post-Script printer, select the name of the application from the top pop-up menu (**Figure 33**). That application's additional options appear (**Figure 24**).

3. Set options as desired.

4. Click OK to save your settings and dismiss the Page Setup dialog box.

✔ Tips

■ Some applications automatically display their own custom Page Setup dialog boxes when you choose Page Setup from their File menus. Microsoft Excel (**Figure 25**) is an example.

■ To learn more about the Page Setup options available in your favorite application, check the documentation that came with the application.

■ If the name of the application does not appear in the pop-up menu at the top of a PostScript printer's Page Setup dialog box (**Figures 27** and **30**), there are no application-specific options to set.

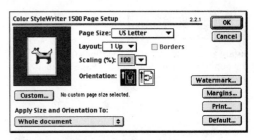

Figure 32 The Page Setup dialog box for a non-PostScript printer displays all options—including application-specific options such as these for Microsoft Word.

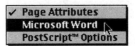

Figure 33 For a PostScript printer, choose the name of the application from the pop-up menu at the top of the Page Setup dialog box.

Figure 34 The Print options for a Color StyleWriter 1500.

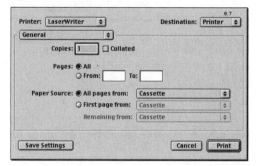

Figure 35 The General options of the Print dialog box for a LaserWriter printer.

Figure 36 Application-specific Print dialog box options for Microsoft Word...

Figure 37 ...and for Microsoft Excel.

The Print Dialog Box

The Print dialog box lets you set printing options and send the print job to the printer. Like the Page Setup dialog box, the Print dialog box is a standard dialog box, but two things can cause its appearance and options to vary:

◆ Print options vary depending on the selected printer driver (**Figures 34**, **35**, and **39**).

◆ Additional options may be offered by specific applications (**Figures 36** and **37**).

In this section, I tell you how to set the basic options—those options available for most printers and most applications—in the Print dialog box.

✔ Tip

■ For information about using Print options specific to an application, consult the documentation that came with the application.

THE PRINT DIALOG BOX

To open the Print dialog box

Choose File > Print (**Figures 38a**, **38b**, and **38c**), or press ⌃ ⌘ P.

✔ Tip

■ To use the Finder's Print command, you must first select the icon for the document that you want to print.

To set QuickDraw printer Print options

1. Open the Print dialog box (**Figures 34**).

2. In the Copies edit box, enter the number of copies of the document to print.

3. In the Pages area, select either the All radio button to print all pages or enter values in the From and To edit boxes (**Figure 39**) to print specific pages.

4. Select a Quality radio button. Some of the options you might see include:

   ▲ **Best** is the best quality. It takes longer to print and uses more ink.

   ▲ **Normal** or **Faster** is standard quality; you'll use it most often.

   ▲ **Draft** prints only the text of the document, in one font and size. It's the quickest print option, but what you get on paper may not match what you see on screen.

5. Select other options specific to your printer, including Paper Type, Paper Feed, Image, and Notification. If you need more information about these options, consult the manual that came with your printer.

✔ Tip

■ Some QuickDraw printers, such as Style-Writer 6000 Series printers, require that you select pop-up menu commands (**Figure 40**) or click buttons to access printing options.

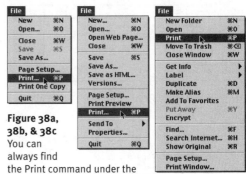

Figure 38a, 38b, & 38c
You can always find the Print command under the File menu. Here are the File menus for SimpleText (left), and Microsoft Word (middle), and the Finder (right).

Figure 39 When you enter values in the From and To edit boxes the From radio button is automatically selected.

Figure 40 The Print dialog box for a Color StyleWriter 6000 Series printer. You have to use a pop-up menu to access come of its printing options.

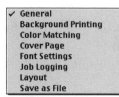

Figure 41
Use the pop-up menu beneath the Printer pop-up menu to select a category of printing options.

Figure 42 Use the Pages area to specify which pages to print.

Figure 43 The Paper Source options make it possible to print the first page of a document on letterhead you manually feed and the rest of the pages on plain paper from the paper cassette.

Figure 44 The Background Printing options in the Print dialog box for a PostScript printer.

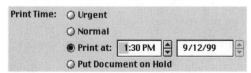

Figure 45 When you select the Print at radio button, you can enter a date and time to print the document.

To set PostScript printer General options

1. In the Print dialog box, choose General from the pop-up menu beneath the Printer pop-up menu (**Figure 41**) to display General options (**Figure 35**).

2. In the Copies edit box, enter the number of copies of the document to print.

3. To collate multiple copies, turn on the Collated check box.

4. In the Pages area, select either the All radio button to print all pages or enter values in the From and To edit boxes to print specific pages (**Figure 42**).

5. Select a Paper Source radio button. If you select First page, you can specify different paper sources for the first page and remaining pages (**Figure 43**).

To set PostScript printer Background Printing options

1. In the Print dialog box, choose Background Printing from the pop-up menu beneath the Printer pop-up menu (**Figure 41**) to display Background Printing options (**Figure 44**).

2. To print while you wait, select the Foreground (no spool file) radio button.

   or

   To print while you continue to work with your computer, select the Background radio button.

3. Select a Print Time radio button:

   ▲ **Urgent** puts the job in the print queue before jobs marked Normal.

   ▲ **Normal** puts the job in the print queue in the order it was received.

   ▲ **Print at** lets you specify a date and time to print the job (**Figure 45**).

   ▲ **Put Document on Hold** puts the job in the print queue but does not schedule it for printing.

To set PostScript printer Color Matching options

1. In the Print dialog box, choose Color Matching from the pop-up menu beneath the Printer pop-up menu (**Figure 41**) to display Color Matching options (**Figure 46**).

2. Choose an option from the Print Color pop-up menu (**Figure 47**):

   ▲ **Black and White** prints in black and white.

   ▲ **Grayscale** prints in shades of gray.

   ▲ **Color/Grayscale** prints in color on a color printer or in shades of gray on a monochrome printer.

   ▲ **ColorSync Color Matching** or **Post-Script Color Matching** prints in color using characteristics of a specific printer. If you choose either of these options, you must also choose options from the Intent and Printer Profile pop-up menus.

✔ Tip

■ Color matching technology is beyond the scope of this book. If you have a color PostScript printer (lucky you!), consult the documentation that came with it for more information.

To set PostScript printer Cover Page options

1. In the Print dialog box, choose Cover Page from the pop-up menu beneath the Printer pop-up menu (**Figure 41**) to display Cover Page options (**Figure 48**).

2. To print a cover page before or after the document, select either the Before Document or After Document radio button. Then use the Cover Page Paper Source pop-up menu (**Figure 49**) to specify the cover page source.

✔ Tips

■ A cover page is a sheet of paper that identifies the source of the print job.

Figure 46 The Color Matching options in the Print dialog box for a PostScript printer.

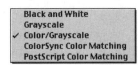

Figure 47 There are five options on the Print Color pop-up menu.

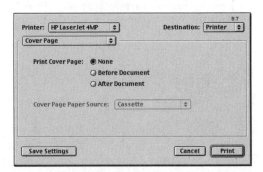

Figure 48 The Cover Page options in the Print dialog box for a PostScript printer.

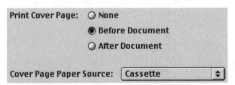

Figure 49 If you decide to print a cover page, you can select a paper source for it.

■ Cover pages waste paper. Unless you're on a network and need to separate your print job from others, don't print a cover page.

Figure 50 The Font Settings options in the Print dialog box for a PostScript printer.

To set PostScript printer Font Settings options

1. In the Print dialog box, choose Font Settings from the pop-up menu beneath the Printer pop-up menu (**Figure 41**) to display Font Settings options (**Figure 50**).

2. Turn on check boxes for desired options:

   ▲ **Annotate Font Keys** includes information about font keys in PostScript output.

   ▲ **Preferred Format** enables you to select the font format you prefer for printing when you have both the PostScript Type 1 and TrueType version of a font.

   ▲ **Always download needed fonts** instructs your computer to download PostScript fonts even when the font already resides on the printer.

   ▲ **Never generate Type 42 format** prevents your computer from generating Type 42 format fonts based on TrueType format fonts.

✔ Tips

■ The Always download needed fonts option helps ensure consistency from one printout to another when a document is printed on a variety of printers.

■ To restore settings to their default values, click the Use Defaults button.

■ I tell you more about fonts in **Chapter 15**.

To set PostScript printer Job Logging options

1. In the Print dialog box, choose Job Logging from the pop-up menu beneath the Printer pop-up menu (**Figure 41**) to display Job Logging options (**Figure 51**).

2. Select one of the radio buttons in the If there is a PostScript™ error area:

   ▲ **No special reporting** does not report PostScript errors.

   ▲ **Summarize on screen** displays Post-Script errors on screen as they occur.

   ▲ **Print detailed report** prints a report of PostScript errors after they occur.

3. Turn on check boxes for desired Job Documentation options:

   ▲ **Generate Job Copy** creates a copy of the job in PostScript format. (This file can later be sent to a PostScript printer to reprint the job without opening the original application.)

   ▲ **Generate Job Log** creates a log that provides information about the print job and printer.

4. To specify the folder in which job documentation should be saved, click the Change button beneath the Job Documentation Folder scrolling window. Then use the dialog box that appears (**Figure 52**) to locate and choose a folder. When you click Choose, the folder you selected appears in the Job Documentation Folder scrolling window (**Figure 53**).

✔ Tips

■ I explain how to use Navigation Services dialog boxes like the one in **Figure 52** in **Chapter 5**.

■ The PostScript files generated by turning on the Generate Job Copy check box can be very large.

Figure 51 The Job Logging options in the Print dialog box for a PostScript printer.

Figure 52 Use a dialog box like this one to locate and choose a folder to store job documentation.

Figure 53 The folder you choose (or create and choose as illustrated here) appears in the Job Documentation Folder scrolling window.

SETTING POSTSCRIPT PRINTER OPTIONS

Figure 54 The Layout options in the Print dialog box for a PostScript printer.

Figure 55
Choose the number of document pages that you want to appear on each printed page.

Figure 56 The Print dialog box displays a sample layout for the number of pages you selected.

Figure 57
Choose an option from the Border pop-up menu to remove or add a border around document pages.

To set PostScript printer Layout options

1. In the Print dialog box, choose Layout from the pop-up menu beneath the Printer pop-up menu (**Figure 41**) to display Layout options (**Figure 54**).

2. Choose the number of document pages that you want to print on each sheet of paper from the Pages per sheet pop-up menu (**Figure 55**).

3. If you select a value higher than 1 in step 3, click a Layout direction button (**Figure 56**) to specify the order in which document pages should appear on the printed pages.

4. To add a border around each document page, choose an option from the Border pop-up menu (**Figure 57**).

✔ Tip

■ Select 2 or 4 from the Pages per sheet pop-up menu (**Figure 55**) to print legible page proofs with less paper.

SETTING POSTSCRIPT PRINTER OPTIONS

To set PostScript printer Save as File options

1. In the Print dialog box, choose Save as File from the pop-up menu beneath the Printer pop-up menu (**Figure 41**) to display Save as File options (**Figure 58**).

2. Choose File from the Destination pop-up menu (**Figure 58**).

3. Choose an option from the Format pop-up menu (**Figure 59**):

   ▲ **PostScript Job** saves the document as a standard PostScript file.

   ▲ **EPS Mac Standard Preview** saves the document as an encapsulated Post-Script file with a bitmap preview.

   ▲ **EPS Mac Enhanced Preview** saves the document as an encapsulated Post-Script file with a PICT preview.

   ▲ **EPS No Preview** saves the document as an encapsulated PostScript file without a preview.

   ▲ **Acrobat PDF** saves the document as an Adobe Acrobat PDF file. This option is only available if you have the full version of Adobe Acrobat (not just Acrobat Reader) installed on your computer.

4. Select a PostScript Level radio button.

5. Select a Data Format radio button.

6. Choose an option from the Font Inclusion pop-up menu (**Figure 60**):

   ▲ **None** does not save any fonts with the file.

   ▲ **All** saves all the fonts with the file.

   ▲ **All But Standard 13** saves all the fonts with the file except the 13 fonts found on most PostScript printers.

   ▲ **All But Fonts in PPD file** saves all the fonts with the file except the fonts listed in printer's PPD file.

Figure 58 The Save as File options in the Print dialog box for a PostScript printer.

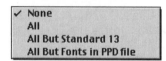

Figure 59 Choose an option from the Format pop-up menu to specify a PostScript file format.

Figure 60 Choose an option from the Font Inclusion pop-up menu to specify which fonts should be included with the file.

✔ Tips

■ If you're not sure how to set these options, leave all of them set to their default values except Font Inclusion, which you should set to All. This produces the most compatible PostScript files.

■ Details about PostScript options are beyond the scope of this book.

SETTING POSTSCRIPT PRINTER OPTIONS

Figure 61 The dialog box confirms that you really do want to save settings for your printer.

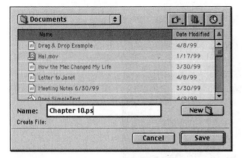

Figure 62 Use this Save As dialog box to enter a name, select a location, and Save a document as a PostScript file.

✔ Tips

- You can normally cancel a print job as it is being spooled to the print queue or printer by pressing ⌘ . . Any pages spooled *before* you press ⌘ . , however, may be printed anyway.

- I tell you how to cancel a print job that has already been spooled to a print queue later in this chapter.

- I tell you how to use the Save As dialog box in **Chapter 5**.

To save PostScript printer Print options

1. Click the Save Settings button at the bottom of the Print dialog box (**Figures 35, 44, 46, 48, 50, 54**, and **58**).

2. A dialog box like the one in **Figure 61** appears. Click OK to save the current settings for the printer.

✔ Tip

- Saving the settings for your printer displays the options you selected as the default options for the printer each time you use the Print dialog box.

To process the print job

1. Click the Print button in the Print dialog box (**Figures 35, 44, 46, 48, 50**, and **54**).

   or

   Click the Save button in the Print dialog box (**Figure 58**).

2. If background printing is turned on, the print job is sent to the print queue, where it waits for its turn to be printed. You can continue working as soon as the spooling window disappears.

   or

   If background printing is turned off, the print job is sent to the printer and printed. You'll have to wait until it's completely spooled to the printer before you can continue working with your computer.

   or

   If you saved the document as a PostScript file, a Save As dialog box appears (**Figure 62**). Use it to enter a name, select a disk location, and save the file.

SAVING PRINT OPTIONS, PROCESSING JOBS

The Print One Command

Some applications include a Print One or Print One Copy command under the File menu (**Figure 63**). This command sends a single copy of the active document to the printer using the current Page Setup and Print options. The print dialog box does not appear.

Figure 63
SimpleText's Print One Copy command does just that—it prints one copy of the active document without displaying the Print dialog box.

✔ Tip

■ The Print One command is a quick way to print one copy of a document, avoiding the Print dialog box.

Desktop Printers

When you use the Chooser to select and set up a printer, Mac OS automatically creates a desktop printer for it. As the name suggests, it appears on the desktop as a printer driver icon (**Figure 64**).

Figure 64
Desktop printer icons. In this illustration, the one on the top is the default printer.

Desktop printers can be used for a number of things:

◆ Identify and change the default printer.

◆ Print documents using drag and drop.

◆ Check or change items in a print queue.

◆ Stop or start a print queue.

I tell you about these things on the following pages.

To identify the default printer

If you have only one desktop printer icon, it represents the default printer.

or

If you have multiple desktop printer icons, the one with the dark border around it represents the default printer (**Figure 64**).

✔ Tip

■ The default printer is the currently selected printer.

PRINT ONE & DESKTOP PRINTERS

Figures 65a & 65b
The commands on the Printing menu vary depending on what desktop printer icon is selected. These Printing menus are for a Color StyleWriter 1500 (left) and a LaserWriter, which is set up as the default printer (right).

Figure 66 Drag the icon for the document that you want to print onto the desktop printer icon for the printer on which you want to print it.

Figure 67
A page icon appears on a desktop printer that has at least one print job queued.

Figure 68 Opening a desktop printer displays its print queue.

To change the default printer

1. Select the desktop printer icon for the printer that you want to set as the default printer.

2. Choose Set Default Printer from the Printing menu (**Figures 65a** and **65b**), or press ⌘⌘L.

To print a document with drag & drop

1. Drag the icon for the document that you want to print onto the desktop printer icon for the printer on which you want to print it (**Figure 66**). If the application that created the document is not already running, Mac OS launches it.

2. Set options in the Print dialog box that appears.

3. Click Print.

✔ Tips

- Drag and drop printing is a great way to print documents on any printer—without changing the default printer.

- When a desktop printer contains one or more documents to be printed, a page icon appears on it (**Figure 67**).

- I tell you about the Print dialog box earlier in this chapter.

To open a desktop printer

Double-click the desktop printer icon.

or

Select the desktop printer icon and choose File > Open or press ⌘⌘O.

The desktop printer's window opens. If any print jobs are waiting to be printed, they appear in a list (**Figure 68**).

CHANGING PRINTERS, DRAG & DROP PRINTING

To change the order of items in a print queue

1. Open the desktop printer for the print queue that you want to change (**Figure 68**).

2. Drag the item that you want to move into a higher (**Figure 69**) or lower position on the list of files to be printed. When you release the mouse button, the item moves (**Figure 70**).

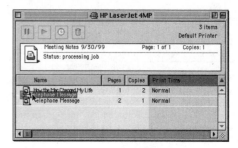

Figure 69 Drag the item that you want to move into a new position in the print queue.

To set print time for a job

1. Open the desktop printer for the print queue that you want to change (**Figure 68**).

2. Select the icon for the print job that you want to schedule (**Figure 70**).

3. Click the Set Time (clock) button. The Set Print time dialog box appears (**Figure 71**).

4. Select the radio button for the time option that you want:

   ▲ **Urgent** puts the job in the print queue before jobs marked Normal.

   ▲ **Normal** puts the job in the print queue in the order it was received.

   ▲ **At Time** lets you specify a date and time to print the job (**Figure 72**).

5. Click OK. The date and time you set appears in the Print Time column of the desktop printer window (**Figure 73**).

To remove a job from a print queue

1. Open the desktop printer for the print queue that you want to change (**Figure 66**).

2. Select the icon for the print job that you want to cancel (**Figure 73**).

3. Click the Remove (trash can) button. The selected print job disappears.

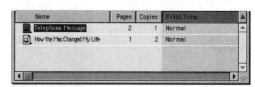

Figure 70 When you release the mouse button, the print job moves.

Figure 71 The Set Print Time dialog box lets you specify when a job should print.

Figure 72 Select the At Time radio button to enter the date and time for a job to print.

Figure 73 The print time column of the desktop printer window displays the date and time a job is scheduled to print.

Figure 74 When you put a print job on hold, the word *Hold* appears in the Print Time column.

Figure 75 The Resume Print Request dialog box lets you specify the page from which to resume printing.

Figure 76 When you stop a print queue, a stop sign appears in the print queue window...

Figure 77
...and on the desktop printer icon.

To put a print job on hold

1. Open the desktop printer for the print queue that you want to change (**Figure 68**).

2. Select the icon for the print job that you want to put on hold (**Figure 73**).

3. Click the Hold (double red bar) button. The word *Hold* appears in the Print Time column of the window (**Figure 74**).

✔ Tip

- A print job on hold will remain on hold until you resume it.

To resume a job

1. Open the desktop printer for the print queue that you want to change (**Figure 68**).

2. Select the icon for a print job on hold that you want to resume (**Figure 73**).

3. Click the Resume (green triangle) button.

4. The Resume Print Request dialog box appears (**Figure 75**). Enter the number of the page on which you want to resume printing, and click OK. The word *Normal* appears in the Print Time column of the window (**Figure 68**).

To stop a print queue

Choose Stop Print Queue from the Printing menu (**Figures 65a** and **65b**). A stop sign icon appears in the print queue window (**Figure 76**) and on the desktop printer icon (**Figure 77**).

✔ Tip

- A stopped print queue will remain stopped until you restart it.

To restart a print queue

Choose Start Print Queue from the Printing menu (**Figures 65a** and **65b**). The stop sign icons disappear.

Troubleshooting Printing Problems

When a printing problem occurs, Mac OS can often give you hints to help you figure out why. Here are some examples:

◆ A dialog box like the one in **Figure 78** appears when your computer can't find the selected printer. Check to make sure the printer is properly connected and turned on.

◆ A dialog box like the one in **Figure 79** appears when your printer is out of paper. Add paper!

◆ The desktop printer's print queue window can often provide information about the printer's status. In **Figure 80**, the printer is off line; touching a button on the printer solves the problem.

✔ Tip

■ If you have printing problems that Mac OS can't help you identify, check the trouble-shooting section of the documentation that came with your printer.

Figure 78 This dialog box appeared when my printer wasn't turned on.

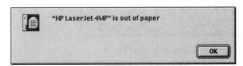

Figure 79 This dialog box appeared when my printer ran out of paper.

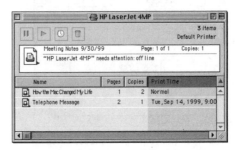

Figure 80 This desktop printer window notes that my printer is off line.

NETWORKING &TELECOMM

Networking & Telecommunications

Mac OS computers offer two ways to connect to other computers:

◆ **Networking** uses direct connections and network protocols to connect your computer to others on a network. Once connected, you can share files, access e-mail, and run special network applications on server computers.

◆ **Telecommunications** uses a modem, telephone line, and communications software to connect your computer to another computer. Once connected, you can exchange files, access e-mail, and work with other features offered by the host computer.

✔ Tips

■ If you use your computer at work, you may be connected to a companywide network; if so, you'll find the networking part of this chapter very helpful. But if you use your computer at home and have only one computer, you won't have much need for the networking information here.

■ Online services, such as America Online, are huge computer systems offering a wealth of information and entertainment for a fee. You can access these systems via modem or Internet connection.

■ You can access the Internet with a network or modem connection. I tell you about connecting to the Internet in **Chapter 11**.

Open Transport & Network Connections

Mac OS 9 includes *Open Transport*, system software that enables a Mac OS computer to connect to virtually any kind of network.

Most networks use one of the following two types of cables and connectors:

◆ **LocalTalk** connectors and standard telephone cables connect to the serial ports of computers and network printers. Devices are *daisy-chained*—linked one after another. LocalTalk is cheap and easy networking, but it is very slow.

◆ **Ethernet** cables connect to the Ethernet ports or Ethernet network interface cards of computers and network printers. Depending on the type of port and size of the network, additional hardware such as *transceivers* and *hubs* may be needed. Ethernet is faster than LocalTalk and is widely used for company and corporate networks.

✔ Tips

■ Details on network configurations are far beyond the scope of this book. The information here is provided primarily to give you an idea of how network connections work and introduce some of the network terms you might encounter when working with your computer and other documentation.

■ If your computer is on a large network, consult the system administrator before changing any network configuration options.

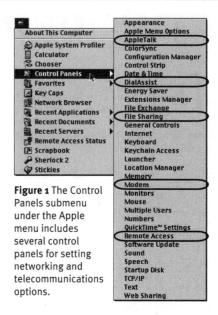

Figure 1 The Control Panels submenu under the Apple menu includes several control panels for setting networking and telecommunications options.

Figure 2 The AppleTalk control panel lets you select the network connection port.

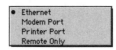

Figure 3 Choose a port from the Connect via pop-up menu.

Figure 4 Click Save in this dialog box if you're sure that you've selected the correct port.

Figure 5
The Apple menu includes several options for accessing networks.

Figure 6 The Chooser window with the AppleShare icon selected. The Chooser window may look different if you're on a multiple-zone network.

Figure 7 If you have to turn AppleTalk on, a dialog box like this reminds you to make sure you're connected to a network.

To select the network connection port

1. Choose Apple menu > Control Panels > AppleTalk (**Figure 1**).

2. In the AppleTalk control panel that appears (**Figure 2**), use the Connect via pop-up menu (**Figure 3**) to select the port to which the network is connected to your computer.

3. Close the AppleTalk control panel.

4. If you changed the configuration, a dialog box like the one in **Figure 4** appears. Click Save.

✔ Tips

- The Mac OS Setup Assistant should automatically configure the network connection for you—if you are connected to the network when you run it. I tell you about the Mac OS Setup Assistant in **Chapter 1**.

- The options that appear in the Connect via pop-up menu (**Figure 3**) will vary depending on your computer model.

- If you select the wrong port in step 2, your network connection will not work.

- I tell you more about control panels in **Chapters 13** and **14**.

To turn on AppleTalk

1. Choose Apple menu > Chooser (**Figure 5**) to display the Chooser window (**Figure 6**).

2. Select the Active radio button at the bottom of the Chooser window. A dialog box like the one in **Figure 7** appears. Click OK.

3. Close the Chooser to save your settings.

✔ Tip

- As the dialog box in **Figure 7** reminds you, you must be connected to an AppleTalk network to activate AppleTalk.

SELECTING A PORT, TURNING ON APPLETALK

Connecting to Another Computer

Mac OS 9 offers two tools to establish a connection to another computer via network:

◆ The **Chooser** (**Figure 8**) is the traditional way of accessing network volumes on a Mac OS computer.

◆ The **Network Browser** (**Figures 15** and **16**) enables you access network volumes using an interface similar to the Open dialog box.

Both tools enable you to select and connect to a computer on the network, then mount one or more network volumes. Once you mount a volume, you can use the Finder to browse and work with its contents.

✔ Tips

■ You can only connect to computers that recognize you as a user or allow guest connections.

■ Although the Chooser and Network Browser refer to other computers as *file servers*, you can connect to any computer on the network that allows connections—not just dedicated file servers.

■ Network volumes are usually disks, but a folder can also be a network volume, depending on how file sharing is set up on the networked computer. I tell you about setting up file sharing later in this chapter.

■ I explain how to use the Open dialog box in **Chapter 5**.

■ You can use Mac OS's alias or Favorites feature to create an alias or Favorite for a frequently mounted network volume. You can then open that volume by opening its alias or choosing it from the Favorites submenu under the Apple menu. I explain how to use aliases and Favorites in **Chapter 4**.

Figure 8 Select the computer to which you want to connect.

Figure 9 Use this dialog box to log onto the computer.

Figure 10 Select the volume or folder to which you want to connect.

Figure 11
The icon for the item to which you are connected appears on the Desktop.

Figure 12 Some computers allow guest connections. If so, the Guest radio button will be available in the connection dialog box.

Figure 13 Enter a server's IP address in this dialog box.

- To select more than one volume in step 9, hold down [Shift] while clicking each one.

- To automatically connect to a volume when you start your computer, turn on the check box beside the volume name (**Figure 10**).

To mount a network volume with the Chooser

1. Choose Apple menu > Chooser (**Figure 5**).

2. Select the AppleShare icon on the left side of the Chooser window (**Figure 6**).

3. If you're on a multiple-zone network, select the name of the zone in which the computer you want to connect to resides.

4. Select the name of the computer to which you want to connect to (**Figure 8**).

5. Click OK.

6. A dialog box like the one in **Figure 9** appears. Enter your name and password in the Name and Password edit boxes.

7. If desired, turn on the Add to Keychain check box (**Figure 9**) to add your login information to your keychain.

8. Click OK.

9. In the list of volumes that appears (**Figure 10**), select the one that you want to open.

10. Click OK. The icon for the item appears on your desktop (**Figure 11**).

11. Close the Chooser window.

✔ Tips

- If you're not sure which zone to select in step 3, ask your system administrator.

- To connect to another computer as a guest, select the Guest radio button in the connection dialog box (**Figure 12**), and click Connect.

- I explain how to use the Keychain feature to store login information in **Chapter 12**.

- To connect to a server using its IP address, click the Server IP Address button in the Chooser window (**Figure 8**). Then enter the server's IP address in the dialog box that appears (**Figure 13**), and click Connect. I tell you about TCP/IP in **Chapter 11**.

USING THE CHOOSER

To mount a network volume with the Network Browser

1. Choose Apple menu > Network Browser (**Figure 1**) to display the Network Browser.

2. If necessary, double-click the AppleTalk option in the Network Browser's Network window (**Figure 14**).

3. If necessary, double-click the name of the AppleTalk zone in which the computer you want to connect to resides.

4. Double-click the name of the computer you want to connect to in the AppleTalk window (**Figure 15**).

5. A dialog box like the one in **Figure 9** appears. Enter your name and password in the Name and Password edit boxes.

6. If desired, turn on the Add to Keychain check box (**Figure 9**) to add your login information to your keychain.

7. Click OK.

8. In the list of volumes that appears (**Figure 16**), double-click the one you want to mount. The icon for the item appears on your desktop (**Figure 11**), and its window opens.

9. Close the Network Browser window.

✔ Tips

- To connect to another computer as a guest, select the Guest radio button in the connection dialog box (**Figure 12**), and click Connect.

- To connect to a server using its IP address, choose Connect to Server from the Shortcut button's menu in the Network Browser window (**Figure 17**). Then enter the server's IP address in the dialog box that appears (**Figure 18**), and click Connect.

- I explain how to use the Keychain feature to store login information in **Chapter 12**.

Figure 14
The Network window displays all networks to which you are connected— including TCP/IP networks.

Figure 15
The AppleTalk window lists the networked computers accessible via AppleTalk.

Figure 16
The window for a specific computer lists all of its volumes.

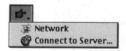

Figure 17 The shortcuts menu enables you to view different Network Browser windows or connect to a server by entering its IP address.

Figure 18
Use this dialog box to enter the IP address for the server you want to connect to.

Figure 19 Enter your old and new passwords in this dialog box.

Figure 20 This dialog box tells you what to do next.

To change your server password

1. Follow steps 1 through 5 in the section titled "To mount a network volume with the Chooser."

   or

   Follow steps 1 through 4 in the section titled "To mount a network volume with the Network Browser."

   A dialog box like the one in **Figure 9** appears.

2. Click the Change Password button to display a dialog box like the one in **Figure 19**.

3. Enter your old password and new password in the edit boxes, and click OK.

4. A dialog box like the one in Figure 20 appears, telling you to reenter your new password for confirmation. Click OK to redisplay the dialog box in **Figure 19**.

5. Enter your new password in the New password edit box, and click OK.

✔ Tips

- To enhance security, it's a good idea to change your password regularly.

- Following these steps changes your password in the server's Users & Groups setup, which I discuss later in this chapter.

- You cannot change your password if your user set on the server does not permit password changes.

To unmount a network volume

Drag the icon for the volume you want to unmount to the Trash.

✔ Tips

- Dragging a server item to the Trash does not delete that item.

- To completely disconnect from a computer, unmount all of its volumes.

Sharing Files with Others

You can share files on your computer with other network users. To do this, you must do two things:

1. Use the File Sharing control panel to set networking options and turn on file sharing.

2. Set privileges for the items that you want to share.

I explain how to do all of these things on the next few pages.

✔ Tip

- File sharing is allowed on an individual or group basis determined by users and groups:

  ▲ A *user* is an individual account consisting of a user name and password.

  ▲ A *group* is a number of users with the same privileges.

Using the File Sharing Control Panel

The File Sharing control panel (**Figures 21**, **28**, and **29**) enables you to do the following:

- Set the network identity for your computer, including the owner name, owner password, and computer name.

- Turn file sharing and program linking on or off.

- See who is connected to your computer and what items are being shared.

- Create users and groups for the people you want to access your computer.

To open the File Sharing control panel

Choose Apple menu > Control Panels > File Sharing (**Figure 1**).

Figure 21 The Start/Stop options for the File Sharing control panel.

To set or change your computer's network identity

1. Open the File Sharing control panel.

2. If necessary, click the Start/Stop tab to display its options (**Figure 21**).

3. Enter your name in the Owner Name edit box.

4. Enter a password to protect your computer in the Owner Password edit box. The characters you type turn to bullet characters when you advance to another edit box.

5. Enter a name for your computer in the Computer Name edit box.

6. Close the File Sharing control panel to save your settings.

✔ Tips

- If you used the Mac OS Setup Assistant to configure your computer after installing Mac OS 9, your computer's network identity will already be set. I tell you about the Mac OS Setup Assistant in **Chapter 1**.

- You can name your computer anything you like. I use model names on my personal network, but you may want to name your computer after yourself so that other network users know it's yours.

- The Computer Name is what identifies your computer in the Chooser and Network Browser windows of other computers on the network.

- Although you can leave the Owner Password edit box blank, doing so enables other users to connect to your computer as you without entering a password.

SETTING THE NETWORK IDENTITY

To turn file sharing on

1. Open the File Sharing control panel.

2. If necessary, click the Start/Stop tab to display its options (**Figure 21**).

3. Click the Start button in the File Sharing area. The status area indicates that sharing is starting up (**Figure 22**). After a moment, it indicates that file sharing is on (**Figure 23**).

4. Close the File Sharing control panel.

✔ Tips

- File sharing enables other users to access files and folders on your hard disk as specified by users and groups settings and access privileges.

- If you are connected to a TCP/IP network and want to allow users on that network to share files with you, you can turn on the check box for Enable File Sharing clients to connect over TCP/IP. Use this option with care! If you are connected to the Internet, you may be opening your computer to users all over the world! I tell you about TCP/IP in **Chapter 11**.

- If there is a Stop button instead of a Start button in the File Sharing area of the File Sharing control panel, file sharing is already turned on (**Figure 23**).

- If AppleTalk is not turned on when you attempt to start file sharing, a dialog box like the one in **Figure 24** appears. Click OK to dismiss the dialog box and turn Apple-Talk on. I explain how to turn AppleTalk on earlier in this chapter.

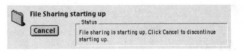

Figure 22 The status area tells you that file sharing is starting up.

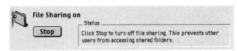

Figure 23 The status area also tells you when file sharing is turned on.

Figure 24 As this dialog box points out, AppleTalk must be turned on before you can turn on file sharing.

To turn program linking on

1. Open the File Sharing control panel.

2. If necessary, click the Start/Stop tab to display its options (**Figure 21**).

3. Click the Start button in the Program Linking area. After a moment, the status area indicates that program linking is on.

4. Close the File Sharing control panel.

✔ Tips

■ Program linking enables other users to link to shared programs on your computer. If you're not sure if an application can be linked, check its documentation.

■ If you are connected to a TCP/IP network and want to allow users on that network to link to shared programs on your computer, you can turn on the check box for Enable Program Linking clients to connect over TCP/IP. Use this option with care! If you are connected to the Internet, you may be allowing users all over the world to run your software! I tell you about TCP/IP in **Chapter 11**.

STARTING PROGRAM LINKING

To turn file sharing or program linking off

1. Open the File Sharing control panel.

2. If necessary, click the Start/Stop tab to display its options (**Figure 21**).

3. Click the Stop button in the File Sharing area (**Figure 23**) or Program Linking area.

4. If you turned off file sharing, a dialog box like the one in **Figure 25** appears. Enter the number of minutes before users are disconnected, and click OK.

5. Close the File Sharing control panel.

✔ Tips

- When you turn off file sharing, connected users see dialog boxes like the ones in **Figures 26** and **27**.

- When file sharing is turned off, all users are automatically disconnected.

To monitor file sharing activity

1. Open the File Sharing control panel.

2. If necessary, click the Activity Monitor tab. It displays connected users and shared items as well as an activity meter (**Figure 28**).

✔ Tips

- You can disconnect a specific user by selecting his name in the Connected Users list and clicking the Disconnect button (**Figure 28**). A dialog box like the one in **Figure 25** lets you enter the number of minutes before the user is disconnected.

- You can check privileges for shared items by selecting the item name in the Shared Items list and clicking the Privileges button (**Figure 28**). I tell you more about privileges later in this chapter.

How many minutes until file sharing is turned off?

Figure 25 Enter the number of minutes before users are disconnected.

"iMac via AppleTalk"

The file server is closing down in 10 minute(s) [4:40 PM on 8/30/99].

Figure 26 When you stop file sharing, connected users see one or more warning messages like this one...

"iMac via AppleTalk"

The file server has closed down [4:40 PM on 8/30/99].

Figure 27 ...before they're disconnected and see a message like this one.

Figure 28 The Activity Monitor tab of the File Sharing control panels lets you see who's connected.

Figure 29 The Users & Groups tab of the File Sharing control panel enables you to maintain accounts for the people who access files on your computer.

Figure 30 You create users with the New User window.

Figure 31 Enter the user's name and password.

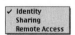

Figure 32 Choose Sharing from the Show pop-up menu.

To create a new user

1. Open the File Sharing control panel.

2. If necessary, click the Users & Groups tab (**Figure 29**).

3. Click the New User button. A New User window appears (**Figure 30**).

4. Enter the user's name in the Name edit box. The name appears in the title bar of the window when you advance to the next field.

5. Enter the user's password in the Password edit box. The characters you type change to bullets (**Figure 31**) when you click outside the Password field.

6. To allow the user to change his password, make sure the Allow user to change password check box is turned on.

7. Choose Sharing from the Show pop-up menu (**Figure 32**). The Sharing options appear (**Figure 33**).

8. To enable file sharing for the user, make sure the Allow user to connect to this computer check box is turned on.

9. To enable program linking for the user, turn on the Allow user to link to programs on this computer check box.

10. Choose Remote Access from the Show pop-up menu (**Figure 32**). The Remote Access options appear (**Figure 34**).

11. To enable the user connect to the computer via modem, turn on the Allow user to dial into this computer check box.

12. To instruct your computer to call back the user when he connects via modem, turn on the check box for Call back at and enter a phone number in the edit box beside it.

Continued on next page...

CREATING NEW USERS

Continued from previous page.

13. Click the window's close box to save your settings. The user's name appears in the list of users and groups (**Figure 35**).

✔ Tips

- I explain file sharing and program linking earlier in this section.

- Remote access options enable users to connect to your computer and an AppleTalk network by using a modem to dial into your computer. This feature must be used in conjunction with the call answering feature of Remote Access. I tell you more about Remote Access later in this chapter.

- The phone number you enter in step 12 should include all digits required to dial the user. This includes any special numbers that must be dialed to get a regular dial tone (if dialing from within an office environment) and, if necessary, a long distance prefix (usually 1) and area code.

Figure 33 Set Sharing options in this window.

Figure 34 Set Remote Access options in this window.

Figure 35 The new user appears in the users and groups list.

Figure 36 Use the New Group window to name a group and add users to it.

Figure 37 Drag a user name from the Users & Groups control panel to the group window.

Figure 38 When you release the mouse button, the user's name appears in the group window.

Figure 39 The group name appears in the Users & Groups control panel window.

To create a group

1. Open the File Sharing control panel.

2. If necessary, click the Users & Groups tab (**Figure 29**).

3. Click the New Group button. A New Group window appears (**Figure 36**).

4. Enter the group's name in the Name edit box. The name appears in the title bar for the window when you click outside the edit box.

5. Drag the icon for a user that you want to include in the group from the Users & Groups control panel window to the group window (**Figure 37**). When you release the mouse button, the user appears in the window (**Figure 38**).

6. Repeat step 5 for each user that you want to include in the group.

7. Click the group window's close box to close it. The group name appears in the list of users and groups (**Figure 39**).

✔ Tips

■ You must create a user before you can add it to a group. I tell you how to create users on the previous page.

■ You can add each user to as many groups as you like.

To modify a user or group

1. Open the Users & Groups tab of the File Sharing control panel (**Figure 29**).

2. Select the name of the user or group that you want to modify (**Figure 40**), and click Open.

   or

   Double-click the name of the user or group that you want to modify.

3. Make changes in the user or group window (**Figures 30**, **33**, **34**, and **38**) as desired.

4. Close the window to save your changes.

To remove a user from a group

1. Open the Users & Groups tab of the File Sharing control panel (**Figure 29**).

2. Double-click the name of the user that you want to remove from a group.

3. Choose Sharing from the pop-up menu at the top of the user window (**Figure 32**).

4. Click the name of the group from which you want to remove the user (**Figure 41**).

5. Press Delete.

6. In the confirmation dialog box that appears (**Figure 42**), click Remove. The user's name disappears from the list.

7. Close the window to save your changes.

or

1. Open the Users & Groups tab of the File Sharing control panel (**Figure 29**).

2. Double-click the name of the group from which you want to remove a user.

3. Click the name of the user that you want to remove from the group.

4. Press Delete.

5. In the confirmation dialog box that appears (**Figure 42**), click Remove.

6. Close the window to save your changes.

Figure 40 Select the name of the user or group that you want to modify.

Figure 41 The sharing settings in the user window list the groups to which the user belongs.

Figure 42 A confirmation dialog box like this appears when you try to remove a user from a group.

MODIFYING USERS & GROUPS

Figure 43 When you duplicate a user or group, the copy appears beneath the original in the list.

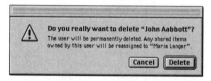

Figure 44 A confirmation dialog box like this one appears when you try to delete a user or group.

To duplicate a user or group

1. Open the Users & Groups tab of the File Sharing control panel (**Figure 29**).

2. Select the name of the user or group that you want to duplicate (**Figure 40**).

3. Click Duplicate. A copy of the item appears beneath the original (**Figure 43**).

✔ Tips

■ Duplicating a user or group is a quick way to create a new user or group with most of the same settings as an existing user or group.

■ Once you duplicate a user or group, you can open its window to modify it. I tell you about modifying users and groups on the previous page.

To delete a user or group

1. Open the Users & Groups tab of the File Sharing control panel (**Figure 29**).

2. Select the name of the user or group that you want to delete (**Figure 40**).

3. Click Delete.

4. A confirmation dialog box like the one in **Figure 44** appears. Click Delete.

✔ Tip

■ If you delete a user or group that owns items on your computer, those items are automatically reassigned to the computer's owner (you).

DUPLICATING & DELETING USERS & GROUPS

Setting Privileges

The final step to sharing items is to specify which items will be shared and how users can access them. A user's access to an item is referred to as his *privileges*.

There are four types of privileges:

◆ **Read & write** privileges allow the user to open and save files.

◆ **Read-only** privileges allow the user to open files, but not save files.

◆ **Write-only** privileges allow the user to save files but not open them.

◆ **None** means the user can neither open nor save files.

Privileges can be set for three categories of users:

◆ **Owner** is the user or group who can set access privileges for the item. You will probably be the owner for most, if not all, of the folders on your computer.

◆ **User/Group** is the user or group that has access to the item. This can be set to None if only the owner should have access.

◆ **Everyone** is everyone else on the network.

You set privileges in the sharing information area of the Info window for a specific folder (**Figure 45**) or disk (**Figure 46**).

✔ Tips

■ A disk or folder with write-only privileges is sometimes referred to as a *drop box* because users can drag and drop files into it but cannot see its contents.

■ It's vital that you set privileges correctly if there are confidential files on your computer. Otherwise those files could be accessible by other users on your network.

Figure 45 The sharing information in the Info window for the Shared Files folder created by the Mac OS Setup Assistant...

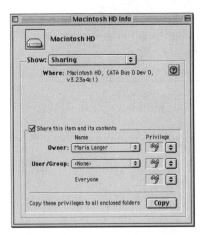

Figure 46 ...and for a disk.

SETTING PRIVILEGES

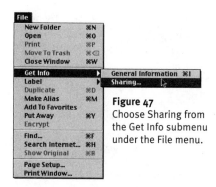

Figure 47
Choose Sharing from the Get Info submenu under the File menu.

Figure 48 If a folder resides inside a shared folder or disk, there will be no Share this item and its contents check box.

To open the Sharing Info window

1. Select the folder or disk for which you want to open the sharing window.

2. Choose File > Get Info > Sharing (**Figure 47**). The sharing information of the Info window appears (**Figures 45** and **46**).

✔ Tip

- You cannot open a sharing window for an individual file.

To turn on sharing

1. Open the Sharing Info window for the folder or disk (**Figures 44** and **45**).

2. Turn on the Share this item and its contents check box. The icon for the item may change (**Figure 45**).

3. Close the Sharing Info window.

✔ Tip

- If the folder is inside a shared folder or disk, the Sharing Info window will look like the one in **Figure 48**. If desired, you can turn on the Use enclosing folder's privileges check box to automatically assume the privileges of the folder or disk in which the folder resides—even if it is moved.

To prevent a shared folder from being moved, renamed, or deleted

1. Open the Sharing Info window for the folder (**Figures 45** and **48**).

2. Turn on the Can't move, rename, or delete this item check box.

3. Close the Sharing Info window.

✔ Tip

- It's a good idea to enable this option if you're concerned about users modifying folders on your hard disk.

SETTING PRIVILEGES

To set privileges

1. Open the sharing window for the folder or disk (**Figures 45**, **46**, and **48**).

2. Choose a user or group name from the Owner pop-up menu (**Figure 49**). Then choose a privilege from the Privilege pop-up menu on the same line (**Figure 50**).

3. If desired, choose a user or group name from the User/Group pop-up menu (**Figure 51**). Then choose a privilege from the Privilege pop-up menu on the same line (**Figure 50**).

4. If desired, choose a privilege from the Privilege pop-up menu on the Everyone line (**Figure 50**).

5. To assign the same privileges to every folder within the folder or disk, click the Copy button. A confirmation dialog box like the one in **Figure 52** appears. Click Copy to copy the privileges.

6. Close the sharing window.

✔ Tips

- The Owner and User/Group pop-up menus include all users and groups in the Users & Groups control panel. I tell you about users and groups earlier in this chapter.

- Confused? These two examples may help you understand how users and groups work.

  ▲ In **Figure 53a**, the item is owned by Maria Langer, who can open and save files. The primary group is Wickenburg Group, whose members can only save files. No one else can access the item.

  ▲ In **Figure 53b**, the item is owned by Maria Langer, who can open and save files. The primary user is John Aabbott, who can also open and save files. Everyone else can only save files.

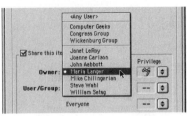

Figure 49 Choose an owner from the Owner pop-up menu.

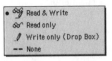

Figure 50 The Privileges pop-up menus list all four types of privileges.

Figure 51 Choose the user from the User/Group pop-up menu.

Figure 52 When you click the Copy button, a confirmation dialog box like this one appears.

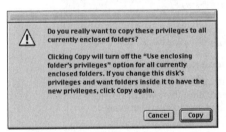

Figures 53a & 53b Two examples of how privileges can be set.

Figure 54 Folder icons indicate file-sharing privileges. (The Desktop folder is always a locked folder.)

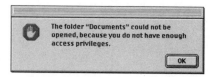

Figure 55 When you try to open a folder you're not allowed to open, a dialog box like this appears.

Figure 56 When you use a drop box, a dialog box like this appears.

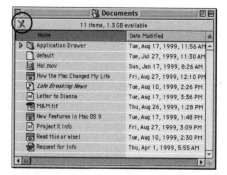

Figure 57 A tiny icon on the left side of the header indicates that this is a read-only folder.

Icons & Windows of Shared Items

The appearance of a shared item provides visual clues to its privilege settings.

◆ Folders that cannot be opened have buckles around them (**Figure 54**). If you try to open of these folders, a dialog box like the one in **Figure 55** tells you why you can't.

◆ A drop-box folder has a down-pointing arrow above it (**Figure 54**). When you drop an item into one of these folders, a dialog box like the one in **Figure 56** reminds you that you won't be able to see it once it's gone.

◆ Folders that cannot be renamed, moved, or deleted display a padlock icon beside them (**Figure 54**).

◆ The window for a read-only folder displays a tiny pencil with a slash icon on the left side of the header (**Figure 57**). When you try to drag an item into it, a dialog box like the one in **Figure 58** tells you why you can't.

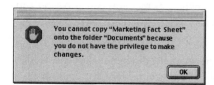

Figure 58 When you try to copy a file to a folder with read-only privileges, a dialog box like this appears.

Modem Connections

You can also use a modem and a standard telephone line to connect to other computers. A *modem* is a hardware device that is either inside your computer (an *internal* modem) or connected to one of your computer's serial ports (an *external* modem). You configure a modem connection with the Modem control panel.

Having a modem isn't enough to connect to another computer. You also need telecommunications software. The software you use depends on the type of system you are connecting to. For example, to connect to a friend's computer, you could use a general-purpose program like ZTerm; to connect to an online service like America Online, you would use the freely distributable America Online client software. Modems usually come with one or more kinds of telecommunications software.

✔ Tips

- Although Mac OS 9 does not include any general purpose telecommunications software, it does include Remote Access, which can be used to connect to the Internet or an Apple Remote Access server. I discuss Internet connections in **Chapter 11** and Remote Access Server connection at the end of this chapter.

- Most of today's modems can also send and receive faxes. Software to utilize this modem feature normally comes with the modem.

- There are many modem makes and models that will work with Mac OS computers— far too many to discuss in detail here. Read the documentation that came with your modem to learn more about using it and its features.

Figure 59
The Modem control panel.

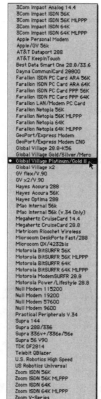

Figure 60
Choose the port to which your modem is connected from the Connect via pop-up menu.

Figure 61
Choose your modem make and model from the Modem pop-up menu.

Figure 62 Click Save to save your settings.

To set modem options with the Modem control panel

1. Choose Apple menu > Control Panels > Modem (**Figure 1**). The Modem control panel appears (**Figure 59**).

2. If necessary, choose an option from the Connect via pop-up menu (**Figure 60**). The options offered in the menu will vary depending on your computer model.

3. Select a modem make and model from the Modem pop-up menu (**Figure 61**).

4. Select one of the Sound radio buttons to turn the modem speaker On or Off.

5. Select one of the Dialing radio buttons to specify whether you have Tone or Pulse dialing.

6. To instruct the modem to dial no matter what the dial tone sounds like, turn on the Ignore dial tone check box.

7. Click the Modem control panel's close box.

8. In the confirmation dialog box that appears (**Figure 62**), click Save.

✔ Tips

- If you cannot find your modem make and model in the Modem pop-up menu (**Figure 61**), try another modem with the same brand name or one of the Hayes modems.

- Turn on the Ignore dial tone check box in step 6 if you have a telephone answering system that changes the sound of a dial tone when messages are waiting.

- The telecommunications software you use with your modem may have other settings. Check the documentation that came with the software for configuration information.

USING THE MODEM CONTROL PANEL

Remote Access

Remote Access is telecommunications software that's part of Mac OS 9. It has two main functions:

◆ Use it to connect to Apple Remote Access (ARA) servers—or Mac OS 9 computers with Remote Access privileges enabled—to access network volumes. I tell you how on the following pages.

◆ Use it to connect to an Internet Service Provider (ISP) via PPP. I tell you how in **Chapter 11**.

✔ Tips

■ Mac OS 9 comes with a special client/ server version of ARA. I explain how to enable Remote Access file sharing features earlier in this chapter.

■ The Remote Access control panel replaces the PPP control panel found in versions of Mac OS prior to 8.5.

To create a Remote Access configuration for connecting to an ARA server

1. Choose Apple menu > Control Panels > Remote Access.

2. The Remote Access control panel window appears (**Figure 63**). If the edit boxes are empty, skip ahead to step 7.

3. Choose File > Configurations (**Figure 64**), or press ⌃ ⌘ K.

4. In the Configurations dialog box that appears (**Figure 65**), select Default and then click Duplicate.

5. In the Duplicate Configuration dialog box that appears, enter a name for the new configuration (**Figure 66**) and click OK.

Figure 63
The Remote Access control panel.

Figure 64
Choose Configurations from the File menu.

Figure 65 The Configurations dialog box lists all Remote Access configurations, including those for Internet connections.

Figure 66
Use this dialog box to rename a duplicate configuration.

Figure 67 Select the configuration you created, and click Make Active.

Figure 68
Here's what the connection information might look like in the Remote Access control panel window.

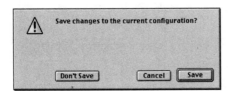

Figure 69 If you close the Remote Access control panel or switch configurations after making changes to the active configuration, a dialog box like this one appears.

6. Back in the Configurations dialog box (**Figure 67**), make sure the configuration you just named is selected and click the Make Active button to return to the Remote Access control panel window.

7. Enter your user name on the remote system in the Name edit box.

8. Enter your password on the remote system in the Password edit box. The password you enter appears as bullet characters (**Figure 68**).

9. To instruct Remote Access to save your password so you don't have to enter it each time you connect, turn on the Save password check box.

10. Enter the telephone number for the remote system in the Number edit box. Be sure to include all numbers that must be dialed, such as long-distance prefixes or codes to disable call waiting.

11. To connect, follow the instructions on the next page.

   or

   To close the Remote Access control panel without connecting, click its close box. If a dialog box like the one in **Figure 69** appears, click Save.

✔ Tips

- You can create a separate configuration for each network to which you connect.

- If the edit boxes in the Remote Access control panel window are not empty, overwrite their contents with correct information. Since the configuration is a duplicate, you don't have to worry about losing information that may have been in the original configuration file.

SETTING UP REMOTE ACCESS

To connect to an ARA server

1. Choose Apple menu > Control Panels > Remote Access.

2. If necessary, choose File > Configurations (**Figure 64**) to open the Configurations dialog box (**Figure 67**). Select the configuration you want to use, and click the Make Active button.

3. Click Connect. The Status area of the window indicates that Remote Access is dialing (**Figure 70**). When you have successfully connected, the Status area shows Send and Receive bars as well as the time connected (**Figure 71**).

4. Follow the instructions in the section titled "Connecting to another computer" near the beginning of this chapter to connect to a computer on the network.

✔ Tips

- These steps enable you to connect to any ARA server, including a Mac OS 9 computer set up for remote access file sharing. I explain how to enable remote access file sharing for a user earlier in this chapter and how to set up Remote Access to answer the phone on the next page.

- You can also use Remote Access Status (**Figure 73**) to monitor the status of a connection. To open this program, choose Apple menu > Remote Access Status (**Figure 5**).

- The Chooser looks and works the same when connecting via Remote Access (**Figure 73**) as it does when connecting from a computer on the network (**Figure 6**).

- Once connected, you can share files and applications and even print just as you would if you were on the network. Access speed, however, will be quite a bit slower.

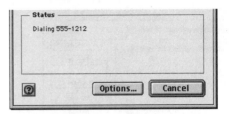

Figure 70 The status area provides connection status information, from the moment Remote Access starts dialing...

Figure 71 ...to the moment it connects and starts sending and receiving information.

Figure 72 Once connected, you can use the Chooser to connect to a network computer and access its volumes.

Figure 73 Remote Access Status offers another way to monitor a Remote Access connection.

Figure 74
Choose Answering from
the RemoteAccess menu.

Figure 75 Use the Answering dialog box
to enable remote access call answering.

Figure 76 The Status area indicates whether
call answering is enabled.

✔ Tips

- Use this feature in conjunction with the
remote file sharing options I discuss earlier
in this chapter to enable users to dial in to
your computer of the network for file
sharing.

- With call answering enabled, your computer
will automatically answer the phone, so it's
a good idea to connect your computer to
its own phone line when using this feature.

To disconnect from an ARA server

1. Drag the icons for shared disks to the trash.

2. Click Disconnect in the Remote Access
control panel window (**Figure 71**).

   or

   Click Disconnect in the Remote Access
window (**Figure 73**).

3. Wait while Remote Access disconnects.

To set up Remote Access to answer the phone

1. Choose Apple menu > Control Panels >
Remote Access to display the Remote
Access control panel (**Figure 68**).

2. Choose RemoteAccess > Answering (**Figure 74**) to display the Answering dialog
box (**Figure 75**).

3. To instruct Remote Access to answer the
phone for incoming file sharing calls, turn
on the Answer Calls check box.

4. To limit the amount of time a user can
remain connected, turn on the Maximum
Connection Time check box and enter the
maximum number of minutes in the check
box beside it.

5. Select a radio button to specify the amount
of access the user has:

   ◆ **Entire network** gives the remote user
   access to the entire network.

   ◆ **This computer** gives the remote user
   access to your computer only.

6. To allow remote users to use TCP/IP when
they connect using PPP, turn on the Allow
TCP/IP clients to connect using PPP check
box.

7. Click OK to save your settings. The status
area of the Remote Access control panel
indicates that call answering is enabled
(**Figure 76**).

DialAssist

DialAssist is a control panel that you can use to set up advanced dialing options. You can then use these options with Remote Access to dial in to other computers or an ISP.

To configure DialAssist

1. Choose Apple menu > Control Panels > DialAssist (**Figure 1**) to display the Dial-Assist window (**Figure 77**).

2. Enter the area code from which you are dialing in the City/Area Code edit box.

3. Choose the country you from which you are dialing from the Country pop-up menu.

4. If necessary, choose a dialing prefix from the Prefix pop-up menu. (A Prefix is dialed before the phone number you are calling and is commonly used to access an outside line from a business or hotel.)

5. If necessary, choose a long distance dialing prefix from the Long Distance Access pop-up menu. (A Long Distance Access code is dialed after the prefix but before the number you are calling and is usually the number *1*.)

6. If necessary, choose a dialing suffix from the Suffix pop-up menu. (A suffix is dialed after the number you are calling and is commonly used for calling card or credit card numbers.)

7. Close the DialAssist window to save your settings.

✔ Tip

■ You can click one of the four buttons at the bottom of the DialAssist window to modify the Country, Prefix, Long Distance, and Suffix pop-up menus. **Figure 78** shows an example of the dialog box that appears when you click the Prefix button.

Figure 77
Use the DialAssist window to configure DialAssist for your complex dialing needs.

Figure 78 Use dialog boxes like this one to edit the pop-up menus in the DialAssist window.

CONFIGURING DIALASSIST

Figure 79 With Remote Access set for Advanced user mode, the Use DialAssist check box is available.

Figure 80 Choose User Mode from the Edit menu.

Figure 81 The User Mode dialog box enables you to switch from one user mode to another.

To dial with DialAssist

1. Choose Apple menu > Control Panels > Remote Access to display the Remote Access window (**Figure 68** or **79**).

2. If the window includes the Use DialAssist check box (**Figure 79**), skip ahead to step 6.

3. Choose Edit > User Mode (**Figure 80**) or press ⌃ ⌘ U to display the User Mode dialog box (**Figure 81**).

4. Select the Advanced radio button.

5. Click OK. The Remote Access changes to include the Use DialAssist check box, as shown in **Figure 79**.

6. Turn on the Use DialAssist check box.

7. Continue using the Remote Access dialog box as discussed earlier in this chapter.

✔ Tip

- The advanced features of Apple Remote Access that are accessible in Advanced and Administration modes are beyond the scope of this book.

DIALING WITH DIALASSIST

CONNECTING TO THE INTERNET

Connecting to the Internet

The *Internet* is a vast, worldwide network of computers that offers information, communication, online shopping, and entertainment for the whole family.

There are two ways to connect to the Internet:

◆ In a *direct* or *LAN connection*, your computer has a live network connection to the Internet all the time. This is costly for individuals, but if your computer is on a companywide network, you may have Internet access through the network.

◆ In a *modem* or *dial-up connection*, your computer uses its modem to dial in to a server at an *Internet Service Provider* (*ISP*), which gives it access to the Internet. This is a cheaper way to connect, but your access speed is limited by the speed of your modem.

In this chapter, I tell you how to configure your system for an Internet connection, connect to the Internet, and use the Internet applications and utilities included with Mac OS 9.

✔ Tips

■ An ISP is an organization that provides access to the Internet for a fee.

■ The *World Wide Web* is part of the Internet. I tell you about the Web and the *Web browser* software you use to access it later in this chapter.

■ I tell you more about modems in **Chapter 10**.

The Internet Setup Assistant

The Internet Setup Assistant is an application that steps you through the process of configuring your computer to connect to the Internet. It has two parts that are launched automatically as you need them:

- ◆ **ISP Referral Assistant** helps you open an account with an Internet Service Provider (ISP). This is the part you'll use if you don't have an account with an ISP and want to open one.

Figure 1 Double-click the Internet Setup Assistant icon in the Assistants folder.

- ◆ **Internet Editor Assistant** helps you add or modify existing Internet configuration settings. This is the part you'll use if you already have an account with an ISP or a direct connection to the Internet.

To start the Internet Setup Assistant

1. Double-click the Internet Setup Assistant icon in the Assistants folder on your hard disk (**Figure 1**). The Internet Setup Assistant's main window appears (**Figure 2**).

2. Click the Yes button to display the second window of the Internet Setup Assistant (**Figure 3**).

Figure 2 The main window of the Internet Setup Assistant.

✔ Tip

- ■ The Internet Setup Assistant is automatically launched when you click the Continue button at the end of a Mac OS 9 installation. I tell you about installing Mac OS 9 in **Chapter 1**.

Figure 3 The second window of the Internet Setup Assistant asks if you already have an Internet connection.

Figure 4 The Introduction window tells you what the assistant does.

Figure 5 The Modem Settings window lets you configure your modem.

Figure 6 The Disclaimer window was obviously inserted by an Apple lawyer.

To register with an ISP

1. In the second window of the Internet Setup Assistant (**Figure 3**), click No.

2. Read the information in the Introduction window that appears (**Figure 4**). Then click the right arrow at the bottom of the window.

3. The Modem Settings window appears next (**Figure 5**). Select the make and model of your modem from the Modem pop-up menu. Use the Port pop-up menu to select the port to which your modem is connected. Select the radio button for either Tone or Pulse dialing. To instruct your computer to dial whether or not it detects a dial tone, turn on the Ignore dial tone check box. To dial certain digits before each call, enter the digits in the Dialing Prefix edit box. Then click the right arrow.

4. The Disclaimer window appears next (**Figure 6**). Read its contents and click the right arrow.

5. Next, the Country and Area Code window appears (**Figure 7**). Choose your Country from the Country pop-up menu. Enter your area code in the Area Code edit box and the first three digits of your phone number in the Phone Prefix edit box. Then click Register.

Continued on next page...

Figure 7 Enter your country, area code, and first three numbers of your phone number.

REGISTERING WITH AN ISP

Continued from previous page.

8. Wait while your computer uses your modem to retrieve a list of ISPs in your area. (It dials a toll-free number.)

9. The Conclusion window appears next (**Figure 8**). Read the information it contains, and click the Go Ahead button.

10. The Connection Status window appears while your modem connects to Apple's ISP server. When you successfully connect, Internet Explorer launches.

11. Wait while the Internet Account Server Web page loads. When it's finished, it'll look something like **Figure 9**.

12. Follow the instructions that appear on screen to choose a service and fill out forms. The information you'll have to provide includes:

   ▲ Your service preferences (if the ISP offers multiple levels of service).

   ▲ Your user ID and password.

   ▲ Billing and payment information.

   During this process, you'll also select the phone number that your modem will dial to connect to the Internet.

13. Wait while the information you entered is processed.

14. An Internet Setup Assistant window like the one in **Figure 10** appears. It contains information about your new account. Click Done.

Figure 8 The Conclusion window tells you what will happen next.

Figure 9 Use Internet Explorer to get more information about various ISPs, select one, and open an account.

Figure 10 At the end of the ISP registration process, the Internet Setup Assistant summarizes your account information.

Figure 11 A dialog box like this may appear when you submit information entered in a Web page form.

✔ Tips

- If your modem's make and model are not listed in the Modem pop-up menu in step 3, try a similar model from the same manufacturer or one of the Hayes models. I tell you more about modems in **Chapter 10**.

- If you click the Show Details button in step 10, you'll see a summary of the information you entered in the previous steps.

- If a security warning dialog box like the one in **Figure 11** appears during step 12, click Send to go on.

- While comparing Internet deals in step 12 (if multiple deals are offered for your area), note the toll-free numbers for the ISPs. You can call any ISP directly if you have more questions.

- If you live in an out-of-the-way place (such as Wickenburg, AZ), the ISPs in step 12 may not have an access number that is local to you. Although you may be able to access an ISP using a toll-free number for an additional hourly charge, this may be costly if you plan to spend a lot of time online. If you can't find a local provider using the Internet Setup Assistant, do some research with the phone book to find the best ISP for you. (I called a local computer consultant; she gave me the name and number of the only local ISP.) Then use the Internet Setup Assistant to set up an Internet connection for an existing ISP account, as discussed on the next few pages.

- In step 14, write down your ISP account log on information and put it in a safe place. Although this information is automatically entered in your system, it's a good idea to have it written down in case you ever need to enter it manually.

REGISTERING WITH AN ISP

To add a dialup configuration

1. In the second window of the Internet Setup Assistant (**Figure 3**), click Yes.

2. Read the information in the Introduction window that appears (**Figure 12**). Then click the right arrow at the bottom of the window.

3. The Configuration name and connection type window appears (**Figure 13**). Enter a name for the connection in the edit box. Then select the Modem radio button and click the right arrow button.

4. The Modem Settings window appears next (**Figure 5**). Select the make and model of your modem from the Modem pop-up menu. Use the Port pop-up menu to select the port to which your modem is connected. Select the radio button for either Tone or Pulse dialing. To instruct your computer to dial whether or not it detects a dial tone, turn on the Ignore dial tone check box. To dial certain digits before each call, enter the digits in the Dialing Prefix edit box. Then click the right arrow.

5. In the Configuration information window that appears next (**Figure 14**), enter the local access number for your ISP in the top

Figure 12 The Introduction window explains what the Internet Setup Assistant does and what information you'll need to use it.

Figure 13 Use the Configuration Name and Connection Type window to provide a name and specify a type of configuration.

Figure 14 In the Configuration Information window, enter the local access number and log on information for your ISP.

Figure 15 Use the PPP Connect Scripts window to indicate whether your ISP requires a PPP connect script.

ADDING A DIALUP CONFIGURATION

Figure 16 Choose a script from the Script pop-up menu.

Figure 17 Use this IP Address window to specify whether you have your own IP address.

Figure 18 Use this IP Address window to enter your IP address if you selected Yes in the previous window.

edit box, your user ID in the middle edit box, and your password in the bottom edit box. Then click the right arrow.

6. The PPP Connect Scripts window appears next (**Figure 15**). Select a radio button to indicate whether your ISP requires a PPP connect script. Click the right arrow.

7. If you selected Yes in step 6, a second PPP Connect Scripts window appears (**Figure 16**). Choose a connect script from the Script pop-up menu, and click the right arrow.

8. The IP Address window appears next (**Figure 17**). Select a radio button to indicate whether your have been assigned your own IP address. Then click the right arrow.

9. If you selected Yes in step 8, another IP Address window appears (**Figure 18**). Enter the IP address in the edit box, and click the right arrow.

10. The Domain Name Servers window appears next (**Figure 19**). Enter the DNS address or addresses in the top edit box. If there is more than one, make sure you press [Return] between each one. Then enter the domain name in the bottom edit box. Click the right arrow.

Continued on next page...

Figure 19 Use the Domain Name Servers window to enter the DNS addresses and domain name for your ISP.

ADDING A DIALUP CONFIGURATION

Continued from previous page.

11. In the E-mail Address and Password window (**Figure 20**), enter your e-mail address in the top edit box and your e-mail password in the bottom edit box. Then click the right arrow.

12. In the E-mail Account and Host Computer window (**Figure 21**), enter the POP account in the top edit box and the SMTP host in the bottom edit box. Click the right arrow.

13. In the Newsgroup Host Computer window (**Figure 22**), enter the NNTP host. Then click the right arrow.

14. The Proxies window that appears next (**Figure 23**) asks if you use a proxy server for Internet connections. Select the appropriate radio button, and click the right arrow.

15. If you selected Yes in step 14, the Proxies window appears (**Figure 24**). Turn on the check boxes for the types of proxies you use, then enter proxy information in the corresponding edit boxes. When you're finished, click the right arrow.

16. The Conclusion window finally appears (**Figure 25**). To connect to the ISP when the settings have been entered, make sure the Connect when finished check box is turned on. Then click Go Ahead.

17. The Internet Setup Assistant window indicates the progress of your configuration. Once completed, if you turned on the Connect when finished check box in step 15, the software attempts to connect to the ISP. Otherwise, it quits.

Figure 20 In the E-mail Address and Password window, enter your e-mail address and password.

Figure 21 In the E-mail Account and Host Computer window, enter the POP account and SMTP host provided by your ISP.

Figure 22 Enter the NNTP host provided by your ISP in the Newsgroup Host Computer window.

Figure 23 This Proxies window asks whether you connect to the Internet through a proxy server.

Figure 24 You can enter your proxy server information in this Proxies window.

Figure 25 The Conclusion window lets you know you're done entering information.

✔ Tips

- If your modem's make and model are not listed in the Modem pop-up menu in step 4, try a similar model from the same manufacturer or one of the Hayes models. I tell you more about modems in **Chapter 10**.

- If your ISP provided a PPP Connect Script, copy it to the PPP Connect Scripts folder inside the Extensions folder in your System Folder before using the Internet Setup Assistant to set up for Internet access. Doing so will automatically display the script in the Scripts pop-up menu in step 4.

- You can get most of the configuration information you need from your ISP or system administrator.

- It is not necessary to enter your password in steps 5 and 11. If you omit it, you'll have to enter it when connecting to your ISP or checking your e-mail.

- If you click the Show Details button in step 17, you'll see a summary of all the information you entered.

ADDING A DIALUP CONFIGURATION

To add a LAN configuration

1. In the second window of the Internet Setup Assistant (**Figure 3**), click Yes.

2. Read the information in the Introduction window (**Figure 12**). Then click the right arrow at the bottom of the window.

3. The Configuration name and connection type window appears (**Figure 13**). Enter a name for the connection in the edit box. Then select the Network radio button, and click the right arrow button.

4. The IP Address window appears next (**Figure 17**). If you have been assigned your own IP address, select the Yes radio button. If not, select the No radio button. Click the right arrow.

5. If you selected Yes in step 4, another IP Address window appears (**Figure 18**). Enter the IP address in the edit box, and click the right arrow.

6. If you selected Yes in step 4, the Subnet Mask and Router Address window appears (**Figure 26**). Enter the subnet mask in the top edit box and router address in the bottom edit box.

7. The Domain Name Servers window appears next (**Figure 19**). Enter the DNS address or addresses in the top edit box. If there is more than one, make sure you press Return between each one. Then enter the domain name in the bottom edit box. Click the right arrow.

8. In the E-mail Address and Password window (**Figure 20**), enter your e-mail address in the top edit box and your e-mail password in the bottom edit box. Then click the right arrow.

9. In the E-mail Account and Host Computer window (**Figure 21**), enter the POP account in the top edit box and the SMTP host in the bottom edit box. Click the right arrow.

Figure 26 Use the Subnet Mask and Router Address window to enter additional information if you have your own IP address on the LAN.

Figure 27 When you're finished, the Conclusion window tells you.

10. In the Newsgroup Host Computer window (**Figure 22**), enter the NNTP host. Then click the right arrow.

11. The Proxies window, which appears next (**Figure 23**), asks if you use a proxy server for Internet connections. Select the appropriate radio button, and click the right arrow.

12. If you selected Yes in step 14, the Proxies window appears (**Figure 24**). Turn on the check boxes for the types of proxies you use, then enter proxy information in the corresponding edit boxes. When you're finished, click the right arrow.

13. The Conclusion window finally appears (**Figure 27**). Click Go Ahead.

14. The Internet Setup Assistant window indicates the progress of your configuration. When it's finished, it quits.

✔ Tips

■ You can get most of the configuration information you need from your LAN administrator.

■ It is not necessary to enter your password in step 8. If you omit it, you can enter it when checking your e-mail.

■ If you click the Show Details button in step 13, you'll see a summary of all the information you entered.

ADDING A LAN CONFIGURATION

TCP/IP, PPP, & Remote Access

Your computer accesses the Internet via a TCP/IP network connection. *TCP/IP* is a standard Internet protocol, or set of rules, for exchanging information.

A TCP/IP connection works like a pipeline. Once established, Internet applications—like your Web browser and e-mail program—reach through the TCP/IP pipeline to get the information they need. When the information has been sent or received, it stops flowing through the pipeline. But the pipeline is not disconnected.

If you have a direct or network connection to the Internet, the Internet is accessible all the time. But if you have to connect via modem, you need to use Apple's Remote Access software. This software, which comes with Mac OS, uses PPP to connect to TCP/IP networks via modem. *PPP* is a standard protocol for connecting to networks.

When you connect via modem using Remote Access, you set up a temporary TCP/IP pipeline. Internet applications are smart enough to automatically use Remote Access to connect to the Internet when necessary. When you're finished accessing Internet services you should tell Remote Access to disconnect.

✔ Tip

■ Remote Access is also used to connect to an Apple Remote Access (ARA) server or another Mac OS 9 computer configured to allow remote file sharing. I tell you more about that in **Chapter 10**.

Setting Internet Configuration Options

Mac OS 9 includes three control panels you can use to manually set up an Internet configuration:

◆ **TCP/IP** enables you to set server IP address and domain name information.

◆ **Remote Access** enables you to set dial-up connection options.

◆ **Internet** enables you to set a wide variety of configuration options, including personal, e-mail, Web, and news information.

Many of these options are configured when you use the Internet Setup Assistant, so you shouldn't have to use these control panels to configure your Internet connection. In this section, however, I show you the configuration options in all three control panels in case you ever need or want to modify settings.

✔ Tips

■ The Remote Access control panel replaces the PPP control panel found in versions of Mac OS prior to 8.5.

■ If your Internet configuration is working fine, don't change it! Internet connections follow one of the golden rules of computing: *If it ain't broke, don't fix it.*

To set options in the TCP/IP control panel

1. Choose Apple menu > Control Panels > TCP/IP (**Figure 28**). The TCP/IP control panel appears (**Figure 29**). The name of the active configuration appears in the title bar.

2. To select a different configuration, choose File > Configurations. In the Configurations window that appears (**Figure 30**), select the configuration that you want to use and click Make Active.

3. If desired, make changes in the TCP/IP control panel window (**Figure 29**).

4. Close the TCP/IP control panel window.

5. If you made changes to the configuration, a dialog box like the one in **Figure 31** appears. Click Save.

✔ Tips

- Do not change settings in the TCP/IP control panel unless you have to. Changes that are incorrect could prevent your Internet connection from functioning properly.

- If you're not sure what to select or enter in the TCP/IP control panel, use the Internet Setup Assistant to create a new Internet connection with the desired settings. Although it may take longer to work with its interface, it's easier to use and understand.

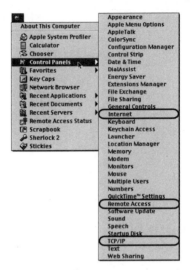

Figure 28 TCP/IP, Remote Access, and Internet can be found under the Control Panels submenu under the Apple menu.

Figure 29 The TCP/IP control panel.

Figure 30 Select the configuration that you want, and click Make Active. This dialog box looks the same for TCP/IP and Remote Access.

Figure 31 Click Save to save your changes.

Figure 32
The Remote
Access
control panel.

Figure 33 Use the Options dialog box to change redialing, connection, and protocol options.

✔ Tips

■ If you have a direct or LAN connection to the Internet, you do not need to set up or modify Remote Access configurations.

■ You can also use the Remote Access control panel to establish a connection to the Internet. I tell you more about connecting to the Internet later in this chapter.

To set options in the Remote Access control panel

1. Choose Apple menu > Control Panels > Remote Access (**Figure 28**). The Remote Access control panel appears (**Figure 32**). It includes the name of the active configuration file in the title bar.

2. To select a different configuration, choose Configurations from the File menu. In the Configurations window that appears (**Figure 30**), select the configuration that you want to use and click Make Active.

3. If desired, make changes in the Remote Access control panel window (**Figure 32**).

4. If desired, click Options to display the Options dialog box (**Figure 33**). Click tabs to display and change redialing, connection, and protocol options. When you are finished, click OK.

5. Close the Remote Access control panel window.

6. If you made changes to the configuration, a dialog box like the one in **Figure 31** appears. Click Save.

■ Do not change settings in the Remote Access control panel unless you have to. Changes that are incorrect could prevent you from successfully connecting to your ISP.

■ If you're not sure what to select or enter in the Remote Access control panel, use the Internet Setup Assistant to create a new configuration for your dial-up connection. Although it may take longer to work with its interface, it's easier to use and understand.

SETTING REMOTE ACCESS OPTIONS

To set options in the Internet control panel

1. Choose Apple menu > Control Panels > Internet (**Figure 28**). The Internet control panel appears (**Figure 34**).

2. To make a different set of options active, choose its name from the Active Set pop-up menu.

3. To edit a set of options, choose its name from the Edit Set pop-up menu.

4. If desired, make changes in the various tabs of the Internet control panel window to modify the set of options displayed in the Edit Set pop-up menu:

   ▲ **Personal** (**Figure 34**) includes your name, e-mail address, and organization (or, in my case, title). You can also enter additional information and an e-mail signature that can appear at the bottom of every e-mail message you send.

   ▲ **E-mail** (**Figure 35**) includes your e-mail configuration information as well as notification options for incoming e-mail and your default e-mail application.

   ▲ **Web** (**Figure 36**) includes the URLs for your default home and search pages as well as the folder for downloaded files, colors to use for Web page links and backgrounds, and your default Web browser application.

   ▲ **News** (**Figure 37**) includes your Internet news configuration information and your default newsreader application.

5. Close the Remote Access control panel window.

6. If you made changes to a set, a confirmation dialog box appears. Click Save to save the changes.

Figure 34 The Personal tab of the Internet control panel includes some basic information about you.

Figure 35 The E-mail tab of the Internet control panel includes a variety of e-mail configuration information.

Figure 36 The Web tab of the Internet control panel includes Web-related configuration options.

Figure 37 The News tab of the Internet control panel has configuration options for accessing Internet news.

Figure 38
Use the Internet control panel's File menu to work with sets of options.

✔ Tips

- The Internet control panel replaces the Internet Config application found in versions of Mac OS prior to 8.5.

- In step 4, you can change a link or background color in the Web tab by clicking a colored box, then using the color picker dialog box that appears to select a new color. I tell you about the color picker in **Chapter 3**.

- Microsoft Outlook and Microsoft Internet Explorer are the e-mail program and Web browser that are bundled with Mac OS 9. You can use the pop-up menus in the E-mail, Web, and News tabs to locate and choose other applications you may have installed on your computer for Internet access.

- You can also use options under the Internet control panel's File menu (**Figure 38**) to create, duplicate, and rename a set of options.

SETTING INTERNET OPTIONS

Connecting to an ISP

There are two ways to establish a PPP connection to your ISP:

◆ Use the Remote Access control panel or Remote Access Status application to dial in whenever you want.

◆ Launch an application that requires an Internet connection (such as Microsoft Internet Explorer); a PPP connection is automatically established.

✔ Tip

■ If you have a direct or LAN connection to the Internet, you don't have to worry about establishing a connection—it's always there.

To connect to an ISP with the Remote Access control panel

1. Choose Apple menu> Control Panels > Remote Access (**Figure 28**) to display the Remote Access control panel (**Figure 32**).

2. If necessary, switch to the configuration with which you want to connect.

3. Click the Connect button. Remote Access initializes your modem and dials. It displays the connection status in its status area (**Figure 39**).

When Remote Access has successfully connected, the Connect button turns into a Disconnect button and the Status area fills with connection information. You can see all this in **Figure 40**.

✔ Tip

■ The Remote Access control panel does not have to be open while you are connected to the Internet.

Figure 39 The Remote Access control panel's Status area keeps you informed about a connection as you connect...

Figure 40 ...and while you're connected.

Figure 41
Choose Remote
Access Status from
the Apple menu.

Figure 42 The tiny Remote Access Status Monitor window.

Figure 43 The Remote Access Status window expands to show connection status.

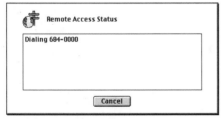

Figure 44 The Remote Access Status dialog box appears when you launch a program that requires an Internet connection but you are not connected to the Internet.

Figure 45 An icon like this blinks over the Apple menu while you are connected to the Internet—no matter how you connected.

To connect to an ISP with Remote Access Status

1. Choose Apple menu > Remote Access Status (**Figure 41**) to display the Remote Access window (**Figure 42**).

2. Click the Connect button. Remote Access Status initializes your modem and dials. It displays the connection status.

   When Remote Access Status has successfully connected, the Connect button turns into a Disconnect button and the status area fills with connection information. You can see all this in **Figure 43**.

✔ Tip

- The Remote Access Status application does not have to be open while you are connected to the Internet.

To automatically connect to an ISP

Launch any program that requires an Internet connection. After the program's splash screen appears, a dialog box like the one in **Figure 44** appears to show connection status. When the PPP connection is established, the dialog box disappears.

To disconnect from an ISP

1. Open or switch to Remote Access or Remote Access Status (**Figure 40** or **43**).

2. Click the Disconnect button. The connection is terminated.

✔ Tip

- You can always tell if you're connected to the Internet by looking at the Apple menu icon. If it blinks with an icon like the one in **Figure 45**, you are connected to the Internet.

CONNECTING TO AN ISP

Internet Applications

Mac OS 9 includes two full-featured applications for accessing the Internet:

◆ **Outlook Express** is a Microsoft program that enables you to send and receive e-mail and participate in Internet newsgroups.

◆ **Internet Explorer** is a Microsoft program that enables you to browse Web sites and download files from FTP sites.

In this section, I provide brief instructions for using these two programs. You can explore the other features of these programs on your own.

✔ Tips

■ Outlook Express and Internet Explorer are set as the default e-mail, newsgroup, and Web browser programs. If you prefer to use other applications, be sure to change the appropriate settings in the Internet control panel, which I discuss earlier in this chapter.

■ Mac OS 9 also comes with Netscape Communicator, another Web browser. Communicator works very much like Internet Explorer does; consult the instructions for using Internet Explorer to learn the same basics that apply to Communicator.

Figure 46
You can open your e-mail and Web browser applications by double-clicking icons on the Desktop.

Figure 47 You can also launch Microsoft Outlook Express or Microsoft Internet Explorer by double-clicking icons in the Internet window.

Launching Internet Applications

There are two main ways to launch an Internet application in Mac OS 9:

◆ Double-click a Desktop icon (**Figure 46**).

◆ Double-click an icon in the Internet folder (**Figure 47**).

To open Outlook Express

Use one of the following techniques:

◆ Double-click the Mail icon on your Desktop (**Figure 46**).

◆ Double-click the Microsoft Outlook Express icon in the Internet folder on your hard disk (**Figure 47**).

✔ Tip

■ Mail launches the default e-mail application set in the Internet control panel (**Figure 35**).

To open Internet Explorer

Use one of the following techniques:

◆ Double-click the Browse the Internet icon on your Desktop (**Figure 46**).

◆ Double-click the Microsoft Internet Explorer icon in the Internet folder on your hard disk (**Figure 47**).

✔ Tip

■ Browse the Internet launches the default Web browser application set in the Internet control panel (**Figure 36**).

LAUNCHING INTERNET APPLICATIONS

Outlook Express

Outlook Express (**Figure 48**) is an e-mail application from Microsoft Corporation. It enables you to send and receive e-mail messages using your Internet account.

In this section, I tell you enough about Outlook Express to get you started sending and receiving e-mail.

✔ Tips

- I explain how to launch Outlook Express on the previous page.

- The first time you launch Outlook Express, a Welcome dialog box like the one in **Figure 49** appears. Click OK to dismiss it.

- The first time you launch Outlook Express, the Preferences dialog box appears (**Figure 50**). All the options for your e-mail setup should already be entered by the Internet Setup Assistant, but you can change them if you need to. Click OK to accept the settings.

- You can reopen the Preferences dialog box (**Figure 50**) by choosing Edit > Preferences.

Figure 48 The Outlook Express main window with the Inbox displayed.

Figure 49 Outlook Express displays this dialog box the first time you launch it.

Figure 50 The Outlook Express Preferences dialog box offers many options.

OUTLOOK EXPRESS

Figure 51 Clicking the New button opens an untitled message window like this one.

Figure 52 Here's a short message ready to be sent.

Figure 53 Outlook Express displays a Progress dialog box like this one when it sends or retrieves messages.

To create & send a message

1. Click the New button at the top of the Outlook Express main window (**Figure 48**). An untitled message window appears (**Figure 51**).

2. Enter the e-mail address of the message recipient in the To edit box.

3. Enter a subject for the message in the Subject edit box.

4. Type your message into the large edit box at the bottom of the window. When you are finished, the window might look like the one in **Figure 52**.

5. Click the Send button near the top of the window. Outlook Express sends the message. It displays a Progress dialog box as it works (**Figure 53**). When it disappears, the message has been sent.

✔ Tips

- You can use Outlook Express's contacts feature to maintain a directory of the people you write to.

- You can click buttons in the area above the message text area to format selected text. Keep in mind, however, that your formatting may not be visible to the recipient.

- In step 5, if you are not connected to the Internet, Outlook Express initiates a connection before sending the message.

- If you prefer to compose e-mail messages while *offline* (not connected to the Internet), click the Send Later button in step 5. Your messages will be stored in the Outbox until you send them. When you're ready to send all messages (and receive new ones), click the Send & Receive button in the main window (**Figure 48**) to connect to the Internet and exchange mail.

CREATING & SENDING MESSAGES

To retrieve e-mail messages

1. Click the Send & Receive button at the top of the main window (**Figure 48**).

2. Outlook Express connects to your e-mail server and downloads messages waiting for you. It displays a Progress dialog box as it works (**Figure 53**). When the dialog box disappears, any incoming messages appear in bold in the Inbox area of the main window (**Figure 54**).

✔ Tips

- The Send & Receive button tells Outlook Express to retrieve all e-mail items waiting on the mail server and send any e-mail items in the Outbox.

- You can view the contents of the Inbox or Outbox by clicking the appropriate icon in the left side of the main Outlook Express window (**Figure 48**).

To read an incoming message

1. In the Inbox window, click the message that you want to read. It appears in the bottom half of the main Outlook Express window (**Figure 55**).

2. Read the message.

✔ Tips

- You can also double-click a message in the Inbox to display it in its own message window (**Figure 56**).

- To reply to the message, click Reply. A preaddressed message window with the entire message quoted appears (**Figure 57**). Type your reply, and click Send.

- To forward the message to another e-mail address, click Forward. A message window containing a copy of the message appears. Enter the e-mail address for the recipient in the To edit box, and click Send.

Figure 54 New incoming messages appear in bold in the Inbox.

Figure 55 Click a message to display its contents in the bottom half of the Outlook Express window.

Figure 56 Double-click a message to open it in its own window.

Figure 57 When you click the Reply button, a preaddressed message window appears.

Figure 58 When you launch Internet Explorer, it connects to the Internet and displays the default home page—in this case, Apple's "Live Page."

Figure 59 Clicking the link in **Figure 58** displays this page.

Internet Explorer

Internet Explorer is a popular Web browser application from Microsoft. It enables you to view, or *browse*, pages on the World Wide Web.

A Web *page* is a window full of formatted text and graphics (**Figures 58**). You move from page to page by clicking text or graphic links or by opening *URLs* (*uniform resource locators*) for specific Web pages. These two methods of navigating the World Wide Web can open a whole world of useful or interesting information.

✔ Tips

- I explain how to launch Internet Explorer earlier in this chapter. If you are not connected to the Internet when you launch Internet Explorer, it automatically connects for you.

- The version of Internet Explorer included with Mac OS has been customized to start with a specific home page and offer buttons with links to Apple and Microsoft pages.

- You can easily identify a link by pointing to it; the mouse pointer turns into a pointing finger (**Figure 58**).

To follow a link

1. Position the mouse pointer on a text or graphic link. The mouse pointer turns into a pointing finger (**Figure 58**).

2. Click. After a moment, the page or other location for the link you clicked will appear (**Figure 59**).

To view a specific URL

1. Choose File > Open Location (**Figure 60**), or press ⌘⌃L.

2. Enter the URL in the Open Internet Address dialog box (**Figure 61**), and click Open.

or

Enter the URL in the edit box near the top of the Internet Explorer window (**Figure 62**), and press Return or Enter.

To return to the home page

Click the Home button at the top of the Internet Explorer window (**Figure 58**).

✔ Tip

■ You can change the default home page by specifying a different page's URL in the Web tab of the Internet control panel. The page you specify will load each time you launch Internet Explorer. I tell you about the Internet control panel earlier in this chapter.

Figure 60
Choose Open Location from the File menu.

Figure 61 Then enter the URL in the Open Internet Address dialog box, and click Open.

Figure 62 Or enter the URL in the edit box at the top of the Internet Explorer window, and press Enter.

Figure 63 Use the Web Sharing control panel to configure and enable Personal Web Sharing.

Personal Web Sharing

Personal Web Sharing is a feature of Mac OS that enables you to create your own Web server. With it, you can use Web pages to share information with others on your network.

Here's how it works. First create one or more Web pages with the information that you want to share. Place them in a folder on your hard disk. Then use the Web Sharing control panel (**Figure 63**) to specify the Web folder and home page, set privileges, and enable Web sharing. When another network user uses his Web browser to open your IP address, the home page you specified appears.

✔ Tips

- To use Personal Web Sharing, you must be connected to a TCP/IP network and have an IP address. I tell you about TCP/IP earlier in this chapter.

- Personal Web Sharing is automatically installed as part of a basic Mac OS 9 installation. I tell you about installing Mac OS in **Chapter 1**.

- Instructions for creating Web pages are far beyond the scope of this book. If you're looking for a program that makes creating Web pages easy and a book to make using the program easy, try Adobe PageMill 3.0 and *PageMill 3 for Macintosh & Windows: Visual QuickStart Guide*.

PERSONAL WEB SHARING

To configure & enable Personal Web Sharing

1. Choose Apple menu > Control Panels > Web Sharing (**Figure 64**). The Web Sharing control panel appears (**Figure 63**).

2. To specify the location of the folder containing your Web pages, click the Select button beside Web Folder. Then use an Open dialog box (**Figure 65**) to locate and select the folder.

3. To specify the home page for your Web site, click the Select button beside Home Page. Then use the dialog box that appears (**Figure 66**) to select the document for your home page.

4. Select a radio button to either give everyone who accesses your Web site read-only access or use file sharing privileges to control access.

5. Click Start. After a moment, the words *Web Sharing On* appear in the bottom half of the Web Sharing control panel (**Figure 67**).

✔ Tips

- Mac OS includes a folder on your hard disk called Web Pages. Inside it, you'll find sample Web pages to get you started.

- I tell you how to use an Open dialog box in **Chapter 5** and how to set File Sharing privileges in **Chapter 10**.

Figure 64 Choose Web Sharing from the Control Panels submenu under the Apple menu.

Figure 65 Use a standard Open dialog box to locate and select the Web folder.

Figure 66 Use a dialog box like this one to select a home page for your Web site.

Figure 67 The words *Web Sharing On* appear in the bottom part of the Web Sharing control panel.

Figure 68 Enter the URL for the site to which you want to connect.

Figure 69 A page published with Personal Web Sharing can look like any other Web page.

To connect to a personal Web site

1. Double-click the Browse the Internet icon on the desktop (**Figure 46**) to launch your Web browser.

2. Choose File > Open Location (**Figure 60**), or press ⌃ ⌘ L.

3. In the dialog box that appears, enter the URL for the site to which you want to connect (**Figure 68**) and click Connect. After a moment, the page appears in your Web browser (**Figure 69**).

✔ Tip

- The URL for a personal Web site consists of the characters *http://* followed by the IP address for the computer (**Figure 68**).

SECURITY & MULTIPLE USERS

12

Security & Multiple Users

Mac OS 9 includes a number of brand new features that control and enhance security and enable you to configure your computer for multiple users:

◆ Keychain Access enables you to create keychain files for storing server, application, and Internet access information. This can speed up access to secure sites.

◆ Security applications, such as Apple File Security and Apple Verifier enable you to encrypt files and verify that files originate from someone you trust.

◆ Multiple Users enables you to configure your computer for use by more than one person. Each user can have his own custom interface for accessing files.

This chapter covers all of these features, as well as the PowerBook Security feature, which enables you to protect your PowerBook from unauthorized access.

Keychain Security

The Keychain Security feature, which is new in Mac OS 9, enables you to create a *keychain file* where you can store passwords and certificates for servers, applications, and Internet locations. Once you open your keychain, you can access any location for which you have saved a password or certificate without manually logging on.

For example, say you access a certain file server every day. When you open the file server, you're prompted to enter your Name and Password. If you store this logon information in a keychain, when the keychain is open, you can access the server without going through the logon process.

✔ Tip

- The Keychain Access feature can be a real timesaver, especially if you access many secure items.

To create a keychain

1. Choose Apple menu > Control Panels > Keychain Access (**Figure 1**).

2. If you have never created a keychain, a dialog box like the one in **Figure 2** appears. Click Create.

   or

   If you have already created a keychain and that keychain is open, the keychain's window appears (**Figure 5**) appears. Choose File > New Keychain (**Figure 3**), or press ⌃ ⌘ N.

3. In the Create Keychain dialog box that appears (**Figure 4**), enter the following information:

   ▲ Keychain Name is the name you want to assign to the keychain.

   ▲ Password is the password that must be entered to open the keychain.

   ▲ Confirm is the same password you entered in the Password edit box.

Figure 1 The Control Panels submenu under the Apple menu.

Figure 2 This dialog box appears when you open the Keychain Access control panel and either you do not have a keychain or your keychain is not open.

Figure 3 Use the File menu to create new keychains or work with open ones.

Figure 4 Use this dialog box to enter a name and password for opening your keychain.

Figure 5 The keychain window for a newly created keychain.

Figure 6 Use this dialog box to select and unlock a keychain.

Figure 7 The Keychains menu lists all of your keychains.

4. Click Create. A window for the keychain opens (**Figure 5**).

✔ Tip

■ In most situations, you should not need more than one keychain file.

To unlock a keychain

1. Choose Apple menu > Control Panels > Keychain Access (**Figure 1**).

2. If your keychain is locked, a dialog box like the one in **Figure 6** appears.

   or

   If your keychain is unlocked, its window opens (**Figure 5**). To unlock another keychain, choose its name from the Keychains menu (**Figure 7**) to display a dialog box like the one in **Figure 6**.

3. If necessary, choose the name of the keychain you want to unlock from the pop-up menu, enter your password in the edit box, and click Unlock. The keychain's window opens (**Figure 5**).

✔ Tips

■ A keychain must be unlocked to be used.

■ If your keychain is open, anyone who uses your computer can access any item in the keychain. If you're in a work environment with many people, you may want to set options to automatically lock your keychain when your computer is idle; I explain how later in this section.

UNLOCKING A KEYCHAIN

To lock a keychain

1. Choose Apple menu > Control Panels > Keychain Access (**Figure 1**). Your keychain window should open (**Figure 5**).

2. If more than one keychain window opens, use the Keychains menu (**Figure 7**) to switch to the keychain you want to lock.

3. Click the Lock button in the keychain window (**Figure 5**).

   or

   Choose File > Lock "*keychain name*" (**Figure 3**), or press ⌃ ⌘ L .

   The window collapses to hide item information, and the Lock button turns into an Unlock button (**Figure 8**).

✔ Tip

- You can lock all unlocked keychains at once by choosing File > Lock All Keychains (**Figure 3**).

To add an item to a keychain

1. Unlock the keychain to which you want to add an item.

2. Follow your usual procedure to access the secure item.

3. In the Connect to (**Figure 9**) or Login dialog box, turn on the Add to Keychain check box. As you complete the access procedure, the item's login information is added to the open keychain (**Figure 10**).

✔ Tip

- If your keychain is locked when you attempt to add an item to it, a dialog box like the one in **Figure 6** appears, allowing you to unlock it. When you unlock the keychain, the item is added.

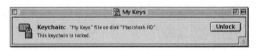

Figure 8 A locked keychain window.

Figure 9 Use the Add to Keychain check box to add login information to your keychain file.

Figure 10 Items added to your keychain appear in the keychain's window.

Figure 11 Use this dialog box to access an item with your keychain—and to set options so the dialog box never appears again.

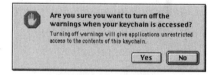

Figure 12 This dialog box appears when you enable any option that turns off warnings.

To access items with your keychain

1. Follow your usual procedure to access the secure item.

2. A dialog box like the one in **Figure 11** appears. If desired, you may set one of two check boxes:

   ▲ **Allow access without warning when using keychain "*keychain name*"** tells your Mac to open items in the keychain without displaying this dialog box if the keychain is unlocked. With this option enabled, the second option is not available.

   ▲ **Allow "*application name*" to access items without warning while running** tells your computer to allow the current application to open items in the keychain without displaying this dialog box if the keychain is unlocked.

3. If you turn on either of the options in step 2, a dialog box like the one in **Figure 12** appears. Click Yes.

4. Click Allow to access the item.

✔ Tip

■ If you click Deny in the access dialog box (**Figure 11**), you will have to access the item the usual way—by providing login information.

243

To set keychain options

1. Open and unlock the keychain for which you want to set options.

2. Choose Edit > "*keychain name*" Settings.

3. In the dialog box that appears (**Figure 13**), enter your password for the keychain and click View. The Change Keychain Settings dialog box appears (**Figure 14**)

4. To change your password, enter a new password in each of the two Password edit boxes.

5. Turn on check boxes for other options you want to enable:

   ▲ **Allow access without warning** allows access to any of the items in the keychain while it is unlocked without displaying a warning dialog box like the one in **Figure 11**.

   ▲ **Lock after *n* minutes of activity** automatically locks the keychain when your computer has been idle for a set number of minutes. If you turn on this option, be sure to enter the desired number of minutes in its edit box.

   ▲ **Lock when system sleeps** automatically locks the keychain when your computer goes to sleep. (I tell you about system sleep in **Chapter 2**.)

6. Click Save to save your settings.

✔ Tip

■ If you use your computer in a work environment with other workers, use one or both of the two locking options in step 5 to enhance security on your computer when you step away from it.

Figure 13 Before you can change settings for a keychain, you must enter the keychain's password in this dialog box.

Figure 14 Use this dialog box to change a keychain's password and set other options.

Figure 15
Mac OS 9 includes two
security programs in
its Security folder.

Figure 16 Drag the icon for a file you want to encrypt
onto the Apple File Security icon.

Figure 17 Enter the same password for
the file in each edit box.

Project X Info

Figure 18
A tiny key appears on the
icon of an encrypted file.

Security Applications

Mac OS 9 introduced two new security software applications:

◆ **Apple File Security** encrypts files so they cannot be opened by others unless they have the file's passphrase. It also compresses encrypted files so they take up less space on disk and can be transferred online more quickly.

◆ **Apple Verifier** verifies the digital signatures that may be present in files. A digital signature can confirm that a file originates from a specific individual or organization.

You can find both of these programs in the Security folder (**Figure 15**) inside the Applications folder on your hard disk

To encrypt a file

1. Drag the icon for the file you want to encrypt onto the Apple File Security icon (**Figure 16**).

2. In the Apple File Security dialog box that appears, enter the same password or *passphrase* for the file in each edit box. The characters you enter are displayed as bullets (**Figure 17**).

3. Click Encrypt. Apple File Security encrypts the file. A tiny key appears on its icon (**Figure 18**).

✔ Tip

■ In step 2, if you leave the Add to Keychain check box turned on in the Apple File Security dialog box (**Figure 17**), the password will automatically be entered in your Keychain file. I tell you more about using keychains in the beginning of this chapter.

ENCRYPTING FILES

To decrypt and open a file

1. Double-click the icon for the encrypted file that you want to open (**Figure 18**).

2. In the Apple File Security dialog box that appears, enter the password or passphrase for the file. The characters you enter appear as bullets (**Figure 19**).

3. Click Decrypt. Apple File Security decrypts the file and the file opens.

✔ Tip

■ When you decrypt a file, it remains decrypted. To secure it again, follow the instructions on the previous page to encrypt it.

To verify a digital signature

1. Drag the icon for a file you want to verify onto the Apple Verifier icon (**Figure 20**).

2. The Verification Results dialog box appears (**Figure 21**). It tells you whether the file was verified. Click OK to dismiss it.

✔ Tip

■ The vast majority of files do not include a digital signature. Don't be alarmed if a file you check cannot be verified—unless you are sure it includes a digital signature.

Figure 19 Enter the file's password in the edit box and click Decrypt.

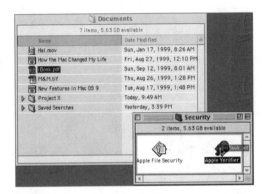

Figure 20 Drag the icon for the file you want to verify onto the Apple Verifier icon.

Figure 21 The Verification Results dialog box indicates whether a signature within the file has been verified.

Figure 22 The Multiple Users control panel window.

Multiple Users

The new multiple users feature enables you to set up your computer for use by more than one person. Each user can set different interface and appearance options and access a different set of files. One person—the owner—has control over access and features. The owner can include security measures that protect applications and documents.

✔ Tip

- The multiple users feature is especially handy in two scenarios:

  ▲ In a workplace, where multiple workers share a single computer.

  ▲ At home, where multiple family members share a single computer.

To enable/disable multiple users

1. Choose Apple menu > Multiple Users (**Figure 1**) to display the Multiple Users control panel window (**Figure 22**).

2. Select one of the radio buttons at the bottom of the window:

   ▲ On enables the multiple users feature.

   ▲ Off disables the multiple users feature.

3. Close the Multiple Users control panel to save your settings.

✔ Tip

- The multiple users feature must be enabled for changes within the control panel to take affect.

OPENING THE MULTIPLE USERS CONTROL PANEL

To set up a new user

1. Choose Apple menu > Multiple Users (**Figure 1**) to display the Multiple Users control panel window (**Figure 22**).

2. Click the New User button to display the Edit User window (**Figure 23**).

3. If necessary, click the triangle beside Show Setup details to expand the window (**Figure 24**).

4. Enter a name and password for the user in the User Name and Password edit boxes.

5. Select one of the Kind of User Account buttons:

   ▲ **Normal** is for users who have access to most of the system.

   ▲ **Limited** is for users who have limited access to the system.

   ▲ **Panels** is for users who have special, simplified access to the system. This option is ideal for children or new users who are unfamiliar with the computer.

6. Click the User Info tab to set additional options for the user:

   ▲ **User Picture** is an icon or picture to represent the user. Use the arrows beside the duckie to select a different picture, or drag a document containing a picture onto the duckie.

   ▲ **User can change password** enables the user to change his password.

   ▲ **Can log in** enables the user to log into the computer. Turning off this check box disables the user's account.

   ▲ **Can manage user account** enables the user to create, delete, or modify other accounts (except the owner's account). Turning on this check box gives the user account manager privileges. This option is only available for Normal users.

Figure 23 The Edit User window with details hidden...

Figure 24 ...and with User Info options displayed.

Figure 25 Use the Applications tab of the Edit User window to specify which applications the user can access.

Figure 26 Use the Privileges tab of the Edit User window to set other access privileges for the user.

▲ **Access by others to user's documents** enables you to specify how other users can view the user's documents: Read & Write, Read Only, and Write Only.

7. If you selected Limited or Panels in step 5, click the Applications tab (**Figure 25**). Then turn on the check box beside each application the user can access.

8. If you selected Limited or Panels in step 5, click the Privileges tab (**Figure 26**). Set options as desired:

   ▲ **CD/DVD-ROMs** enables the user to access CD-ROM and DVD-ROM discs. If you turn on this check box, you can select one of the radio buttons beneath it. Any gives the user access to all discs; List for restricted users gives the user access to only the discs on a list you can create. (I tell you how later in this section.)

   ▲ **Other removable media** enables the user to access other removable media, including floppy disks, Zip and Jaz disks, and any other removable storage media.

   ▲ **Shared Folder** enables the user to access a shared folder set up for the computer.

   ▲ **Chooser and Network Browser** enables the user to work with the Chooser and Network Browser for choosing printers and accessing the network.

   ▲ **Control Panels** enables the user to open and change settings in control panels.

   ▲ **Other Apple Menu Items** enables the user to work with items on the Apple menu.

Continued on next page...

SETTING UP A NEW USER

Continued from previous page.

▲ User Can Print enables the user to print. If you turn on this check box, you can also select All Printers or a specific printer from the Allowed Printer pop-up menu.

9. Close the window to save your settings. The new user appears in the Multiple Users control panel window (**Figure 27**).

10. Repeat steps 2 through 9 for each user you want to create.

11. Close the Multiple Users control panel to save your settings.

✔ Tips

■ You can create as many as 40 user accounts and one guest account.

■ The Panels option displays an interface similiar to that of At Ease, an Apple software package designed to limit access to shared computers.

To log out of a shared computer

1. In the Finder, choose Special > Logout (**Figure 28**) or press ⌃⌘Q.

2. In the dialog box that appears (**Figure 29**), click Yes.

✔ Tip

■ Logging out prevents access to the computer using your user account. It also locks any unlocked keychains.

■ It's a good idea to log out of a shared computer when you leave it.

■ If you don't click anything in step 2 above, you'll automatically be logged out in 90 seconds.

■ When you log out, a window like the one in **Figure 30** appears, enabling users to log into the computer.

Figure 27 When you create a new user, his name and icon (or picture) is added to the Multiple Users window.

Figure 28 With the multiple users feature enabled, a Logout command appears on the Special menu.

Are you sure you want to quit and logout?

(This message will be automatically accepted within 90 seconds.)

No   Yes

Figure 29 Click Yes in this dialog box to confirm that you want to log out.

Figure 30 This Welcome window appears when you log out of or start a shared computer.

250

Figure 31 Select your account name in the Welcome window.

Figure 32 Enter your password in the Password edit box.

Figure 33 A dialog box like this may appear while Mac OS prepares the computer for your use.

Figure 34 A Users folder appears on the hard disk for a computer with multiple users.

To log in to a shared computer

1. If necessary, start the computer.

2. In the Welcome window, select your account name (**Figure 31**) and click the Log in button.

3. Enter your password in the dialog box that appears (**Figure 32**), and click OK.

4. A Login dialog box like the one in **Figure 33** may appear briefly. When it disappears, you can use the computer.

✔ Tips

- When you log in to a shared computer, it appears the same way it looked when you logged out—even if other users accessed the computer since your last session.

- Normal and Limited users can access their files and folders, as well as shared files, in the Users folder that appears in the hard disk window (**Figure 34**).

- Panel users see an interface like the one in **Figure 35**.

Figure 35 The Panels interface is highly simplified and offers access only to the items that appear in the panel windows.

To set global multiple users options

1. Choose Apple menu > Multiple Users (**Figure 1**) to display the Multiple Users control panel window (**Figure 27**).

2. Click the Options button to display the Global Multiple Users Options dialog box.

3. Click the Login tab to display its options (**Figure 36**). Set options as desired:

   ▲ **Welcome message** enables you to enter a custom message to appear in the Welcome window (**Figure 37**).

   ▲ **Allow Alternate Password** enables you to set up Multiple Users for Voice Verification. To use this option, each user must record a phrase to be used for voiceprint verification.

   ▲ **Users may speak their names** enables users to say rather than select or type their names. To use this option, Speakable Items software must be installed and enabled in the Speech control panel. (I cover the Speech control panel in **Chapter 15**.)

   ▲ **If the user is idle for _n_ minutes** enables you to specify what should happen when the user is idle for the number of minutes you specify. If you turn on this check box, enter a value in the minutes edit box and select one of the radio buttons: Log out user or Lock the screen.

4. Click the CD/DVD-ROM Access tab to display its options (**Figure 38**). To create a list of restricted CDs or DVDs, insert a disc into the computer and click the Add to List button. You can then turn on check marks beside individual items on the disc that restricted users can access (**Figure 39**).

5. Click the Other tab to display its options (**Figure 40**). Set options as desired:

Figure 36 The Login options in the Global Multiple User Options dialog box.

Figure 37 A custom welcome message appears near the top of the Welcome window.

Figure 38 The CD/DVD-ROM options in the Global Multiple User Options dialog box.

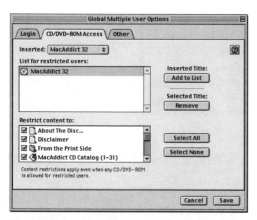

Figure 39 You can specify exactly which items on a restricted disc can be viewed by users.

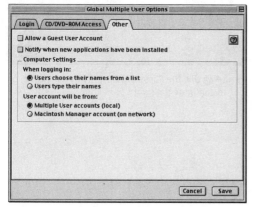

Figure 40 The Other options in the Global Multiple User Options dialog box.

Figure 41 For added security, you can require that users type both their name and their password to log in to a shared computer.

▲ **Allow a Guest User account** creates a Guest User account. You can then edit settings for the user to specify access privileges for a guest.

▲ **Notify when new applications have been installed** informs you when a new application has been installed so you can allow or prevent user access to it.

▲ **When logging in** options specify how the Welcome window should appear for a user to log in. The Users choose their names from a list option displays a Welcome window like the one in **Figure 27**; the Users type their names option displays a Welcome window like the one in **Figure 41**.

▲ **User account will be from** options specify which kinds of user accounts can log into the computer. The Multiple User accounts option enables users created with the Multiple Users control panel to log in; the Macintosh Manager account option enables users created over the network with Macintosh Manager software to log in.

6. Click Save to save your changes.

✔ Tip

■ If you're not sure how to set a specific option in the Global Multiple User Options dialog box, leave it set to the default setting.

PowerBook Password Security

The Password Security control panel (**Figure 42**) protects your PowerBook from unauthorized use. You can set it up to require a password for access when starting up and waking from sleep mode.

✔ Tip

■ The Password Security control panel is only installed on PowerBook computers.

To set up password protection

1. Choose Apple menu > Control Panels > Password Security. The Password Security control panel appears (**Figure 42**).

2. Click the Setup button to display the Password Security Setup dialog box (**Figure 43**).

3. Enter the same password in the top two edit boxes.

4. Enter a hint for remembering the password in the third edit box.

5. To also require a password for access when the computer wakes, turn on the Also ask when waking from sleep check box.

6. To display your name and contact information in the dialog box that prompts for a password, turn on the Show ownership information check box. Then fill in the edit boxes to provide contact information.

7. Click OK.

8. Close the window to save your settings.

✔ Tip

■ You may be prompted to enter a password (**Figure 44**) in steps 2 and 7. Enter the password, and click OK to continue.

Figure 42
The Password Security control panel.

Figure 43 Use the Password Security Setup dialog box to configure password protection.

SETTING UP PASSWORD PROTECTION

Figure 44 Use this dialog box to enter your password when prompted.

Figure 45 If you enter an incorrect password, this dialog box tells you.

To enable password protection

1. Choose Apple menu > Control Panels > Password Security. The Password Security control panel appears (**Figure 42**).

2. Select the On radio button.

3. In the Password dialog box that appears (**Figure 44**) enter your password to confirm that you know it and click OK.

4. Close the window to save your settings.

5. If password protection is configured to require a password when the computer wakes, restart the computer.

To access a password-protected PowerBook

1. Start or wake the PowerBook.

2. A password dialog box like the one in **Figure 44** appears. Enter your password, and click OK.

✔ Tips

- If you enter an incorrect password, a dialog box like the one in **Figure 45** appears. Click OK, and try again.

- If you do not enter a password within a minute or so, the computer automatically shuts down or goes back to sleep.

To disable password protection

1. Choose Apple menu > Control Panels > Password Security. The Password Security control panel appears (**Figure 42**).

2. Select the Off radio button.

3. In the Password dialog box that appears (**Figure 44**), enter your password to confirm that you know it and click OK.

4. Close the window to save your settings.

5. If password protection was configured to require a password when the computer wakes, restart the computer.

USING PASSWORD PROTECTION

255

USING SHERLOCK 2

Figure 1 Sherlock enables you to search for files on mounted disks and information on the Internet.

Figure 2 You can launch Sherlock by choosing Sherlock 2 from the Apple menu, ...

Figure 3 ...by choosing the Find or Search Internet commands from the File menu, ...

Figure 4
...or by double-clicking the Sherlock 2 icon on the desktop.

Sherlock 2

Sherlock 2 (**Figure 1**) is the second-generation release of Apple's powerful search utility. With a brand new interface in Mac OS 9, it enables you to perform the following searches:

◆ Search your internal hard disk and other mounted volumes for files.

◆ Search the Internet for information found on Web sites all over the world, as well as contact information for people you know.

In this chapter, I explain how to use Sherlock's search features, as well as how to customize Sherlock so it works the way you want it to.

✔ Tips

■ I explain what a mounted disk or volume is in **Chapter 3**.

■ Internet access is required to use Sherlock to search the Internet for information and e-mail addresses. I tell you about accessing the Internet with Mac OS 9 in **Chapter 11**.

To launch Sherlock 2

Use one of these techniques:

◆ Choose Apple menu > Sherlock 2 (**Figure 2**).

◆ Choose File > Find (**Figure 3**), or press ⌃ ⌘ F.

◆ Choose File > Search Internet (**Figure 3**), or press ⌃ ⌘ H.

◆ Double-click the Sherlock 2 icon on the Desktop (**Figure 4**).

Finding Files

Sherlock enables you to search your internal hard disk or other mounted volumes, including CD-ROM, floppy, and networked disks, for files based on a variety of search criteria:

◆ **File Names** enables you to search for files based on all or part of the file name.

◆ **Contents** enables you to search for files based on any part of the document's contents.

◆ **Custom** criteria enables you to search for files based on any combination of criteria, including file name, contents, and other file attributes.

✔ Tips

■ I tell you more about file attributes later in this section.

To find files by name

1. With Sherlock active, choose Find > Find Files (**Figure 5**), or press ⌃ ⌘ F, to display Sherlock's Files channel (**Figure 1**).

2. Select the File Names radio button.

3. Enter all or part of the name of the file you want to find in the edit box near the top of the window (**Figure 6**).

4. Turn on the check box beside each mounted volume you want to search.

5. Click the magnifying glass button to begin the search. Sherlock searches the specified disks, displaying its status while it works. One of two things happens:

   ▲ If Sherlock finds matches to your criteria, it lists them in the bottom half of its window (**Figure 7**).

   ▲ If Sherlock does not find any matches, it displays a dialog box like the one in **Figure 8**. You can then click OK and repeat steps 2 through 5 to try again.

Figure 5
Use Sherlock's Find menu to select the type of thing you want to search for.

Figure 6 Here's an example of search criteria for searching by name...

Figure 7 ...and here's what the search results might look like.

Figure 8 If Sherlock can't find any matches, it tells you.

Figure 9 Here's the criteria set up for searching by content. The only problem is, the volume to be searched has not yet been indexed.

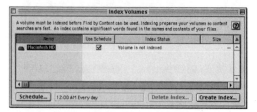

Figure 10 Use the Index Volumes window to select the disks you want to index.

Figure 11 This dialog box warns you that creating an index can take some time.

Figure 12 A dialog box like this appears while your computer creates the index.

To find files by content

1. With Sherlock active, choose Find > Find by Content (**Figure 5**), or press ⌘ ⌘ G, to display Sherlock's Files channel with the Contents radio button selected (**Figure 9**).

2. Enter the text you are searching for within the file's contents in the edit box near the top of the window (**Figure 9**).

3. Turn on the check box beside each mounted volume you want to search. If all of the checked volumes have been indexed (as noted beside the volume name), skip ahead to step 9.

4. Choose Find > Index Volumes (**Figure 5**), or press ⌘ ⌘ L.

5. In the Index Volumes window that appears (**Figure 10**), select the volumes you want to index and click the Create Index button.

6. A dialog box like the one in **Figure 11** appears. Click the Create button.

7. Wait while the disks are indexed. The Indexing Progress dialog box appears while it works (**Figure 12**). When it disappears, the indexing is finished.

8. Close the Index Volumes window to return to the Sherlock window. As shown in **Figure 13**, the volume's Index Status changes to reflect the recent indexing.

9. Click the magnifying glass button to begin the search. Sherlock searches the specified disks, displaying its status while it works. One of two things happens:

   ▲ If Sherlock finds matches to your criteria, it lists them in the bottom half of its window (**Figure 14**).

   ▲ If Sherlock does not find any matches, it displays a dialog box like the one in **Figure 8**. You can then click OK and repeat steps 2 through 9 to try again.

Continued on next page...

FINDING FILES BY CONTENT

Continued from previous page.

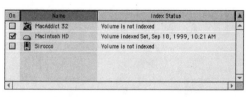

Figure 13 The Index Status changes to indicate when the volume was last indexed.

✔ Tips

- The Find by Content feature searches the index, not the actual files. Therefore, it cannot find files that match criteria if the files were created or modified after the index was last updated.

- You can automatically index your hard disk using a predetermined schedule. I explain how later in this chapter.

- When displaying the results of a search by content, Sherlock includes a Relevance column (**Figure 14**) that indicates how many times the search criteria appeared in the content of the file. Found files are sorted by relevance, so the most likely matches appear at the top of the list.

To find files by custom criteria

1. With Sherlock active, choose Find > Find Files (**Figure 5**), or press ⌘F, to display Sherlock's Files channel (**Figure 1**).

2. Select the radio button beside the Custom pop-up menu.

3. Click the Edit button, choose Find > More Options (**Figure 5**), or press ⌘M.

4. In the More Search Options dialog box that appears (**Figure 15**), turn on check boxes and enter search criteria for the attributes you want to use to search for files. Here are your options:

   ▲ **File name** is the name of the file. Choose an option from the pop-up menu (**Figure 16**), and enter all or part of the file name beside it.

   ▲ **Content includes** enables you to specify text to find within a file's contents. Enter the text in the edit box. (The volume must be indexed to find by content; see the section titled "To find by content" for details.)

Figure 14 Here's an example of items found when searching by contents. Note the Relevance column.

Figure 15 Use the More Search Options dialog box to set up custom search criteria.

Figure 16
Use this pop-up menu to specify how a file's name should match your entry.

Figure 17
Use a pop-up menu like this one to specify how a date you enter should match the creation or modification date of a file.

Figures 18, 19, & 20 Pop-up menus like these enable you to specify how criteria such as comments (left); size (middle); and kind, label, and version (right) should match your entries.

Figure 21 Use this pop-up menu to specify the type of file you want to find.

Figure 22 Use this pop-up menu to specify the label assigned to the file you want to find.

Figures 23 & 24
Use these pop-up menus to specify attributes for the folder and file (left) or folder (right) you want to find.

▲ **Date created** is the date the file was created. Choose an option from the pop-up menu (**Figure 17**), and enter a date beside it.

▲ **Date modified** is the date the file was last changed. Choose an option from the pop-up menu (**Figure 17**), and enter a date beside it.

▲ **Comments** are comments entered into the Info window for the file. Choose an option from the pop-up menu (**Figure 18**), and enter the comment text you want to search for. (I tell you about comments and the Info window in **Chapter 4**.)

▲ **Size** is the size of the file in kilobytes (K). Choose an option from the pop-up menu (**Figure 19**), and enter a size value beside it.

▲ **Kind** is the type of file. Choose an option from the first pop-up menu (**Figure 20**), and then choose a type from the pop-up menu beside it (**Figure 21**). (I tell you about file types in **Chapter 2**.)

▲ **Label** is the label applied to the file. Choose an option from the first pop-up menu (**Figure 20**), and then choose a label from the pop-up menu beside it (**Figure 22**). The options that appear on this menu may differ if you created custom labels. (I tell you about labels in **Chapters 3** and **4**.)

▲ **Version** is the version number assigned to the file. Choose an option from the pop-up menu (**Figure 20**), and enter a version number beside it.

▲ **File/folder** is whether the folder is locked or unlocked. Choose an option from the pop-up menu (**Figure 23**).

Continued on next page...

FINDING BY CUSTOM CRITERIA

▲ **Folder** refers to folder attributes. Choose an option from the first pop-up menu (**Figure 20**), and then choose an attribute from the pop-up menu beside it (**Figure 24**).

5. When you are finished setting up search criteria (**Figure 25**), click OK to return to the Sherlock window. The criteria appears in the bottom of the window (**Figure 26**).

6. Turn on the check box beside each mounted volume you want to search.

7. Click the magnifying glass button to begin the search. Sherlock searches the specified disks, displaying its status while it works. One of two things happens:

▲ If Sherlock finds matches to your criteria, it lists them in the bottom half of its window (**Figure 27**).

▲ If Sherlock does not find any matches, it displays a dialog box like the one in **Figure 8**. You can then click OK and repeat steps 2 through 7 to try again.

✔ Tips

■ Sherlock finds files that match *all* search criteria in the More Search Options dialog box (**Figure 25**). The more criteria you include, the fewer files you will find.

■ The Advanced Options area of the More Search Options dialog box (**Figure 25**) enables you to set additional search criteria for finding files. These options are technical in nature and far beyond the scope of this book.

Figure 25 Here's what the More Search Options dialog box looks like with some criteria set,...

Figure 26 ...here's what the same criteria looks like in the Sherlock window,...

Figure 27 ...and here's what the items found list might look like for that criteria.

Figure 28 Use this dialog box to name and save a set of custom search criteria so you can use it again and again.

Figure 29
When you save custom search criteria, its name appears in the Custom pop-up menu in the Sherlock window.

Figure 30 Use this dialog box to select and delete sets of custom search criteria you no longer use.

To save custom criteria

1. Follow steps 1 through 4 in the section titled "To find files by custom criteria" to set up criteria in Sherlock's More Search Options dialog box (**Figure 25**).

2. Click the Save button.

3. Enter a name for the set of search criteria in the Save Custom Settings dialog box that appears (**Figure 28**).

4. Click Save to save the settings and return to the Sherlock window.

✔ Tips

- Once you've saved custom search criteria, you can use it any time by choosing its name from the Custom pop-up menu in the Sherlock window (**Figure 29**).

- Sherlock's Custom pop-up menu (**Figure 29**) includes other commonly used, pre-defined custom search criteria.

- You can remove a set of custom search criteria by choosing Delete from the Custom menu (**Figure 29**). Select the criteria set you want to delete in the Delete Custom Search Settings dialog box that appears (**Figure 30**), and click Delete.

SAVING CUSTOM CRITERIA

263

To work with the items found list

1. Scroll through the list of items found (**Figures 7**, **14**, and **27**) to locate an item that interests you.

2. Click the item to select it (**Figure 31**). Then:

   ▲ To see where the item is located, consult the bottom part of the window for the complete path to its location (**Figure 31**).

   ▲ To open the item, double-click it, choose File > Open (**Figure 32**), or press ⌘O.

   ▲ To open the folder in which the item is stored, choose File > Open Enclosing Folder (**Figure 32**) or press ⌘E.

   ▲ To print the item (if it is a printable file), choose File > Print (**Figure 32**) or press ⌘P. (I tell you more about printing files in **Chapter 9**.)

   ▲ To move the item, drag it from the Sherlock window to a disk, folder, or window in the Finder (**Figure 33**). When you release the mouse button, the item still appears in the Sherlock window, but its path at the bottom of the window changes (**Figure 34**).

   ▲ To delete the item, drag it from the Sherlock window to the Trash, choose File > Move to Trash (**Figure 32**), or press ⌘Delete. The item still appears in the Sherlock window, but its path at the bottom of the window shows that it is in the Trash (**Figure 35**).

   ▲ To open the Info window for the item, choose one of the commands from the Get Info submenu under the File menu (**Figure 36**). (I tell you about the Info window in **Chapters 4**, **5**, and **10**.)

Figure 31 When you select a found item, the complete path to its location appears in the bottom of the Sherlock window.

Figure 32 Sherlock's File menu offers all kinds of commands for working with selected items.

Figure 33 You can move an item by dragging it from the Sherlock window to a new place on disk.

Figure 34 When you release the item, its path changes.

WORKING WITH ITEMS FOUND

Figure 35 When you move an item to the Trash, its new location appears in the path.

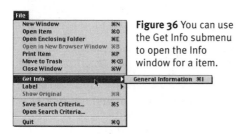

Figure 36 You can use the Get Info submenu to open the Info window for a item.

Figure 37 The Label submenu enables you to assign a label to a selected item.

Figure 38 When you use the Find Similar Files command, Sherlock conducts another search based on the selected item.

▲ To assign a label to the item, choose a label from the Label submenu under the File menu (**Figure 37**). (I cover labels in **Chapter 3**.)

▲ To view the original for the item (if it is an alias), choose File > Show Original or press ⌘⌘R. (I discuss aliases in **Chapter 4**.)

▲ To find files that are similar to the item, choose Find > Find Similar Files (**Figure 5**). Sherlock performs another find based on the selected file's contents and attributes and displays the results in its window (**Figure 38**).

✔ Tips

■ To select more than one found item at a time, hold down Shift while clicking each one. The paths for the items do not appear at the bottom of the Sherlock window when more than one item is selected.

■ You can sort the items found list in the Sherlock window (**Figure 31**) by clicking one of its column headings. You can reverse the sort order by clicking the button at the top of the vertical scroll bar for the list.

■ To remove the items found list so you can perform a new search, choose one of the first four commands on the Find menu (**Figure 5**).

■ To open a separate Sherlock window to perform a new search (without disturbing the items found list), choose File > New Window or press ⌘⌘N.

Searching the Internet

If you have Internet access, you can use Sherlock to search for Web pages with information about topics that interest you. Unlike other Internet search engines, Sherlock can search multiple directories (or *search sites*) at once. Best of all, you don't need to know special search syntax. Just enter a search word or phrase in plain English, select the search sites you want to use, and put Sherlock to work. It displays matches in order of relevance, so the most likely matches appear first.

To search the Internet

1. With Sherlock active, choose Find > Search Internet (**Figure 5**) or press ⌃ ⌘ H to display Sherlock's Internet channel (**Figure 39**).

2. Enter a search word or phrase in the edit box near the top of the window.

3. Turn on the check box beside each search site you want to use to search.

4. Click the magnifying glass button to begin the search. Sherlock searches the Internet, displaying its status while it works.

5. After a moment, the matches begin to appear. You can begin working with matches immediately or wait until Sherlock has finished searching (**Figure 40**).

✔ Tips

- When entering words in step 2, enter at least two or three words you expect to find in documents about the topic you area searching for. This helps narrow down the search, resulting in more useful matches.

- The more search sites you select the longer the search will take.

- Ads appear at the bottom of the Sherlock window. Click an ad to open a corresponding Web page in your Web browser.

Figure 39 Use Sherlock's Internet channel to search the Internet for information.

Figure 40 Sherlock displays matches, in order of relevance, in its window.

Figure 41 Select a Web page to display information about it.

Figure 42 Double-clicking the name of a Web page displays the page in your Web browser window. Here's my favorite Web site for my favorite western town.

To work with the items found list

1. Scroll through the list of items found (**Figure 40**) to locate an item that interests you.

2. Click the item to select it (**Figure 31**). Then:

   ▲ To learn more about the item, consult the information that appears beneath the items found list (**Figure 41**).

   ▲ To open the item's Web page, double-click it, choose File > Open, or press ⌘O. Your Web browser launches and displays the item in its window (**Figure 42**).

✔ Tip

■ To open a Web page in new Web browser window (rather than in the currently open Web browser window), choose File > Open in New Browser Window or press ⌘B.

■ You can sort the items found list in the Sherlock window (**Figure 40**) by clicking one of its column headings. You can reverse the sort order by clicking the button at the top of the vertical scroll bar for the list.

■ To remove the items found list so you can perform a new search, choose one of the first four commands on the Find menu (**Figure 5**).

Searching for People

If you have Internet access, you can use Sherlock to find the e-mail address and other contact information for people you know. This feature searches the entries in several popular e-mail directories to find matches.

To search for a person's e-mail address

1. With Sherlock active, choose Find > Find People (**Figure 5**) or press ⌃ ⌘ J to display Sherlock's People channel (**Figure 43**).

2. Enter the complete name for the person in the edit box near the top of the window.

3. Turn on the check box beside each search site you want to use to search.

4. Click the magnifying glass button to begin the search. Sherlock searches the directories you selected, displaying its status while it works.

5. After a moment, the matches begin to appear. You can begin working with matches immediately or wait until Sherlock has finished searching (**Figure 44**).

6. To get all the information about a matched item, click it once. The information appears in the area beneath the list (**Figure 45**).

✔ Tip

- In most cases, the only information that appears for an entry is the e-mail address.

- Although Sherlock can find e-mail addresses for people, the search sites it uses may not have up-to-date data. For example, all of the e-mail addresses shown in **Figure 44** were once valid for me, but I do not currently use any of them. Oddly enough, none of my current e-mail addresses appear on the list.

Figure 43 Use Sherlock to search for people you know.

Figure 44 Sherlock displays a list of all matches for the name you entered.

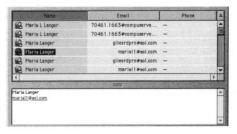

Figure 45 Click an item to see its details in the bottom of the window. (Don't use any of these old addresses to send e-mail to me; I won't get it!)

Files   People   News   Reference

Internet   Shopping   Apple   My
                                    Channel

Figure 46 Sherlock's default channels.

Figure 47
You can switch to a channel by choosing its name from the Channels menu.

Working with Channels

Sherlock's interface includes a feature called *channels*, which enables you to organize search sites based on the types of information they can find for you. Sherlock comes preconfigured with 8 channels:

◆ **Files** is for searching mounted volumes for files. It is the only channel that does not require Internet access to use.

◆ **Internet** is for searching the Internet for general information.

◆ **People** is for searching the Internet for the e-mail addresses and other contact information of people you know.

◆ **Shopping** is for searching online stores for items you may want to purchase.

◆ **News** is for searching news and information sites for news articles.

◆ **Apple** is for searching Apple computer for product and technical information.

◆ **Reference** is for searching reference libraries for information.

◆ **My Channel** is an empty channel you can use to organize your own search sites.

Other than the Files channel, all channels require Internet access to use and work very much as discussed in the section titled "Searching the Internet" earlier in this chapter.

To switch to a specific channel

Click the icon for the channel at the top of the Sherlock window (**Figure 46**).

or

Choose the name of the channel from the Channels menu (**Figure 47**).

WORKING WITH CHANNELS

Saving Searches

Sherlock enables you to save search files with the details of frequently used searches. This makes it possible to repeat a search by simply opening a Sherlock search file icon.

To save a search

1. Use Sherlock as described throughout this chapter to set up search criteria and perform a search.

2. Choose File > Save Search Criteria (**Figure 5**), or press ⌘⌥S.

3. Use the Save dialog box that appears (**Figure 48**) to select a disk location and enter a name for the search file.

4. Click Save. The search criteria is saved as a file on disk.

To use a saved search

Double-click the icon for a saved search file (**Figure 49**). Sherlock opens and performs the search, displaying the results in its window.

or

1. Choose File > Open Search Criteria (**Figure 5**).

2. Use the Open dialog box that appears to locate, select, and open the saved search criteria file.

   Sherlock performs the search, displaying the results in its window.

Figure 48 Use a standard Save As dialog box to save search criteria as a file on disk.

terms contain "Wickenburg AZ"

Figure 49 A Sherlock search file's icon looks like this.

Figure 50 You can open a search file from within Sherlock, using a standard Open dialog box.

SAVING SEARCH CRITERIA

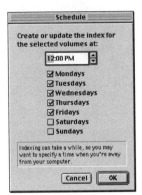

Figure 51
The Schedule dialog box enables you to set up a schedule for automatically indexing a volume.

Automatically Indexing Volumes

As discussed earlier in this chapter, to search for files by content, you must index the volume you want to search. The amount of time it takes to index a volume varies depending on how many files are on the volume and how fast your computer is. For example, my 266 MHz iMac can index its 2,700 items in less than 10 minutes, while my 300 MHz G3 takes about an hour to index its 24,000 items.

In most cases, when you want to perform a search, you don't want to wait any longer than necessary. For this reason, you may want to set up Sherlock to automatically index volumes regularly, based on a schedule you set up.

To set up an indexing schedule for a volume

1. Choose Find > Index Volumes (Figure 5) or press ⌃ ⌘ L to display the Index Volumes window (**Figure 10**).

2. Select the volume for which you want to set up a schedule.

3. Click the Schedule button to display the Schedule dialog box (**Figure 51**).

4. Set the time of day you would like the volume indexed. For best results, this should be a time when you're likely to be away from your computer, such as lunch time or the end of the work day.

5. Turn on the check box beside each day of the week that you want indexing to be completed.

6. Click OK to return to the Index Volumes window.

7. Click the Index Volumes window to dismiss it.

Fine-Tuning Functionality 14

Fine-Tuning Mac OS Functionality

The Mac OS System software includes a number of programs—primarily system extensions and control panels—that enable you to fine-tune the way your computer works. These programs perform a variety of tasks, from providing shortcuts to changing the amount of RAM available to the CPU.

In this chapter, I provide a closer look at the system extensions and control panels that enable you to customize your computer's functionality.

✔ Tips

- Some functionality options explored elsewhere in this book that are not repeated here include:
  - ▲ Finder preferences in **Chapter 4**.
  - ▲ Application memory allocation in the Info window in **Chapter 5**.
  - ▲ File Exchange in **Chapter 8**.
  - ▲ Chooser and desktop printers, in **Chapter 9**.
  - ▲ AppleTalk, File Sharing, Users & Groups, Modem, and Remote Access control panels, in **Chapter 10**.
  - ▲ TCP/IP, Remote Access, and Internet control panels, in **Chapter 11**.
  - ▲ Keychain Access and Multiple Users, in **Chapter 12**.
  - ▲ Balloon Help, in **Chapter 16**.
- You can usually customize the operation of a specific application by using its Preferences or Options dialog box. Check the application's Edit menu for a Preferences or Options command or consult its documentation for details. I tell you more about applications in **Chapter 5**.
- I discuss control panels for customizing the appearance of Mac OS, as well as installing fonts, in **Chapter 15**.

The System Folder

The software that makes up Mac OS 9 resides in the System Folder on your hard disk (**Figure 1**). The system software consists primarily of the System, Finder, and Mac OS ROM files, and the following types of items:

◆ **Extensions** are files that add features or extend the functionality of the system. Their features are preset and cannot be modified—just install them and they work. You can find them in the Extensions folder.

◆ **Drivers** are files that enable your computer to use hardware devices such as printers and CD-ROM drives. Like extensions, their features are preset and cannot be modified—install them and the devices they control become available for use. You can find them in the Extensions folder.

◆ **Control panels** are files that either add features to the system or enable you to set system options. They offer an interface you can use to modify their settings. You can find them in the Control Panels folder.

◆ **Fonts** are typefaces that are used to display text on screen and in printed documents. When you install them properly, they're available for use in every application that can access fonts. You can find them in the Fonts folder. (I cover fonts in **Chapter 15**.)

◆ **Startup Items** are items that open when you start your computer. You can find them in the Startup Items folder, which is empty by default.

◆ **Shutdown Items** are items that open when you shut down your computer. You can find them in the Shutdown Items folder, which is empty by default.

Figure 1
The standard contents of a Mac OS 9 System Folder.

✔ Tips

■ Do not remove any item from your System Folder or a folder within it unless you know what you are doing or are instructed by someone who knows what he or she is doing. Removing a required item in error could prevent your computer from starting!

■ To prevent extensions, control panels, and startup items from loading, hold down (Shift) while the computer is starting up.

THE SYSTEM FOLDER

Figure 2 The Extensions Manager control panel.

Figure 3 The Control Panels submenu under the Apple menu offers many customization options.

Extensions Manager

Extensions Manager (**Figure 2**) is a control panel that enables you turn individual extensions, drivers, control panels, startup items, and shutdown items on or off. An item that is turned off does not load at startup so it is disabled.

Extensions Manager also lets you create sets of item settings. By creating a variety of sets for different purposes, you can change settings quickly and easily by selecting a menu item.

✔ Tip

■ After making changes in the Extensions Manager control panel, you must restart your computer for the changes to take effect.

To open Extensions Manager

Choose Apple menu > Control Panels > Extensions Manager (**Figure 3**).

To open Extensions Manager during startup

Hold down Spacebar while the computer is starting up. Do not release Spacebar until the Extensions Manager window appears (**Figure 2**).

✔ Tip

■ If you open Extensions Manager during startup and make changes, it is not necessary to restart your computer for the changes to take effect. The changes take effect as the startup process finishes after you close Extensions Manager.

OPENING EXTENSIONS MANAGER

275

To toggle item settings

1. Open the Extensions Manager control panel (**Figure 2**).

2. Click the check box to the left of an item name to turn it on or off (**Figure 4**).

3. Repeat step 2 for each item whose setting you want to toggle.

✔ Tip

■ To start over with the settings that were in the Extensions Manager window when you first opened it, click Revert.

To turn all items on or off

1. Open the Extensions Manager control panel (**Figure 2**).

2. To turn all items on, choose Edit > All On (**Figure 5**).

   or

   To turn all items off, choose Edit > All Off (**Figure 5**).

To save settings

To save the settings and immediately restart your computer, click Restart.

or

To save your settings without restarting your computer, close the Extensions Manager window.

✔ Tips

■ If you opened Extensions Manager while the computer was starting up, click Continue; there is no Restart button.

■ You can also save settings to the current set by switching to another set. I tell you about sets next.

Folder with some items turned on and others turned off

Item turned off

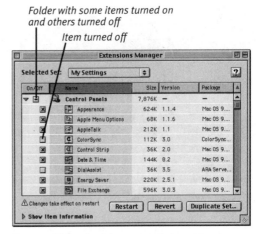

Figure 4 Click a check box to toggle its setting.

Figure 5 Use the All On or All Off commands under the Edit menu to quickly turn all items on or off.

Figure 6 The Selected Set pop-up menu lists all settings.

Figure 7
The File menu includes commands to create, duplicate, rename, and delete sets.

Figure 8 Enter a name for the set in the New Set dialog box.

To choose a set

In the Extensions Manager control panel (**Figure 4**), choose the set that you want from the Selected Set pop-up menu (**Figure 6**). The settings for the set are applied.

✔ Tips

- Extensions Manager comes configured with three sets:

  ▲ **Mac OS 9.0 All** consists of all the Mac OS 9 items that are installed.

  ▲ **Mac OS 9.0 Base** consists of the items that make up a basic Mac OS 9 system.

  ▲ **My Settings** starts with all items turned on but can be changed.

- You cannot change the settings in or delete the Mac OS 9.0 All or Mac OS 9.0 Base sets.

To create a set

1. Open the Extensions Manager control panel (**Figure 2**).

2. Choose File > New Set (**Figure 7**).

3. Enter a name for the set in the New Set dialog box that appears (**Figure 8**), and click OK. The name of the set appears in the Select Set pop-up window.

4. Toggle item check boxes as desired for the set.

✔ Tip

- Other commands under the File menu (**Figure 7**) let you delete, rename, and duplicate the currently selected set.

WORKING WITH SETS

To show information about items

Click the Show Item Information triangle in the Extensions Manager window (**Figure 4**). The window expands. When you select an item, its description appears in the expanded area (**Figure 9**).

✔ Tip

- You can click the Hide Item Information triangle in the Extensions Manager window (**Figure 9**) to hide information about selected items.

To sort items

In the Extensions Manager window (**Figure 4**), click the heading at the top of the column by which you want to sort. The item order changes (**Figure 10**).

To hide the items in a folder

In the Extensions Manager window (**Figure 4**), click the triangle to the left of the folder whose items you want to hide. The items disappear (**Figure 11**).

✔ Tip

- You can click the triangle to the left of a folder with hidden items in the Extensions Manager window (**Figure 11**) to display the items.

Figure 9 When you expand the Extensions Manager window, information about a selected item is displayed in the expanded area.

Figure 10 Click a heading to sort by its contents.

Figure 11 Click the triangle to the left of a folder to hide its items.

Figure 12
The Apple menu offers quick and easy access to just about anything you want. These are the Apple menu items that were automatically installed on my iMac.

Apple Menu Options

The Apple menu (**Figure 12**) offers easy access to whatever applications, documents, folders, or other items you want to put there. It also automatically keeps track of recently used documents, applications, and network servers.

You can customize the way the Apple menu works by changing settings in the Apple Menu Options control panel. You can also add or remove items from the Apple menu so it displays the items you use most.

✔ Tips

- The Mac OS Installer installs the Apple menu items that are compatible with your computer. Because of this, your Apple menu may include more or fewer items than what you see in **Figure 12**.

- I explain how to use items that appear under the Apple menu throughout this book.

Operating System Trivia

Back in the days before System 7, when the average Macintosh had only 1 MB of RAM, the Apple menu offered users access to little programs called *desk accessories* that could be opened and used at any time—even when another program was running. Although it doesn't sound impressive now, back then it was a very big deal.

APPLE MENU OPTIONS

To set Apple menu options

1. Choose Apple menu > Control Panels > Apple Menu Options (**Figure 3**). The Apple Menu Options control panel appears (**Figure 13**).

2. To display the contents of folders on the Apple menu as submenus, select the On radio button under Submenus.

   or

   To display the folders on the Apple menu as items without submenus, select the Off radio button under Submenus.

3. To have Mac OS automatically track recently used items, make sure the Remember recently used items check box is turned on. Then enter values in the three edit boxes to specify the number of recent items Mac OS should track.

4. Close the Apple Menu Options control panel window to save your settings.

✔ Tips

■ I tell you about recently used items in **Chapter 4**.

■ The submenus feature, which is often referred to as *hierarchical folders*, can display up to five levels of folders (**Figure 14**).

Figure 13
The Apple Menu Options control panel gives you some control over the way the Apple menu works.

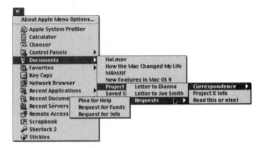

Figure 14 You can display up to five levels of folders as submenus under the Apple menu.

Figure 15 Drag the item that you want to add to the Apple menu into the Apple Menu Items folder in your System Folder.

Figure 16
The item is added to the Apple menu.

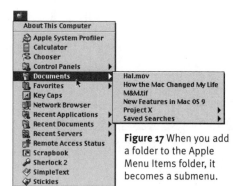

Figure 17 When you add a folder to the Apple Menu Items folder, it becomes a submenu.

To add items to the Apple menu

1. Open the icon for your computer's startup disk.

2. Locate and open the icon for the System Folder.

3. Drag the item that you want to add to the Apple menu into the Apple Menu Items folder in your System Folder (**Figure 15**). The item is added to the Apple menu (**Figure 16**).

✔ Tips

- Adding items to the Apple menu is a great way to make them quick and easy to access.

- Your computer's startup disk is normally its internal hard disk.

- It's a good idea to add an alias of an item to the Apple Menu Items folder rather than the original item. This makes it easy to keep applications and documents where they belong so they're easy to find and back up. To add an alias to the Apple Menu Items folder, follow the above steps, but hold down ⌘ Option while dragging the icon. When you release the mouse button, an alias is automatically created and added to the Apple Menu Items folder. I tell you about aliases in **Chapter 4**.

- The Favorites feature of Mac OS enables you to add aliases of items to the Favorites folder, which appears under the Apple menu. I tell you about Favorites in **Chapter 4**.

- When you add a folder or an alias to a folder to the Apple Menu Items folder, a submenu with the folder's contents is automatically created (**Figure 17**).

- To remove an item from the Apple menu, simply drag its icon out of the Apple Menu Items folder in your System Folder.

ColorSync

ColorSync is a color matching technology developed by Apple computer and supported by many applications and hardware devices. You can use the ColorSync control panel to set device and document profiles, as well as color matching methods for your computer.

✔ Tip

■ ColorSync is primarily of interest to graphic designers who do a lot of color output. If color matching is not vital to your work, leave the ColorSync control panel set as is.

To set ColorSync options

1. Choose Apple menu > Control Panels > ColorSync (**Figure 3**) to open the ColorSync control panel.

2. Click the Profile tab and choose Profiles for Standard Devices from the top pop-up menu (**Figure 18**). Then choose appropriate options from the Input, Display, Output, and Proofer pop-up menus.

3. Choose Default Profiles for Documents from the top pop-up menu (**Figure 19**). Then choose appropriate options from the RGB Default, CMYK Default, Gray Default, and Lab Profile pop-up menus.

4. Click the CMMs tab to display its options (**Figure 20**). Then choose an option from the Preferred CMM pop-up menu: Automatic, Heidelberg CMM, or Apple CMM.

5. Click the ColorSync control panel's close box. In the dialog box that appears (**Figure 21**), click Save to save your settings.

✔ Tip

■ For detailed information about using ColorSync with specific software or hardware products, consult the documentation for those products.

Figure 18 The device profile options determine how ColorSync works with your hardware.

Figure 19 The document profile options determine how ColorSync works with your documents.

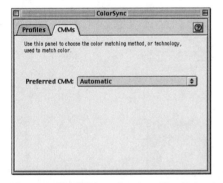

Figure 20 The CMMs options specify which color management method ColorSync should use.

Figure 21 Click Save to save your settings.

Figure 22
The Control Strip control panel window.

Energy Settings
Monitor BitDepth
Sound Volume
AppleTalk Switch
Keychain Strip
Printer Selector
Web Sharing

Play a CD
Apple Location Manager
Remote Access
File Sharing
Monitor Resolution
Sound Strip

Figure 23 The control strip. The modules that appear on your control strip may differ from these.

Figure 24
If you select the Hot key to show/hide radio button, you can click Define hot key...

Figure 25
...to display this dialog box. Then change the hot key to show and hide the control strip.

Figure 26
Use the Font pop-up menu to select a font.

Control Strip

The Control Strip control panel (**Figure 22**) enables you to set options for the control strip that appears at the bottom of your screen (**Figure 23**).

✔ Tips

■ The control strip consists of *modules* that display pop-up menus for quick and easy access to many Mac OS features. The modules that appear on your control strip vary depending on your computer model and Mac OS options installed. Additional control strip modules are available from third-party developers.

■ You can collapse and expand the control strip by clicking the tab at its right end.

To set control strip options

1. Choose Apple menu > Control Panels > Control Strip (**Figure 3**). The Control Strip control panel appears (**Figure 22**).

2. Select a Show/Hide radio button:

   ▲ **Show Control Strip** displays the control strip.

   ▲ **Hide Control Strip** does not display the control strip.

   ▲ **Hot key to show/hide** enables the Define hot key button (**Figure 24**), which you can click to display a dialog box for changing the hot key (**Figure 25**). Pressing the keystroke in this dialog box toggles the display of the control strip.

3. Choose a font from the Font pop-up menu (**Figure 26**).

4. Choose a font size from the Size pop-up menu.

5. Close the window to save your settings.

SETTING CONTROL STRIP OPTIONS

Energy Saver

Energy Saver is a control panel that enables you to set energy saving options:

◆ **Sleep Setup (Figures 27** and **28)** enables you to specify when your system, display, and hard disk should sleep.

◆ **Schedule (Figure 29)** enables you to set the days and times for your computer to automatically start up and shut down.

Figure 27 The Sleep Setup options of the Energy Saver control panel window.

✔ Tips

■ Computers that do not support sleep mode do not support Energy Saver. On these computers, the Mac OS Installer installs Auto Power On/Off **(Figure 32)**, which offers the same functionality as Energy Saver's Scheduled Startup & Shutdown options.

■ The Energy Saver control panel offers different options for PowerBook users, as I explain later in this section.

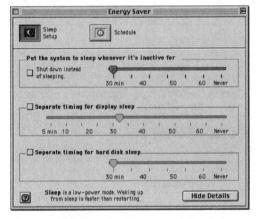

Figure 28 Click Show Details to expand the window to show more options.

To set automatic sleep options

1. Choose Apple menu > Control Panels > Energy Saver **(Figure 3)**.

2. If necessary, click the Sleep Setup button at the top of the Energy Saver window that appears **(Figure 27)**.

3. Use the slider to set the amount of idle time before the computer goes to sleep.

4. To set the computer so it shuts down instead of going into sleep mode, turn on the Shut down instead of sleeping check box.

5. To set different options for display (monitor) sleep and hard disk sleep, click Show Details. The window expands to show two additional sliders. Turn on the check box beside each slider you want to set, and set the sliders **(Figure 28)**.

6. Close the window to save your settings.

✔ Tip

■ I tell you about sleep mode and shutting down the computer in **Chapter 2**.

Figure 29 The Schedule options of the Energy Saver window.

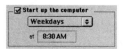

Figure 30 Turn on the Start up the computer check box to choose a day and time.

Figure 31
Choose a day or group of days from the pop-up menu in the dialog box.

Figure 32 The Auto Power On/Off control panel window.

To schedule start up & shut down times

1. Choose Apple menu > Control Panels > Energy Saver (**Figure 3**).

2. If necessary, click the Schedule button at the top of the Energy Saver window that appears (**Figure 29**).

3. To start the computer at a specific time, turn on the Start up the computer check box (**Figure 30**). Use the pop-up menu beneath it (**Figure 31**) to select the day or days on which the computer should automatically start. Enter a time in the at edit box beneath the pop-up menu.

4. To shut down the computer at a specific time, turn on the Shut down the computer check box. Use the pop-up menu beneath it (**Figure 31**) to select the day or days on which the computer should automatically shut down. Enter a time in the at edit box beneath the pop-up menu.

5. Close the window to save your settings.

✔ Tips

- You can use this feature to start your computer before you arrive at work so it's ready and waiting for you.

- You can also use this feature to automatically shut down at a certain time so you don't work too long.

- If your computer has Auto Power On/Off installed rather than Energy Saver, choose Apple menu > Control Panels > Auto Power On/Off. Then set options in the Auto Power On/Off control panel (**Figure 32**). The interface is slightly different from Energy Saver but works the same way.

SCHEDULING START UP & SHUT DOWN TIMES

To set energy use options on a PowerBook

1. Choose Apple menu > Control Panels > Energy Saver.

2. If necessary, click the Idle Sleep button and the Hide Details button in the Energy Saver control panel that appears so the control panel window looks like the one in **Figure 33**.

3. Choose an option from the Settings for pop-up menu (**Figure 34**) to specify which setting should be modified:

   ▲ **Battery** is for settings that should be applied when the PowerBook is running on battery power.

   ▲ **Power Adapter** is for settings that should be applied when the PowerBook is plugged in.

4. Drag the slider in the Energy Use area to a desired position between Better Conservation (less power consumption) or Better Performance (more power consumption).

5. Close the control panel window to save your settings.

✔ Tips

■ The PowerBook version of the Energy Saver control panel replaces the PowerBook control panel in versions of Mac OS prior to 8.5.

■ The Energy Saver control panel offers different options when installed on a PowerBook because power consumption is a major concern of PowerBook users who often depend on batteries for power.

■ Detailed options for the Energy Saver control panel on a PowerBook are basically the same as those for any other Macintosh model.

Figure 33 Basic Idle Sleep options in the Energy Saver control panel on a PowerBook.

Figure 34 Use this pop-up menu to specify whether settings should apply to the computer when running on battery power or plugged in.

Figure 35 Advanced Settings options in the Energy Saver control panel on a PowerBook.

To set advanced options on a PowerBook

1. Choose Apple menu > Control Panels > Energy Saver.

2. If necessary, click the Advanced Settings button in the Energy Saver control panel that appears (**Figure 35**).

3. Choose an option from the Settings for pop-up menu (**Figure 34**) to specify which setting should be modified.

4. Set Network Connections options as desired by toggling check boxes:

   ▲ **Reconnect to servers on wakeup** automatically reconnects to any servers to which the PowerBook was connected when it went to sleep.

   ▲ **Remember my passwords** reconnects to servers without prompting you for a password.

   ▲ **Wake when the modem detects a ring** wakes the computer when its modem detects an incoming call. This option is not supported by all PowerBook models.

5. Set Additional Power Savings options as desired by toggling check boxes:

   ▲ **Allow processor cycling** switches your PowerBook's processor to a reduced power mode when idle.

   ▲ **Turn off the PowerBook display instead of dimming it** shuts off the display when idle for the amount of time specified for display dimming.

   ▲ **Turn off power to inactive PC Cards** cuts power to installed PCMCIA cards that are not in use.

   ▲ **Reduce processor speed** saves power by changing the processor speed. This option is not supported by all Power-Book models.

6. Close the control panel to save your settings.

SETTING ADVANCED ENERGY SAVER OPTIONS

General Controls

The General Controls control panel (**Figure 36**) enables you to set a variety of options that affect the way your computer works.

To set General Controls control panel options

1. Choose Apple menu > Control Panels > General Controls (**Figure 3**). The General Controls window appears (**Figure 36**).

2. To display the icons on your Desktop while other applications are active, turn on the Show Desktop when in background check box.

3. To automatically display the Launcher control panel when the computer starts, turn on the Show Launcher at system startup check box.

4. To have your computer inform you at start up when it was shut down improperly, turn on the Warn me if computer was shut down improperly check box. Enabling this option also instructs Disk First Aid to automatically check your hard disk when you start up after an improper shut down.

5. To keep items in the System Folder or Applications folder from being renamed or removed, turn on the appropriate check boxes in the Folder Protection area.

6. To set the rate at which the insertion point blinks, select a radio button in the Insertion Point Blinking area. The sample to the left of the radio buttons shows you the effect of your change.

7. To set the number of times a selected menu item blinks before the menu disappears, select a Menu Blinking radio button.

8. To set the default folder location in a Save As dialog box, select a Documents radio button.

9. Close the window to save your settings.

Figure 36 The General Controls control panel window.

SimpleText

Figure 37 With folder protection enabled, item icons include tiny padlocks...

You cannot move "SimpleText" to the "Desktop", because Application Folder Protection is on. To move this item, first turn off Application Folder Protection in the General Controls panel.

OK

Figure 38 ...and a dialog box like this appears when you try to move one.

✔ Tips

■ I tell you about Disk First Aid in **Chapter 6**, about Launcher on the next page, and about the Save As dialog box in **Chapter 5**.

■ You cannot change folder protection options if file sharing is turned on. I discuss file sharing in **Chapter 10**.

■ With folder protection turned on, icons in protected folders appear with tiny padlocks beside them (**Figure 37**). A dialog box like the one in **Figure 38** appears if you try to move something out of a protected folder.

■ If you select Documents folder in step 8 but do not have a Documents folder, Mac OS creates one for you.

SETTING GENERAL CONTROLS OPTIONS

Figure 39 The Launcher window appears at the bottom of the screen.

Figure 40 Hold down ⌘ while clicking in the Launcher window to display a menu of button sizes.

Figure 41 To add an item, drag its icon into the Launcher window.

Figure 42 A button for an alias of the item is added to the Launcher window.

Launcher

Launcher displays a special window with buttons you can click to open specific items. You can add and remove items as desired to include only the items you access frequently.

✔ Tip

- Launcher works with aliases, which I discuss in **Chapter 4.**

To open Launcher

Choose Apple menu > Control Panels > Launcher (**Figure 3**). The Launcher window appears (**Figure 39**).

✔ Tips

- To have Launcher automatically appear at start up, turn on the Show Launcher at system startup check box in the General Controls control panel (**Figure 36**). I discuss General Controls on the previous page.

- To change the size of the buttons in the Launcher window, hold down ⌘ while clicking in the window to display a menu of button sizes (**Figure 40**). Choose the size you want.

To add items to Launcher

Drag the icon for an item that you want to include in Launcher into the Launcher window (**Figure 41**). When you release the mouse button, a button for the item appears in the Launcher window (**Figure 42**). The original item remains where it was.

To remove items from Launcher

Hold down Option while dragging the item to the Trash.

Keyboard

The Keyboard control panel (**Figure 43**) enables you to select keyboard layouts to appear on the Keyboard menu, set key repeat options for keyboard operation, and assign items to function keys.

To set basic keyboard options

1. Choose Apple menu > Control Panels > Keyboard (**Figure 3**) to display the Keyboard window (**Figure 43**).

2. Turn on the check box beside each keyboard layout that you want to include on the Keyboard menu (**Figure 44**).

3. Use the Key Repeat Rate slider to set how fast a key repeats when held down.

4. Use the Delay Until Repeat slider to set how long a key must be pressed before it starts to repeat.

5. Close the window to save your settings.

✔ Tips

- You can use the keyboard layout feature to type using the keyboard layout for another language. If you select more than one keyboard layout in step 2 above, a keyboard menu appears beside the application menu (**Figure 44**). Choose the keyboard layout for the language you want to type in.

- At least one keyboard layout must be selected. That's why the check box for U.S. is gray in **Figure 43**.

- The Scripts pop-up menu is for use with systems that have WorldScript, a multi-language feature of Mac OS, installed.

- You can click the Options button (**Figure 43**) to set additional options for using multiple keyboard layouts (**Figure 45**).

- Key Repeat settings are especially useful for heavy-handed typists.

Figure 43
The Keyboard control panel window.

Figure 44 When you select more than one language in the Keyboard Layouts area, a keyboard menu appears beside the application menu.

Figure 45 Use the Options dialog box to set options for switching from one keyboard layout to another.

Figure 46 Use the Hot Function Keys dialog box to assign items to function keys.

Figure 47 Drag the item from a Finder window into the box for a function key.

Figure 48 When you release the mouse button, the item you dragged is assigned to the function key.

To assign items to function keys

1. Choose Apple menu > Control Panels > Keyboard (**Figure 3**) to display the Keyboard window (**Figure 43**).

2. Click the Function Keys button to open the Hot Function Keys dialog box (**Figure 46**).

3. Drag an item you want to assign to a function key to the box beside the function key (**Figure 47**). When you release the mouse button, the item appears in the box (**Figure 48**).

4. Repeat step 3 for each item you want to assign to a function key.

5. To set up the function keys so you have to hold down [Option] when using them as hot keys, turn on the Use F1 through F12 as Function Keys check box. This enables you to use the function keys as assigned within applications (without holding down [Option]).

6. Click OK.

7. Close the Keyboard window.

✔ Tips

■ If the Function Key button is not visible in the Keyboard control panel (**Figure 43**), your computer does not support this feature.

■ Once you assign an item to a function key, pressing the function key opens the item.

ASSIGNING ITEMS TO FUNCTION KEYS

Mouse & Trackpad

The Mouse control panel (**Figure 49** or **50**) enables you to set options that control the way the mouse pointer works. The Trackpad control panel (**Figure 52**) enables you to control the way the trackpad works on a PowerBook.

To set mouse options

1. Choose Apple menu > Control Panels > Mouse (**Figure 3**). The Mouse control panel window appears (**Figure 49** or **50**).

2. To set the speed of the mouse movement on your screen, drag the Mouse Tracking slider (**Figure 49** or **50**).

3. To set the amount of time between each click of a double-click, drag the Double-Click Speed slider (**Figure 49** or **50**). The leftmost position is for longer time between clicks, and the rightmost position is for shorter time between clicks.

4. To set the mouse tracks option on a Power-Book, drag the Mouse Tracks slider (**Figure 50**). The Off position (left) turns off this feature, and the rightmost position displays the longest mouse tracks.

5. To make the I-beam pointer more visible on a PowerBook, turn on the Thick I-beam check box (**Figure 50**).

6. Close the window to save your settings.

✔ Tip

- If you're just learning to use a mouse, you may find it helpful to set the mouse speed and double-click rates to slower than the default settings shown in **Figure 49** or **50**.

Figure 49
The Mouse control panel window on an iMac...

Figure 50
...and on a PowerBook.

Figure 51
The Trackpad control panel.

Figure 52 To turn on the Dragging and Drag lock check boxes, you must turn on the check boxes above them.

To set PowerBook Trackpad options

1. Choose Apple menu > Control Panels > Trackpad. The Trackpad control panel appears (**Figure 51**).

2. To change the speed at which the mouse pointer moves, select a Tracking Speed radio button.

3. To change time between double-click clicks, select a Double-Click Speed radio button. The option on the left is for more time between double-clicks, and the option on the right is for less time.

4. To use the trackpad for clicking, dragging, and drag lock, turn on the appropriate check boxes in the Use Trackpad for area.

5. Close the Trackpad window to save your settings.

✔ Tips

■ To turn on the Dragging or Drag lock check box, you must turn on the check box above it (**Figure 51**).

■ To use the trackpad dragging feature, tap the item you want to drag, then tap and move your finger on the trackpad to drag it. When Drag lock is enabled, you must tap again to release the item.

SETTING POWERBOOK TRACKPAD OPTIONS

Memory

The Memory control panel (**Figure 53**) enables you to set options that determine how RAM is used in your computer. On most computers, it controls the following three options:

◆ **Disk cache** is RAM set aside for storage of frequently used computer instructions. The recommended disk cache setting is 32 kilobytes (K) of cache for each megabyte of installed RAM.

◆ **Virtual memory** is hard disk space used as RAM. For efficient performance on a computer with a PowerPC processor, virtual memory should be turned on and set to default settings.

◆ **RAM disk** is RAM used as disk space. If set up and used properly, it can benefit Power-Book users by reducing the computer's power consumption, thus increasing battery life.

✔ Tips

■ I tell you more about RAM in **Chapter 5**.

■ The options that appear in the Memory control panel vary depending on the computer model.

Figure 53 The Memory control panel window.

Figure 54 About This Computer tells you about the amount of RAM that is installed and in use.

To set memory options

1. Choose Apple menu > Control Panels > Memory (**Figure 3**). The Memory control panel window appears (**Figure 53**).

2. To set the disk cache size, select the Custom setting radio button. In the warning dialog box that appears, click the Custom button. Then click the arrows beside the Size after restart edit box that appears in the Memory control panel window to change the value.

3. To turn virtual memory on or off, select the appropriate Virtual Memory radio button. If you select On, choose a hard disk from the pop-up menu and click the arrows beside the edit box to set the total amount of RAM that you want.

4. To turn a RAM disk on or off, select the appropriate RAM Disk radio button. If you select On, use the slider to set the RAM disk size.

5. Close the window to save your settings.

6. If you changed settings in the Memory window, restart your computer.

✔ Tips

■ Don't change the memory options unless you know what you are doing or are following detailed instructions provided by someone who knows what he or she is doing. These are powerful options that can negatively affect your computer's performance if set improperly. When in doubt, click the Use Defaults button to use the default settings for your computer.

■ You can learn how much RAM is installed in your computer by choosing Apple menu > About This Computer (when the Finder is active). A window like the one in **Figure 54** appears. It specifies the amount of installed (built-in) RAM, virtual memory, and largest unused block of RAM as well as the amount of RAM in use by applications.

Startup Disk

The Startup Disk control panel enables you to specify which disk or volume should be used to start the computer.

Figure 55
The Startup Disk window shows all bootable high-capacity media, including those available via network.

✔ Tips

- Any *bootable disk*—a disk with a correctly configured System Folder on it—can be a startup disk.

- You don't need to use the Startup Disk control panel to start from a bootable floppy disk (like a Disk Tools disk). Just insert the disk before starting up.

To set the startup disk

1. Choose Apple menu > Control Panels > Startup Disk (**Figure 3**). The Startup Disk window appears (**Figure 55**).

2. Select the icon for the disk that should be used as the startup disk the next time the computer is started.

3. Close the Startup Disk window.

✔ Tip

- The Startup Disk control panel window displays all mounted bootable disks.

To start from a bootable CD

Hold down C right after hearing the computer's startup tone. You can release this key when you see the Welcome to Mac OS window. It is usually not necessary to use the Startup Disk control panel to start from a bootable CD.

The type of connection appears here.

Figure 56
The Infrared control panel.

Figure 57
The Options dialog box for the Infrared control panel, which is only available if your computer supports both IrDA and IRTalk.

Figure 58
The AppleTalk control panel.

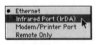

Figure 59 Select Infrared Port (IrDA) from the Connect via pop-up menu.

Figure 60
The Infrared control panel indicates connection status.

✔ Tip

■ The Infrared control panel also displays the status of the IrDA connection (**Figure 60**).

Infrared

Some Mac models, including many PowerBooks and the original iMac, have infrared communication capabilities. If you have one of these computers, you can use the infrared port to communicate with other computers or devices that have infrared networking capabilities, using one of the following infrared options:

◆ **IrDA** enables you to connect to a network using infrared communication. This option is available on all Mac models with infrared capabilities.

◆ **IRTalk**, a proprietary Apple protocol, enables you to exchange files with another Macintosh computer that that has infrared capabilities and supports IRTalk.

To set up IrDA

1. Choose Apple menu > Control Panels > Infrared. The Infrared control panel appears (**Figure 56**).

2. If IrDA does not appear in the upper left corner of the window, click Options. Select the IrDA radio button in the Options dialog box (**Figure 57**) and click OK.

3. Close the Infrared control panel. Click Save or OK in any confirmation or warning dialog boxes that appear.

4. Choose Apple menu > Control Panels > AppleTalk (**Figure 3**) to display the Apple-Talk control panel (**Figure 58**).

5. Select Infrared Port (IrDA) from the Connect via pop-up menu (**Figure 59**).

6. Close the AppleTalk control panel. Click Save or OK in any confirmation or warning dialog boxes that appear.

7. Position the infrared port on your computer within 3 feet of the LAN access device. You can now utilize network services.

SETTING UP IRDA

To set up IRTalk

1. Choose Apple menu > Control Panels > Infrared. The Infrared control panel appears (**Figure 56**).

2. If IRTalk does not appear in the upper left corner of the window, click Options. Select the IRTalk radio button in the Options dialog box (**Figure 57**), and click OK.

3. Close the Infrared control panel. Click Save or OK in any confirmation or warning dialog boxes that appear.

4. Choose Apple menu > Control Panels > AppleTalk (**Figure 3**) to display the Apple-Talk control panel (**Figure 58**).

5. Select Infrared Port (IRTalk) from the Connect via pop-up menu (**Figure 61**).

6. Close the AppleTalk control panel. Click Save or OK in any confirmation or warning dialog boxes that appear.

7. Open the Apple IR File Exchange folder in the Apple Extras folder on your hard disk (**Figure 62**).

8. Double-click the Apple IR File Exchange application icon. You are now ready to send and receive files via IRTalk.

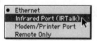

Figure 61 Select Infrared Port (IRTalk) from the Connect via pop-up menu.

Figure 62 The contents of the Apple IR File Exchange folder.

Figure 63
The main window of the QuickTime Settings control panel.

Figure 64
The AutoPlay options of the QuickTime Settings control panel.

Figure 65
The Connection Speed options in the QuickTime Settings control panel.

Figure 66
The QuickTime Exchange option in the QuickTime Settings control panel.

QuickTime Settings

The QuickTime settings control panel (**Figure 63**) controls the way QuickTime and your CD-ROM drive work. In this section, I explain how to set some commonly used options.

✔ Tips

- You can also use the QuickTime Settings control panel to register QuickTime Pro, as I discuss in **Chapter 6**.

- I discuss QuickTime in **Chapter 6**.

To set CD & QuickTime options

1. Choose Apple menu > Control Panels > QuickTime Settings (**Figure 3**). The Quick-Time Settings control panel appears (**Figure 63**).

2. To set CD autoplay options, choose Auto-Play from the pop-up menu to display the AutoPlay options (**Figure 64**). Toggle check box settings as desired:

   ▲ **Enable Audio CD AutoPlay** automatically plays audio CDs when they are inserted.

   ▲ **Enable CD-ROM AutoPlay** automatically starts CD-ROM discs when they are inserted.

3. To set the connection speed for playing back QuickTime files over the Web, choose Connection Speed from the pop-up menu. Then select the radio button for your usual Internet connection speed (**Figure 65**). You may also be able to turn on the Apple Multiple Simultaneous Streams to play multiple streaming channels at once.

4. To easily open QuickTime-compatible media files created on any platform, choose QuickTime Exchange from the pop-up menu. Then turn on the Enable QuickTime Exchange check box (**Figure 66**).

5. Close the window to save your settings.

✔ Tips

- Not all CD-ROM discs utilize the CD-ROM autoplay feature.

- Some Mac OS users have reported computer virus problems when enabling the CD-ROM autoplay feature. If your computer does not have virus protection, consider keeping this option turned off.

Date & Time

The Date & Time control panel (**Figure 67**) enables you to set the date, time, and time zone for your computer. If you have Internet access, you can also use a network time server to set your computer's clock to the exact time.

To manually set the date & time

1. Choose Apple menu > Control Panels > Date & Time (**Figure 3**). The Date & Time control panel window appears (**Figure 67**).

2. To change the date, click the numbers that make up the date and use the arrow buttons to change them.

3. To change the time, click the numbers that make up the time and use the arrow buttons to change them (**Figure 68**).

4. Close the window to save your settings.

To use the time server

1. Choose Apple menu > Control Panels > Date & Time (**Figure 3**). The Date & Time control panel window appears (**Figure 67**).

2. Turn on the Use a Network Time Server check box.

3. Click the Server Options button.

4. In the Server Options dialog box that appears (**Figure 69**), select one of the Update the time radio buttons:

   ▲ **Automatically, when the system clock is different from the time server** changes the time when you are connected to the Internet and your computer's time is different from the time server's time.

   ▲ **Every** enables you to set the number of hours, days, weeks, or months between updates.

   ▲ **Manually** updates the time when you click the Set Time Now button.

Figure 67 The Date & Time control panel window.

Figure 68 Click the digits that you want to change, then click the arrow buttons to change them.

Figure 69 Use the Server Options dialog box to set options for using a time server.

5. Click Set Time Now to update the time immediately. (Your computer will connect to the Internet if necessary.)

6. Click OK to save the Server Options settings.

7. Close the Date & Time window to save your settings.

Figure 70 The Date Formats dialog box lets you customize date formats.

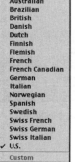

Figure 71
Use the Region pop-up menus to choose one of the preconfigured date, time, and number formats.

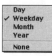

Figure 72
Choose a long date component from this menu.

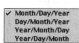

Figure 73
Choose a short date format from this pop-up menu.

Figure 74
The Time Formats dialog box lets you customize the time format.

To set date & time formats

1. Choose Apple menu > Control Panels > Date & Time (**Figure 3**). The Date & Time control panel window appears (**Figure 67**).

2. To change the date format, click Date Formats. The Date Formats dialog box appears (**Figure 70**).

3. Choose an option from the Region pop-up menu (**Figure 71**).

4. Modify the long date format by choosing options from the Long Date pop-up menus (**Figure 72**) and entering punctuation in the edit boxes. If desired, turn on the Leading zero for day check box.

5. Choose a short date format from the Short Date pop-up menu (**Figure 73**). If desired, change the separator character and turn on check boxes to include a leading zero for the day, a leading zero for the month, and the century as part of the year.

6. Click OK to save your changes.

7. To change the time format, click Time Formats. The Time Format dialog box appears (**Figure 74**).

8. Choose an option from the Region pop-up menu (**Figure 71**).

9. Select radio buttons in the Clock area to set clock preferences.

10. If desired, change the suffixes and separator in the Before noon, After noon, and Separator edit boxes and turn on the Use leading zero for hour check box.

11. Click OK to save your changes.

12. Close the Date & Time window to save your settings.

✔ Tip

■ You can check the custom formats you create by looking at the sample area in the Date Formats and Time Format dialog boxes (**Figures 70** and **74**).

To set time zone options

1. Choose Apple menu > Control Panels > Date & Time (**Figure 3**). The Date & Time control panel window appears (**Figure 67**).

2. Click Set Time Zone. A dialog box like the one in **Figure 75** appears. Select a city in your time zone, and click OK.

3. Set check boxes in the Time Zone area:

    ▲ **Set Daylight-Saving Time Automatically** enables your computer to automatically adjusts the clock for daylight saving time twice a year.

    ▲ **Daylight-Saving Time is in effect**, which is only available when the Set Daylight-Saving Time Automatically check box is turned off, enables you to manually specify whether daylight saving time is in effect.

4. Close the window to save your settings.

To set menu bar clock options

1. Choose Apple menu > Control Panels > Date & Time (**Figure 3**). The Date & Time control panel window appears (**Figure 67**).

2. Select a Menu Bar Clock radio button to display (On) or hide (Off) the menu bar clock.

3. If you choose On, click the Clock Options button to display the Clock Options dialog box (**Figure 76**). Set options as desired, and click OK.

4. Close the window to save your settings.

✔ Tips

■ The menu bar clock appears near the right end of the menu bar (**Figure 77**).

■ If you use another program which also puts a clock in the menu bar, set the Menu Bar Clock option to Off in the Date & Time window (**Figure 67**).

Figure 75 Use this dialog box to select a city in your time zone.

Figure 76 Use the Clock Options dialog box to configure the menu bar clock.

Figure 77 The menu bar clock appears at the far-right end of the menu bar, just to the left of the Application menu.

Figure 78 You must turn on the Chime on the hour check box to set Chime Settings options.

■ You must turn on the Chime on the hour check box in the Clock Options dialog box (**Figure 76**) to set options in the Chime Settings area (**Figure 78**).

■ You can check the Sample area of the Clock Options dialog box (**Figure 76**) to see the results of your changes before saving them.

SETTING TIME ZONE & MENU BAR CLOCK

Figure 79 The Numbers control panel window.

Figure 80
The Text control panel window.

Figure 81
Text behaviors are based on languages.

Numbers & Text

The Numbers control panel enables you to set formatting options for numbers. The Text control panel enables you to set text behaviors for WorldScript and sorting. Both control panels are designed primarily for localization settings.

To set number formats

1. Choose Apple menu > Control Panels > Numbers (**Figure 3**). The Numbers control panel window appears (**Figure 79**).

2. Choose a region from the Number Format pop-up menu (**Figure 71**).

3. If desired, customize the format by changing the contents of the edit boxes and selecting a different Currency radio button.

4. Close the window to save your settings.

✔ Tip

- You can check a custom number format you create by looking at the sample area in the Numbers control panel (**Figure 79**).

To set text behavior

1. Choose Apple menu > Control Panels > Text (**Figure 3**). The Text control panel window appears (**Figure 80**).

2. Choose an option from the Behavior pop-up menu (**Figure 81**).

3. Close the window to save your settings.

✔ Tip

- The Script pop-up menu may offer options when WorldScript, a multiple language feature of Mac OS, is installed. You can obtain WorldScript from Apple Computer.

SETTING NUMBER FORMATS & TEXT BEHAVIORS

Location Manager

The Location Manager control panel (**Figure 82**) enables you to create *locations*—groups of computer settings for a specific place or purpose.

The settings you can include in a location depend on Location Manager modules installed in your computer. The modules that come with Mac OS 9 let you include the following settings:

◆ **AppleTalk & TCP/IP** switches between configurations of AppleTalk and TCP/IP (**Chapter 10**).

◆ **Auto-Open Items** are the items to open at startup (**Chapter 14**).

◆ **Default Printer** is the default printer (**Chapter 9**).

◆ **Extension Set** is the name of the Extension Manager set (**Chapter 14**).

◆ **File Sharing State** is the on or off setting for File Sharing (**Chapter 10**).

◆ **Internet Set** is the Internet control panel setting (**Chapter 11**).

◆ **QuickTime Speed** is the connection speed settings in the QuickTime Settings control panel (**Chapter 14**).

◆ **Remote Access** is the Remote Access configuration (**Chapter 11**).

◆ **Sound Level** is the sound out volume in the Monitors & Sound control panel (**Chapter 15**).

◆ **Time Zone** is the time zone setting in the Date & Time control panel (**Chapter 14**).

To open Location Manager

Choose Apple menu > Control Panels > Location Manager (**Figure 3**). Location Manager's window appears (**Figure 82**).

Click here to toggle the display of editing options.

Figure 82 The Location Manager control panel with editing options displayed.

✔ Tip

■ To toggle the display of editing options in the Location Manager control panel window, click the triangle beside Edit Locations (**Figure 82**).

Figure 83
Location
Manager's
File menu.

Figure 84 Enter a name for the new location, and click the Save button.

Figure 85 When you select a setting, its current values appear in the right side of the Location Manager window.

Figure 86 The Get Info button displays additional information about a setting.

Figure 87 Follow the instructions in dialog boxes like this one to change settings, then apply changes to the location being edited.

To create a location

1. Choose File > New Location (**Figure 83**).

2. In the dialog box that appears (**Figure 84**), enter a name for the Location and click the Save button.

   The Location Manager window expands to show editing options for the Location you added (**Figure 82**).

✔ Tip

■ Commands under the File menu (**Figure 83**) also enable you to Duplicate, Rename, Delete, Import, and Export locations.

To edit a location

1. If necessary, click the Edit Locations triangle in the Location Manager window to display editing options (**Figure 82**).

2. Choose the location that you want to edit from the Edit Location pop-up menu.

3. Turn on the check boxes beside the settings that you want to include.

4. Choose File > Save Location (**Figure 83**) to save the location's settings.

✔ Tips

■ To display the value for a setting, click its name to select it. Its value appears on the right side of the window (**Figure 85**).

■ To learn more about a setting, click its name to select it, then click the Get Info button. A dialog box with additional information appears (**Figure 86**).

■ To edit a setting, click its name to select it, then click the Edit button. Follow the instructions in the dialog box that appears (**Figure 87**).

To switch to a location

1. In the Location Manager window, choose a location from the Current Location pop-up menu (**Figure 88**).

2. A dialog box like the one in **Figure 89** appears. It indicates the progress of switching from one location to another. When it's finished (**Figure 90**), you can scroll through the comments in the window to review the changes made.

3. Click OK to dismiss the dialog box.

✔ Tip

■ If switching to another location requires switching to a different Extensions Manager set, you must restart the computer for the new set of extensions and control panels to load.

Figure 88
Choose a location to switch to from the Current Location pop-up menu.

Figure 89 Location Manager displays this dialog box as it switches from one location to another...

Figure 90 ...and it tells you when it's finished switching so you can review the changes made.

Figure 91 The PowerBook SCSI Disk Mode control panel.

PowerBook SCSI Disk Mode

The PowerBook SCSI Disk Mode control panel (**Figure 91**), which is available only on PowerBook computers with a SCSI port, enables you to set the SCSI ID number assigned to the PowerBook when it is attached to another computer via a SCSI cable.

✔ Tip

- This feature does not affect the PowerBook in any way if it is not connected to another computer via a SCSI cable.

To set the PowerBook's SCSI ID number

1. Choose Apple menu > Control Panels > PowerBook SCSI Disk Mode. The PowerBook SCSI Disk Mode control panel appears (**Figure 91**).

2. Select the radio button for the SCSI ID number that you want.

3. Close the control panel to save your settings.

✔ Tips

- When attaching your PowerBook to another computer via SCSI cable, it's vital that the PowerBook's ID number be different than all other connected SCSI devices.

- You must turn off password protection when attaching your computer to another computer via SCSI cable. I tell you about password protection in **Chapter 12**.

SETTING POWERBOOK SCSI DISK MODE OPTIONS

File Synchronization

The File Synchronization control panel (**Figure 92**) enables you to synchronize specific items or the contents of specific folders that exist on both a desktop computer and a PowerBook. This helps ensure that you are always working with the most current version of files.

✔ Tips

- File Synchronization requires that you have a network connection between your Power-Book and desktop computer. I tell you about networks in **Chapter 10**.

- To make the most of File Synchronization, you should use it every time you return from a trip with your PowerBook and every time you prepare to leave for a trip with your PowerBook.

- The File Synchronization control panel replaces the File Assistant application that was part of Mac OS prior to version 8.5.

Figure 92 The File Synchronization control panel window.

Figure 93 Drag the icon for the item you want to synchronize to the File Synchronization area.

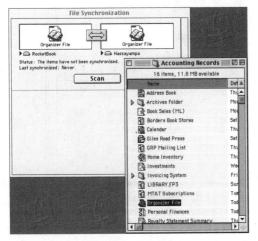

Figure 94 The icon for the second file that you dragged appears beside the first.

Figure 95
Use the Synchronize menu to select a synchronization direction and choose other synchronization options.

To set up a synchronization

1. Establish a network connection to the desktop computer's hard disk.

2. Choose Apple menu > Control Panels > File Synchronization. The File Synchronization control panel appears (**Figure 92**).

3. If necessary, choose File > New or press ⌘N to create an empty synchronization pair.

4. Drag the icon for a file or folder on the PowerBook to the left side *drag item here (or double-click)* area of the File Synchronization window (**Figure 93**). Its icon appears where you dragged it.

5. Drag the icon for the corresponding file or folder on the desktop computer to the right side *drag item here (or double-click)* area of the File Synchronization window. Its icon appears where you dragged it (**Figure 94**).

6. Choose a synchronization direction for the file from the Synchronize menu (**Figure 95**):

   ▲ **In Both Directions** (the default selection) updates either file in the pair when the other file changes.

   ▲ **Left to Right** only updates the file on the right when the file on the left changes.

   ▲ **Right to Left** only updates the file on the left when the file on the right changes.

7. Repeat steps 3 through 6 for each synchronization pair you want to create.

✔ Tips

■ If desired, you can double-click the folder icon in steps 4 and 5 to use a standard Open dialog box for locating and selecting files to synchronize.

■ With In Both Directions synchronization selected, if both files change, File Synchronization cannot synchronize them.

SETTING UP SYNCHRONIZATIONS

To synchronize files

1. Establish a network connection to the desktop computer's hard disk.

2. Choose Apple menu > Control Panels > File Synchronization. The File Synchronization control panel appears (**Figure 92**).

2. Choose Synchronize > Synchronize (**Figure 95**), or press ⌃ ⌘ G.

3. Wait while the files are synchronized. The Synchronizing dialog box appears (**Figure 96**) to indicate the synchronization progress.

4. When synchronization is complete, a dialog box like the one in **Figure 97** appears. Click OK.

   The synchronization date and time appear in the File Synchronization window (**Figure 98**).

✔ Tips

- To synchronize just one pair of files, click the Synchronize button beneath them (**Figure 98**).

- If there is an error during synchronization, a dialog box appears to report it.

- To automatically synchronize files every time your PowerBook connects to the desktop computer while File Synchronization is open, choose Synchronize > Automatic (**Figure 95**) or press ⌃ ⌘ T. This turns on automatic synchronization.

Figure 96 The Synchronizing dialog box appears while files are being synchronized.

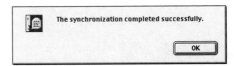

Figure 97 A dialog box like this appears when synchronization has been successfully completed.

Figure 98 The date and time of the last synchronization appears in the File Synchronization window for each pair of files.

Startup & Shutdown Items

The System Folder includes two folders you can use to automatically open items:

◆ **Startup Items** automatically open right after your computer starts up.

◆ **Shutdown Items** automatically open just before your computer shuts down.

✔ Tips

■ Need some ideas for using the Startup Items and Shutdown Items folders? Try these:

▲ Put an alias of your calendar or to-do list document in the Startup Items folder so your calendar or to-do list opens when you're ready to get to work.

▲ Put a sound file in the Startup Items folder so your computer can greet you with a recorded sound.

▲ Put an alias of your backup application in the Shutdown Items folder so you're automatically given an opportunity to back up your work before quitting for the day.

■ It's a good idea to use aliases instead of original items in the Startup Items and Shutdown Items folder. This helps keep originals where they're easy to find and back up. I tell you about aliases in **Chapter 4**.

To set an item to automatically open at start up or shut down

Drag the item (or an alias of the item) into the Startup Items or Shutdown Items folder inside your System Folder.

Software Update

Mac OS 9 introduced Software Update, a control panel that you can use to automatically update your system software.

✔ Tip

- You must have Internet access to use the Software Update control panel.

To manually check for software updates

1. Choose Apple menu > Control Panels > Software Update (**Figure 3**) to display the Software Update control panel window (**Figure 99**).

2. A dialog box like the one in **Figure 100** appears. Click OK.

3. Wait while your computer connects to the Internet and checks for updates. While it works, it displays a dialog box like the one in **Figure 101**.

4. If updates to your software exist, the Install Software dialog box appears (**Figure 102**). Turn on the check box beside each update that you want to install, and click the Install button. Then follow the instructions that appear on screen to complete the installation, and if necessary, restart your computer.

   or

   If no updates to your system software are available, Software Update displays a dialog box like the one in **Figure 103**. Click OK to dismiss it, then close Software Update.

✔ Tip

- If you select the name of an update in the Install Software dialog box (**Figure 102**), information about that item appears in the bottom half of the dialog box.

Figure 99 The Software Update control panel.

Figure 100 Use this dialog box to confirm that you really do want to check for updates.

Figure 101 Your computer displays a dialog box like this while it looks for updates.

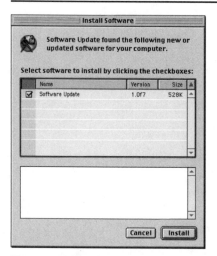

Figure 102 If any software updates are available, they are listed in a dialog box like this one.

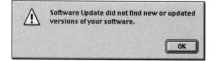

Figure 103 If no software updates are available, a dialog box like this appears.

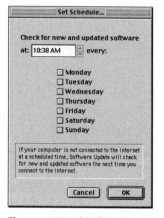

Figure 104 Use this dialog box to set up a schedule for automatically updating software.

To automatically check for software updates

1. Choose Apple menu > Control Panels > Software Update (**Figure 3**) to display the Software Update control panel window (**Figure 99**).

2. Turn on the Update software automatically check box.

3. Click the Set Schedule button.

4. In the Set Schedule dialog box that appears (**Figure 104**), set the time and check off the days that you want your Mac to automatically check for software updates.

5. Click OK to save your settings.

6. To download software updates automatically, without a dialog box, turn off the Ask me before downloading new software check box.

7. Close the Software Update control panel to save your settings.

✔ Tips

■ If you are not connected to the Internet when it's time for an automatic update, your computer will wait until the next time you connect to check for software.

■ You shouldn't have to check for software updates more than once a week.

CHECKING FOR SOFTWARE UPDATERS

313

CUSTOMIZING APPEARANCE

Customizing Mac OS Appearance

One of the great things about Mac OS is the way its appearance can be customized to look the way you want it to. You can change colors, background patterns (or pictures), monitor resolution, and speech options. You can also install or remove fonts.

In this chapter, I explain how to do all of these things—and more.

✔ Tips

- Some appearance customization options explored elsewhere in this book that are not repeated here include:

  ▲ Window views, in **Chapter 3**.

  ▲ Finder preferences and the Info window, in **Chapter 4**.

  ▲ SimpleSound, in **Chapter 6**.

- **Chapter 14** covers a number of other customization features, some of which may indirectly affect the appearance of Mac OS. Be sure to check out that chapter to see what other customization options are available to you.

Appearance

The Appearance control panel includes six tabs you can use to set options that determine how your Mac looks and sounds:

◆ **Themes** (**Figure 1**) enables you to select a group of predefined settings that combine all other appearance options.

◆ **Appearance** (**Figure 3**) enables you to choose an appearance option, highlight color, and variation color.

◆ **Fonts** (**Figure 6**) enables you to choose the fonts for menus, headings, explanatory text, labels, lists, and icons. It also enables you to turn on *anti-aliasing*, to smooth the appearance of fonts on screen.

◆ **Desktop** (**Figure 10**) enables you to select a desktop pattern or picture.

◆ **Sound** (**Figure 14**) enables you to choose a sound track—a group of sound effects for common tasks. It also enables you to disable sounds for certain tasks.

◆ **Options** (**Figure 15**) enables you to set scroll bar and window collapsing options.

✔ Tip

■ Mac OS 9 comes with a number of built-in themes, a sound set, and desktop pictures and patterns. Others are available from Apple and third-party developers.

To open the Appearance control panel

Choose Apple menu > Control Panels > Appearance (**Figure 2**).

Figure 1 The Themes tab of the Appearance control panel.

Figure 2
The Control Panels submenu under the Apple menu.

Figure 3 The Appearance tab of the Appearance control panel.

Figure 4
The Highlight Color
pop-up menu.

Figure 5
The Variation
pop-up menu.

✔ Tip

■ If you choose Other from the Highlight Color pop-up menu (**Figure 4**), you can use a color picker dialog box to select a custom color. I tell you about the color picker in **Chapter 3**.

To select a theme

1. In the Appearance control panel, click the Themes tab to display its options (**Figure 1**).

2. Use the scroll bar in the window to scroll through the available themes.

3. When you see a theme you like, click it to select it.

4. Close the Appearance control panel to save your selection.

✔ Tips

■ Themes include the appearance, fonts, desktop pattern or picture, sound, and window options settings in the Appearance control panel.

■ To customize a theme, select it, make changes in the other tabs of the Appearance control panel, and click the Save Theme button in the Themes tab. Use the dialog box that appears to name and save your custom theme.

To set appearance options

1. In the Appearance control panel, click the Appearance tab to display its options (**Figure 3**).

2. Choose an option from the Appearance pop-up menu to set the overall appearance of menus, icons, windows, and controls.

3. Choose a color from the Highlight Color pop-up menu (**Figure 4**) to set the color of highlighted text.

4. Choose a color from the Variation pop-up menu (**Figure 5**) to set the accent color of menus and controls.

5. Close the Appearance control panel to save your settings.

To choose system fonts

1. In the Appearance control panel, click the Fonts tab to display its options (**Figure 6**).

2. Choose a font from the Large System Font pop-up menu (**Figure 7**) to set the font for menus and headings.

3. Choose a font from the Small System Font pop-up menu to set the font for explanatory text and labels.

4. Choose a font from the Views Font pop-up menu (**Figure 8**) to set the font for lists and icon names. You can also enter a size for the font in the Size edit box beside the pop-up menu.

5. To enable anti-aliasing, turn on the Smooth all fonts on screen check box and enter a minimum font size for anti-aliasing in the Size edit box beside it.

6. Close the Appearance control panel to save your settings.

✔ Tip

- **Figures 9a** and **9b** show examples of onscreen text with anti-aliasing turned off and on.

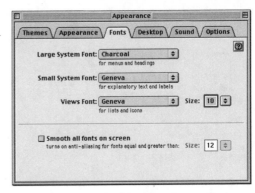

Figure 6 The Fonts tab of the Appearance control panel.

Figure 7
The Large System Font pop-up menu.

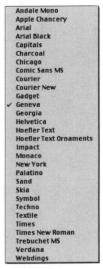

Figure 8
The Views Font pop-up menu.

Courier 12 Points
Courier 18 Points
Courier 24 Points

Helvetica 12 Points
Helvetica 18 Points
Helvetica 24 Points

Times 12 Points
Times 18 Points
Times 24 Points

Courier 12 Points
Courier 18 Points
Courier 24 Points

Helvetica 12 Points
Helvetica 18 Points
Helvetica 24 Points

Times 12 Points
Times 18 Points
Times 24 Points

Figures 9a & 9b Examples of on-screen text with anti-aliasing turned off (left) and on (right).

CHOOSING SYSTEM FONTS

Figure 10 The Desktop tab of the Appearance control panel.

Figure 11 The Open dialog box shows the contents of the Desktop Pictures folder.

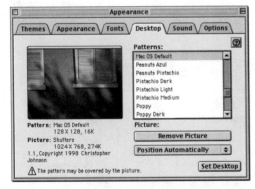

Figure 12 When you choose a picture, it appears in the Desktop tab of the Appearance control panel.

Figure 13
Choose a positioning option for the picture from this menu.

To set the Desktop pattern

1. In the Appearance control panel, click the Desktop tab to display its options (**Figure 10**).

2. Click each of the items in the Patterns scrolling list to see a preview in the left side of the window.

3. When you have selected a pattern you like, click the Set Desktop button. The pattern is applied to the desktop.

To set the Desktop picture

1. In the Appearance control panel, click the Desktop tab to display its options (**Figure 10**).

2. Click the Place Picture button. An Open dialog box showing the contents of the Desktop Pictures folder appears (**Figure 11**).

3. Use the dialog box to locate and select the picture you want.

4. Click Open. The picture appears in the sample area inside the Desktop tab of the Appearance control panel (**Figure 12**).

5. Choose a positioning option from the pop-up menu beneath the Remove Picture button (**Figure 13**).

6. When the picture is just the way you want it, click the Set Desktop button. The picture is applied to the desktop.

✔ Tips

- In step 3, you can click the Show Preview button to see what a selected picture looks like before you choose it.

- A desktop picture appears in place of any desktop pattern.

- You can remove a desktop picture by clicking the Remove Picture button in the Desktop tab of the Appearance control panel (**Figure 12**).

SETTING THE DESKTOP PATTERN OR PICTURE

To set sound options

1. In the Appearance control panel, click the Sound tab to display its options (**Figure 14**).

2. To turn on system sounds, choose an option from the Sound track pop-up menu.

3. Click to toggle check boxes on or off to select the events for which you want to hear sounds.

4. Close the Appearance control panel to save your settings.

✔ Tip

■ To disable sounds, choose None from the Sound track pop-up menu.

To set window options

1. In the Appearance control panel, click the Options tab to display its options (**Figure 15**).

2. To display double-scroll arrows and proportional scroll boxes in the scroll bars of windows, turn on the Smart Scrolling check box. **Figure 16** illustrates a window with this option turned on.

3. To collapse or expand a window by double-clicking its title bar, turn on the Double-click title bar to collapse windows check box.

4. Close the Appearance control panel to save your settings.

Figure 14 The Sound tab of the Appearance control panel.

Figure 15 The Options tab of the Appearance control panel.

Figure 16 Here's what the scroll bars in a window look like with Smart Scrolling turned on.

Figure 17 Use the Monitor options of the Monitors control panel to set basic options for your monitor. This illustration shows options for an iMac monitor.

Monitors

The Monitors control panel (**Figure 17**) enables you to set options for your video display, including depth, resolution, and brightness.

✔ Tips

- The Monitors control panels replaces half of the Monitors & Sound control panel that was installed in previous versions of Mac OS. (The Sound control panel, which is discussed on the next page, replaces the other half.)

To set monitor options

1. Choose Apple menu > Control Panels > Monitors (**Figure 2**) to display the Monitors control panel. As illustrated in **Figure 17**, this control panel's title bar will be named for the type of monitor connected to your computer.

2. If necessary, click the Monitor button to display its options (**Figure 17**).

3. Select a color depth from the list in the Color Depth area. If you choose 256, you can select the Grays radio button to switch to grayscale.

4. Select a resolution from the list in the Resolution area. The higher the resolution, the more information displays on screen.

5. Drag the two sliders in the Contrast and Brightness area to adjust the display's contrast and brightness.

6. Close the window to save your settings.

✔ Tips

- The options that appear in **Figure 17** vary depending on the type of monitor and amount of VRAM (video RAM) installed in your computer. If other options are available, set them as desired.

- If the options in the Monitors control panel look very different from what you see here, check the documentation that came with your monitor.

Sound

The Sound control panel enables you to set sound options for your computer:

◆ **Alert Sounds** (**Figure 18**) enables you to select, add, and change the volume of alert sounds.

◆ **Input** (**Figure 19**) enables you to select a device for sound input.

◆ **Output** (**Figure 20**) enables you to select a device and other options for sound output.

◆ **Speaker Setup** (**Figure 18**) enables you to set speaker options.

Figure 18 Use the Alert Sounds option of the Sound control panel to select an alert sound and set its volume.

✔ Tip

■ The options that appear in the Sound control panel vary depending on your computer model and the input and output devices connected to it. All Sound control panel illustrations in this book show the options for an iMac computer.

To set alert sound options

1. Choose Apple menu > Control Panels > Sound (**Figure 2**).

2. If necessary, select the Alert Sounds option on the left side of the window that appears (**Figure 18**).

3. Select the sound that you would like to hear as your alert sound from the alert sound list.

4. Drag the Alert Volume slider to change the volume of the alert sound.

5. Close the window to save your settings.

✔ Tip

■ You can click the Add button (**Figure 18**) to record your own sounds. I explain how to use the Recording dialog box in **Chapter 6** when I tell you about SimpleSound.

Figure 19 Use the Input options of the Sound control panel to set a sound input source.

Figure 20 Use the Output options of the Sound control panel to select a sound output device and set its volume.

Figure 21 Use the Speaker Setup options of the Sound control panel to select the speakers you want to use and adjust their balance.

To set input, output, & speaker options

1. Choose Apple menu > Control Panels > Sound (**Figure 2**).

2. If necessary, select the Input option on the left side of the window that appears (**Figure 19**).

3. Select one of the devices in the sound input device list.

4. If desired, set other options in the area below the device list.

5. Select the Output option on the left side of the Sound control panel window (**Figure 20**).

6. Select one of the devices in the sound output device list.

7. Drag the Volume slider to set the system sound output volume. To disable the sound, turn on the Mute check box.

8. Select the Speaker Setup option on the left side of the Sound control panel window (**Figure 21**).

9. Select the speakers you want to use.

10. To adjust the speaker balance, click the Start Test button and then drag the sliders until all the speakers sound equally loud. Then click the Stop Test button.

11. Close the Sound control panel window to save your settings.

SETTING INPUT, OUTPUT, & SPEAKER OPTIONS

Speech

The Speech control panel enables you to set options for speech synthesis:

♦ **Voice** options (**Figure 22**) control the voice and speech rate.

♦ **Talking Alerts** options (**Figure 24**) controls whether your computer reads alert dialog boxes to you.

To set voice options

1. Choose Apple menu > Control Panels > Speech (**Figure 2**).

2. If necessary, choose Voice from the Options pop-up menu at the top of the Speech window that appears (**Figure 22**).

3. Choose a voice from the Voice pop-up menu (**Figure 23**).

4. If desired, use the slider to change the speaking rate.

5. Close the window to save your settings.

✔ Tip

■ To hear what the selected voice sounds like, click the speaker icon to the right of the Voice pop-up menu (**Figure 22**).

Figure 22 The Voice options of the Speech control panel.

Figure 23
Choose a voice from the Voice pop-up menu.

SETTING VOICE OPTIONS

Figure 24 The Talking Alerts options of the Speech control panel.

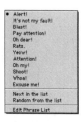

Figure 25
Choose a phrase from the Speak the phrase pop-up menu.

To set talking alerts options

1. Choose Apple menu > Control Panels > Speech (**Figure 2**).

2. If necessary, choose Talking Alerts from the Options pop-up menu at the top of the Speech window that appears (**Figure 24**).

3. To hear your computer speak a phrase instead of playing an alert sound, turn on the Speak the phrase check box. Then choose a phrase from the pop-up menu (**Figure 25**).

4. To hear your computer speak the text in alert dialog boxes, turn on the Speak the alert text check box.

5. If desired, use the Wait before speaking slider to set a delay.

6. Close the window to save your settings.

✔ Tips

- To hear a demo of the talking alerts settings, click the icon beside the Wait before speaking slider (**Figure 24**).

- With a clean installation of Mac OS 9, Talking Alerts is turned on by default.

SETTING TALKING ALERTS OPTIONS

Fonts

Fonts are typefaces that appear on screen and in printed documents. When properly installed in the Fonts folder inside the System Folder (**Figure 26**), they appear on all Font menus (**Figure 27**).

There are three kinds of fonts:

◆ *TrueType fonts* are scalable fonts that appear clear on screen and in print, no matter what size or printer you use. They come in suitcase files (**Figure 26**).

◆ *Bitmapped fonts* are single-size fonts that appear clear on screen only when used in the correct size. They also come in suitcase files (**Figures 28** and **29**).

◆ *PostScript fonts* are scalable fonts that appear clear in print when printed on a PostScript printer, no matter what size you use. With the help of a utility called Adobe Type Manager (ATM), PostScript fonts can also appear clear on screen and in print no matter what size or printer they use. They come in individual font files but must be accompanied by a corresponding bitmapped font (**Figure 28**) to appear on Font menus.

✔ Tips

■ You can open a suitcase file to view the fonts inside it (**Figure 29**). Bitmapped fonts names include numbers.

■ You can open a font file within a suitcase to see a sample of the font's characters (**Figures 30** and **31**). Bitmapped fonts display only one size, and TrueType fonts display three sample sizes.

■ If you're interested in learning more about fonts than what's on these two pages, check out these two Peachpit Press books: *How to Boss Your Fonts Around, Second Edition* and *The Macintosh Font Book, Third Edition*.

Figure 26 The TrueType fonts that are installed with Mac OS 9 can be found in the Fonts folder.

Figure 27 SimpleText's Font menu is just one of the menus that lists installed fonts.

Figure 28 Fonts can come as individual font files (left) or in suitcases (right).

Figure 29 This suitcase contains both TrueType and bitmapped fonts.

Figure 30
Open one of the font files inside a suitcase to see a sample of the font's characters. This is a bitmapped font...

Figure 31
...and this is a TrueType font.

Figure 32 Drag all of the font's files onto the System Folder icon.

Figure 33 Click OK when this dialog box appears.

To install a font

1. Drag all suitcases and files that are part of the font onto the System Folder icon. When the System Folder becomes highlighted (**Figure 32**), release the mouse button.

2. A dialog box like the one in **Figure 33** appears to inform you that fonts must be stored in the Fonts folder. Click OK.

✔ Tips

- You can see a freshly installed font in the Font menu of an application like Simple-Text (**Figure 34**) or your favorite word processor. You can also view the characters in any installed font using Key Caps, which I discuss in **Chapter 6**.

- If an application is running when you install a font, you'll have to quit the application and restart it to see the font in that application's Font menu.

To uninstall a font

1. Quit all applications.

2. Drag all suitcases and files that are part of the font out of the Fonts folder in the System Folder.

Figure 34
The font you installed appears on the Font menus of your applications.

INSTALLING & UNINSTALLING FONTS

GETTING HELP &
TROUBLESHOOTING 16

Figure 1
The Finder's
Help menu.

Getting Help

Mac OS offers several ways to get additional information and answers to questions while you work with your computer:

- ◆ **Balloon Help** identifies screen items as you point to them.

- ◆ **Help Center** provides information about using installed Mac OS components, such as Mac OS and AppleScript.

- ◆ **Mac Help** provides information about using Mac OS.

- ◆ **Guide help** provides information about using specific applications.

- ◆ **Application online help**, which is included in many third-party applications, provides information about the application.

All of these help features can be accessed using commands on the Help menu (**Figure 1**). In this chapter, I tell you how to get help when you need it.

Balloon Help

Balloon Help identifies screen elements that you point to by providing information in cartoon balloon-shaped windows (**Figures 2**, **3**, and **4**).

✔ Tips

- Although Balloon Help might be too annoying to keep turned on all the time, you might find it useful when first starting out with Mac OS 9 or a new software application.

- Balloon Help works in the Finder, all applications and utilities that come with Mac OS 9, and many third-party applications.

To turn on Balloon Help

Choose Help > Show Balloons (**Figure 1**).

To use Balloon Help

Point to an item for which you want more information. A balloon appears with information about the item (**Figures 2**, **3**, and **4**).

To turn off Balloon Help

Choose Help > Hide Balloons (**Figure 5**).

Figure 2 Balloon Help displays a cartoon balloon with information about items you point to.

Figure 3 With Balloon Help turned on, you can learn about almost anything on your screen, including window parts...

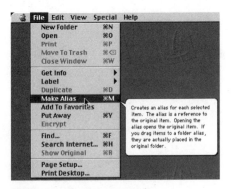

Figure 4 ...and menu commands.

Figure 5
To turn off Balloon Help, choose Hide Balloons from the Help menu.

Figure 6 The Help Center is a centralized starting point for getting help about Mac OS components.

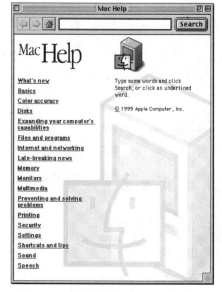

Figure 7 The Mac OS Help main window.

The Help Center & Mac Help

The Help Center (**Figure 6**) offers access to information about Mac OS components installed on your computer. Mac Help (**Figure 7**) offers information and step-by-step instructions for using your Mac. Both of these help features are displayed using Apple's Help Viewer application, so they work similarly.

You can use these features in two ways:

◆ Click blue underlined links to browse help topics and learn more about a topic that interests you.

◆ Search for a specific word or phrase to display a list of topics that discuss that word or phrase. Then click blue underlined links to learn more about the topic that interests you.

To open the Help Center

Choose Help > Help Center (**Figure 1**). The Help Center window appears (**Figure 6**).

To open Mac Help

Choose Help > Mac Help (**Figure 1**), or press ⌃ ⌘ ?.

or

Click the Mac Help link in the Help Center window (**Figure 6**).

The Mac Help main window appears (**Figure 7**).

To browse Mac Help topics

1. On the left side of the Mac Help window (**Figure 7**), click an underlined topic link.

2. On the right side of the Mac Help window, click an underlined topic link (**Figure 8**).

3. Information about the topic appears in a window (**Figure 9**). Read the window's contents to learn more about the subtopic.

✔ Tips

■ When viewing information about a topic, you can click underlined links to learn about related topics.

■ You can use the navigation buttons at the top of the Mac Help window to view windows you have already seen:

   ▲ **Back** displays the previous window.

   ▲ **Forward** displays the next window.

   ▲ **Home** displays the Help Center window.

To search Mac Help topics

1. Enter a search word or phrase in the edit box at the top of the Mac Help window (**Figure 10**).

2. Click Search.

3. After a moment, the Mac Help window fills with a list of search results (**Figure 11**). Click an underlined link to display information about the topic in a window (**Figure 9**).

✔ Tips

■ The asterisks to the left of a topic name in the Search Results list indicate how well the topic matches your search criteria.

■ You can search for help from the Help Center Window, too. Just follow these instructions in that window.

Figure 8 Clicking the Memory link on the left side of the window displays memory topics on the right.

Figure 9 Clicking a topic in the right side of the window displays a window full of information about the topic.

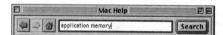

Figure 10 Enter a search word or phrase in the edit box at the top of the window.

Figure 11 Search results appear in a window like this.

Figure 12 These illustrations show step-by-step instructions to walk you through the process of changing the amount of RAM required by an application. First quit the application if it's open,...

Figure 13 ...then open the application's Info window,...

Figure 14 ...then change the Preferred Size value,...

To follow step-by-step instructions

1. In a topic's information window (**Figure 9**), click a link beginning with the words *Help me*.

   A window with instructions appears. Red circles or lines may also be drawn on screen to help you locate items referenced in the instructions. You can see all this in **Figure 12**.

2. Follow the instructions that appear in the window and click the right-pointing triangle at the bottom of the window to advance to the next step. **Figures 12** through **15** show the three steps for creating a folder.

3. Repeat step 2 until the task has been completed.

✔ Tip

■ Step-by-step instructions are created using Apple Guide technology.

Figure 15 ...and finally, close the Info window.

Guide Help

Apple Guide technology forms the basis for help within specific applications, including most applications and utilities that come with Mac OS 9. Opening an application's Guide Help offers information and step-by-step instructions similar to what's available in Mac Help but for a specific application.

✔ Tip

- I tell you all about Mac Help on the previous few pages.

To open Guide Help for an application

Choose Help > *Application* Guide (**Figures 16a** and **16c**) or Help > *Application* Help (**Figure 16b**). The program's Guide Help window appears (**Figures 17a**, **17b**, and **17c**).

✔ Tips

- As shown in **Figures 16a**, **16b**, and **16c**, the exact name of the command to open Guide Help depends on the application name.

- Most Guide Help windows enable you to browse topics, browse an index, or search for specific information. If a Guide Help window does not include Topics and Index buttons (**Figure 17c**), you can browse only the displayed help phrases.

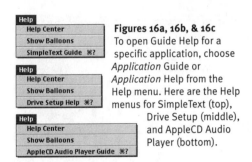

Figures 16a, 16b, & 16c
To open Guide Help for a specific application, choose *Application* Guide or *Application* Help from the Help menu. Here are the Help menus for SimpleText (top), Drive Setup (middle), and AppleCD Audio Player (bottom).

Figures 17a, 17b, & 17c
Here are the corresponding Guide Help windows: SimpleText Guide (top), Drive Setup Help (middle), and AppleCD Audio Player Guide (bottom).

OPENING GUIDE HELP

Figure 18 When you click the Topics button, a list of topics appears on the left side of the window.

Figure 19 When you click a topic, a list of help phrases appears in the right side of the window.

Figure 20 Click a help phrase and click OK to display information about the phrase.

To browse Guide Help topics

1. Click the Topics button in the Guide Help window (**Figures 17a** and **17b**).

2. In the list of topics that appears on the left side of the window (**Figure 18**), click the topic that interests you.

3. In the list of help phrases that appears in the right side of the window (**Figure 19**), click the phrase for the explanation you're looking for.

4. Click OK.

5. Read the explanation or follow the instructions in the window that appears (**Figure 20**).

6. If necessary, click the right-pointing triangle to advance through the help windows.

7. When you're finished reading help information, click the window's close box to dismiss it.

BROWSING GUIDE HELP TOPICS

To browse the Guide Help index

1. Click the Index button in the Guide Help window (**Figures 17a** and **17b**).

2. On the alphabetical index bar that appears (**Figure 21**), click the letter for the term that interests you.

3. In the list of terms that appears in the right side of the window (**Figure 22**), click the term that interests you.

4. In the list of help phrases that appears in the right side of the window (**Figure 23**), click the phrase for the explanation you're looking for.

5. Click OK.

6. Read the explanation or follow the instructions in the window that appears (**Figure 24**).

7. If necessary, click the right-pointing triangle to advance through the help windows.

8. When you're finished reading help information, click the window's close box to dismiss it.

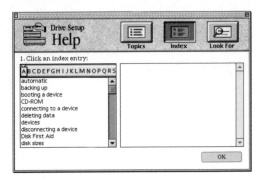

Figure 21 When you click the Index button, an alphabetical index bar and term list appear.

Figure 22 Click a letter to display terms beginning with that letter.

Figure 23 Click a term to display a list of phrases.

Figure 24 Click a phrase and click OK to display information.

Figure 25 When you click the Look For button, a search form appears.

Figure 26 Enter a search word or phrase in the edit box and click Search to display a list of help phrases.

Figure 27 Click a phrase and click OK to display information.

To search Guide Help

1. Click the Look For button in the Guide Help window (**Figures 17a** and **17b**).

2. Click the right-pointing triangle on the left side of the dialog box (**Figure 25**).

3. Enter a search word or phrase in the edit box beside the triangle.

4. Click Search.

5. In the list of help phrases that appears in the right side of the window (**Figure 26**), click the phrase for the explanation you're looking for.

6. Click OK.

7. Read the explanation or follow the instructions in the window that appears (**Figure 27**).

8. If necessary, click the right-pointing triangle to advance through the help windows.

9. When you're finished reading help information, click the window's close box to dismiss it.

SEARCHING GUIDE HELP

337

Application Help

Many applications include extensive online help. The help features of various applications look and work differently, so I can't cover them in detail here. I can, however, tell you how to access help in other applications and assure you that most online help features are easy to use.

Figures 28a & 28b
The Help menus for FileMaker Pro 4.1 (left) and Microsoft Word 98 (right) offer a variety of online help options.

✔ Tips

■ Some applications, like the Microsoft Office suite of products, include an entire online manual that is searchable and printable.

■ Not all applications include online help. If you can't locate an online help feature for an application, check the documentation that came with the application to see if it has one and how you can access it.

To access an application's online help

Choose a command from the Help menu within that application (**Figures 28a** and **28b**).

or

Click a Help button within a dialog box.

Troubleshooting

Occasionally, you might experience problems using your Mac. Here are some examples:

◆ An error message appears on screen when you attempt to perform a task.

◆ An application "unexpectedly quits" while you are using it.

◆ An application simply won't work correctly.

◆ You can't open a certain file.

◆ Your computer "freezes" or "locks up"— either at startup or while working with an application— making it impossible to move the mouse pointer, quit an application, or even properly restart the computer.

These are examples of problems you might experience. Although these problems may be caused by any number of things, there are some techniques you can use to narrow down the cause and fix the problem. That's what troubleshooting is all about.

This part of the chapter will provide some basic troubleshooting information you can use to diagnose and solve many problems on your Macintosh.

✔ Tip

■ Although the information in this section can solve many problems, it can't solve all of them. For a thorough guide to trouble-shooting Macintosh hardware and software problems, check out *Sad Macs, Bombs, and Other Disasters*, a Peachpit Press book by Ted Landau.

■ For more troubleshooting information, including late-breaking information about specific compatibility problems, visit these Web sites:

▲ **MacFixIt** http://www.macfixit.com/

▲ **MacInTouch**
http://www.macintouch.com/

TROUBLESHOOTING

The First Nine

I used to teach a two-day Macintosh trouble-shooting course written by John Bradley. The first thing the course covered was what John called "The First Six"—the first six things you should try when you encounter problems on your Macintosh. I added three things to the list. Here are all nine of these techniques, in the order I suggest trying them:

◆ **Restart.** This can solve RAM-related problems.

◆ **Rebuild the Desktop.** This can solve orphan document problems.

◆ **Restart with extensions disabled.** This can identify conflict problems.

◆ **Trash application preferences.** This can solve problems that occur when an application's preferences file is corrupted.

◆ **Zap the PRAM.** This can solve missing hardware or network device problems.

◆ **Use diagnostic software.** This can identify and repair disk-related problems.

◆ **Reinstall the application.** This can solve problems related to corrupted application files.

◆ **Reinstall the system software.** This can solve problems related to corrupted system software. Be sure to do a clean installation!

◆ **Upgrade software or hardware.** This can solve problems related to incompatibilities between an application and the installed system software or your computer itself.

I've found that one or more of these nine techniques will solve 90 percent of the problems you encounter with your Macintosh.

✔ Tip

■ The rest of this chapter provides further explanations for these problems and techniques.

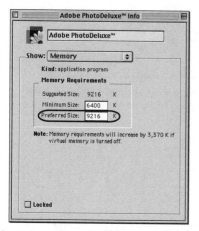

Figure 29 Sometimes you can solve memory errors that occur with a specific application by changing the Preferred Size in the Memory area of the Info window for the application. The inclusion of a Note in this window identifies this application as PowerPC-native.

Figure 30 In this illustration of the Memory control panel, Virtual Memory is properly set for best performance with most PowerPC-native applications: Virtual Memory is turned on and set to the default setting.

Memory Problems

Some problems, including "Not Enough Memory" and "Application has Unexpectedly Quit" error messages, are caused by memory problems. Here are some possible causes:

◆ Your Macintosh may not have enough memory to run an application. Check the system requirements to make sure your computer meets them. If you don't have enough RAM, consider upgrading or using virtual memory. (I tell you about virtual memory in **Chapter 14**.)

◆ Your computer's RAM may be *fragmented*— a situation that occurs when you launch and quit many applications during a work session. Restarting your computer clears out RAM and solves this problem.

◆ The application may require more RAM than what is set in its current memory settings. This happens sometimes when you attempt to open very large or complex documents. Try increasing the value in the Preferred Size edit box of the Info window (**Figure 29**). I explain how in **Chapter 5**.

✔ Tips

■ The term *memory* almost always refers to RAM (Random Access Memory)—*not* hard disk space. I tell you more about RAM in **Chapters 5** and **14**.

■ In general, you can get good performance and minimize the amount of RAM used by *PowerPC-native* applications—those written specifically to take advantage of a Power Macintosh's PowerPC processor—by turning on virtual memory and setting it to the default setting. You do this in the Memory control panel (**Figure 30**), which I cover in **Chapter 14**; click the Use Defaults button to set the default value. You can identify a PowerPC-native application by whether a Note appears in the Memory area of its Info window (**Figure 29**).

MEMORY PROBLEMS

Disk & File Corruption Problems

Some problems, including system "freezes" and files that won't open, may be caused by disk or file corruption:

◆ All kinds of problems can be caused by disk corruption. This can occur when the computer is improperly shut down—especially if the computer was writing a file to disk when the shutdown occurred. Although you can avoid this by always using the Shut Down command to shut off your Macintosh, it's tougher to prevent improper shutdowns due to power outages. Use a program like Disk First Aid (discussed in **Chapter 6**) or Symantec's Norton Utilities for Macintosh to diagnose and repair disk corruption problems.

◆ Problems with a specific application can be caused by corrupted application or preferences files. Try trashing the preferences files for the application first. If the problem doesn't go away, try reinstalling the application from original installation disks.

◆ Problems with many applications can be caused by corrupted system software. Try deleting the Finder Preferences file and restarting. If that doesn't work, try doing a clean installation of the system software as discussed in **Chapter 1**.

◆ If double-clicking a document icon won't open the document with the correct application when the application is properly installed on disk, the disk's invisible Desktop files may be corrupted. To rebuild the Desktop for your internal hard disk, hold down ⌘ Option while restarting the computer. Keep those keys held down until a dialog box like the one in **Figure 31** appears. Click OK, and wait while the Desktop is rebuilt.

◆ An "Error 39" or "Error 43" message when opening a file indicates that the file is corrupted. You'd better have a backup copy!

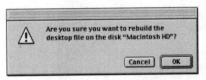

Figure 31 This dialog box appears when you hold down ⌘ Option while starting up or inserting a disk.

✔ Tips

■ You can usually find preferences files in the Preferences folder inside your System Folder.

■ You can rebuild the Desktop on removable media by holding down ⌘ Option while inserting the disk.

Conflict Problems

Conflicts between two or more installed software products or software and hardware can prevent your computer or certain applications from running properly.

◆   If, after installing new software, problems start occurring, chances are the new software conflicts with the system software or some other software in your computer. Remove the new software to see if the problem goes away.

◆   "Init" conflicts are caused by items installed in your Extensions or Control Panels folder conflicting with other software. These conflicts can cause all kinds of problems with your system and applications. You can test for these conflicts by restarting your Macintosh with Shift held down, thus disabling all extensions and control panels (as well as certain other System Folder items). If the problem goes away with extensions and control panels disabled, one of your extensions or control panels is causing the problem.

◆   If an application simply won't run on your Macintosh, it may not be compatible with your computer or Mac OS 9.

◆   If you believe a software product conflicts with other software or Mac OS 9, check with the software developer to learn about updates. *Always* obtain and install free updates to software products when they are available—you can find them on a software developer's Web site. If an upgrade requires a fee, be sure you understand what the revised software can do for you. Then decide whether the improvements are worth the upgrade fee.

Hardware Problems

Hardware problems—such as severely damaged disks and bad computer components—can be a real nightmare because things may not work at all.

♦ If certain peripheral devices don't work properly and you're sure that all device drivers are properly installed, begin by shutting down the computer and checking all cable connections. Then restart. If that doesn't work, zap the PRAM (parameter RAM) by pressing ⌃ ⌘ Option P R while restarting the computer. Release the keys after the startup tone has sounded twice.

♦ A question mark icon at startup means your Mac can't find a bootable disk. This could be caused by a severely damaged or "crashed" hard disk or corrupted system files. Restart the computer from an emergency disk (a Disk Tools floppy or the system software CD-ROM disc). If you can see your hard disk icon on the Desktop, breathe a sigh of relief—it hasn't crashed. Use Disk First Aid to diagnose and repair any problems; if that doesn't solve the problem, reinstall the system software, doing a clean installation as discussed in **Chapter 1**.

♦ If you can't see your hard disk icon on the Desktop, try using Drive Setup to update the disk's driver. Restart to see if the disk reappears. If the hard disk icon does not appear, even after trying all of the techniques listed in "The First Nine" earlier in this chapter, you will probably have to bring the computer to an Apple dealer for servicing.

✔ Tip

■ Zapping the PRAM clears out parameter RAM, forcing your computer to check all connected devices. You may have to reset certain monitor and network settings after zapping the PRAM.

Help & Troubleshooting Advice

Here's some additional advice for getting help with and troubleshooting problems.

◆ **Join a Macintosh user group.** Joining a user group and attending meetings is probably the most cost-effective way to learn about your computer and get help. You can find a users' group near you by consulting the User Group page at Apple's Web site (http://www.apple.com/usergroups/) or calling 1-800-SOS-APPL.

◆ **Visit Apple's Web site.** If you have access to the Web, you can find a wealth of information about your computer right online. Start at http://www.apple.com/ and follow links or search for the information you need.

◆ **Visit the Web sites for the companies that develop the applications you use most.** A regular visit to these sites can keep you up to date on updates and upgrades to keep your software running smoothly. These sites can also provide technical support for problems you encounter while using the software. Learn the URLs for these sites by consulting the documentation that came with the software.

◆ **Read Macintosh magazines.** A number of magazines, each geared toward a different level of user, can help you learn about your computer: *Macworld, Mac Addict, Mac Today*, and *Mac Home Journal* are the most popular. Stay away from PC-centric magazines; the majority of the information they provide will not apply to your Macintosh and may confuse you.

◆ **Check out *Macintosh Tips & Tricks.*** This freely distributable newsletter from Giles Road Press is available on the Web at http://www.gilesrd.com/.

Menus & Keyboard Commands

Menus & Keyboard Commands

This appendix illustrates all of the Mac OS 9 Finder's menus—both Simple Finder (left) and standard Finder (right)—and provides a list of corresponding keyboard commands.

To use a keyboard command, hold down the modifier key (usually ⌥⌘), while pressing the keyboard key for the command. The only keyboard command that works when Simple Finder is turned on is ⌥⌘? (Help).

I tell you all about using menus and keyboard commands in **Chapter 2**.

File Menu

⌥⌘N	New Folder
⌥⌘O	Open
⌥⌘P	Print
⌥⌘Delete	Move to Trash
⌥⌘W	Close Window
⌥⌘Option W	Close All Windows
⌥⌘I	Get Info (General Information)
⌥⌘D	Duplicate
⌥⌘M	Make Alias
⌥⌘Y	Put Away
⌥⌘F	Find
⌥⌘H	Search Internet
⌥⌘R	Show Original

Edit Menu

⌘ Z	Undo
⌘ X	Cut
⌘ C	Copy
⌘ V	Paste
⌘ A	Select All

View Menu

(no command keys)

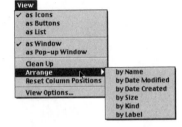

Special Menu

⌘ E	Eject

Help Menu

⌘ ?	Mac Help

Other Command Keys

⌘ Shift 1	Eject floppy disk
⌘ Shift 3	Create picture of screen
⌘ Shift 4	Create picture of selection

iBook
Considerations

iBook Considerations

Apple's new iBook computer (**Figure 1**) takes the simplicity and affordability of the iMac computer on the road. With a stylish, durable case, built-in modem and networking capabilities, and everything great about Mac OS, the iMac is a great choice for anyone interested in computing on the go.

In this appendix, I explain some of the differences between iBook computers and other Macintosh models. If you have an iBook, be sure to read this chapter to learn some of the things that make your computer special.

✔ Tip

- Unfortunately, iBooks were not generally available when this book went to press. Although the information in this appendix is correct, it may not be complete. For updates on this appendix in Adobe Acrobat PDF format, visit the companion Web site for this book at http://www.gilesrd.com/macosvqs/ or send an e-mail message to info@gilesrd.com with the word *iBook* in the subject line.

Figure 1 The iBook is not only funky-looking, but it's durable enough to tote around in your backpack.

Display

The iBook features a bright 12.1-inch TFT
active matrix display (**Figure 2**). The display
supports two resolutions: 800 x 600 pixels and
640 x 480 pixels.

✔ Tip

- You can change the resolution and other
  settings for the iBook display with the
  Monitor control panel. I explain how in
  Chapter 15.

Keyboard

The iBook includes a full-size, full-function
keyboard (**Figure 3**) with two interesting
features:

◆ **Predefined Function Keys.** The F1
through F6 function keys are predefined to
handle specific hardware tasks, such as
changing the monitor brightness and
sound volume. The other six function keys
(F7 through F12) are user-programmable.

◆ **Lockable Keyboard.** The Number Lock
LED key includes a translucent retaining
screw that can be turned with a regular
flat-blade screwdriver to lock the keyboard
down. This helps prevent theft of the
computer's memory chips or Airport
wireless card, both of which are accessible
under the keyboard.

✔ Tip

- You can use the Keyboard control panel to
  program function keys. I tell you how in
  Chapter 14.

Figure 2 The iBook features a bright 12.1-inch display.

Figure 3 The iBook's full-size keyboard includes
predefined function keys and a keyboard lock.

Figure 4 The AirPort base station enables you to network your iBook from up to 150 feet away—even through walls!

Modem

The iBook comes with a built-in 56K modem that you can use to dial in to the Internet (or any other computer system to which you have access) and send and receive faxes.

✔ Tips

- Use the Modem control panel, which is discussed in **Chapter 10**, to set options for the iBook modem.

- I explain how to connect to the Internet via modem in **Chapter 11**.

- To send and receive faxes, you need fax processing software. The iBook comes with FAXstf for this purpose.

Networking

The iBook enables you to connect to a network two ways:

- ◆ **10/100 BASE-T Ethernet.** This is a standard network connection method supported by most computers.

- ◆ **AirPort.** This is a new, wireless networking solution codeveloped by Apple Computer and Lucent Technologies. To use AirPort for networking, you must have an AirPort card installed inside your iBook (required antennas are already installed) and an AirPort base station (**Figure 4**) connected to a phone line or network.

The iBook comes with all the software you need to use either network connection method.

✔ Tips

- I explain how to set up an Ethernet network in **Chapter 10**.

- Use the AirPort Setup Assistant, which works very much like the Mac OS Setup Assistant I discuss in **Chapter 1**, to configure an AirPort connection.

iBook Modem & Networking

Indicator Lights

The iBook uses two different lights to communicate about its hardware:

◆ **Charge Lighting.** When the iBook is
plugged into AC power, its power adapter
port glows green when the battery is fully
charged or amber when the battery is being
charged.

◆ **Beacon Sleep Lighting.** When the iBook
is sleeping, a light below the display dims
and brightens slowly—like the gentle
breathing of a sleeping computer. The light
is visible whether the computer is open or
closed.

✔ Tips

■ The iBook battery can last up to 6 hours
between charges.

■ I discuss system sleep in **Chapter 2**.

Bundled Software

The iMac comes with the following software
products:

◆ Mac OS

◆ Microsoft Internet Explorer

◆ Microsoft Outlook Express

◆ Netscape Communicator

◆ America Online

◆ EarthLink TotalAccess

◆ AppleWorks

◆ FAXstf

◆ Adobe Acrobat Reader

◆ Palm Desktop

◆ EdView Internet Safety Kit Family Edition

◆ World Book Encyclopedia

◆ Nanosaur

◆ Bugdom

✔ Tip

■ *Visual QuickStart Guides* like this one are
available for several of these software
products. Visit the Peachpit Press Web site
at http://www.peachpit.com/ for details.

INDEX

INDEX

Other Visual QuickStart Guides for Mac OS Users

Word 98 for Macintosh: Visual QuickStart Guide

Maria Langer

With the release of Word 98, Word promises to not only remain but continue to grow as the leading word processor on the Macintosh platform. It's been dramatically reworked to more fully utilize and integrate with the Mac OS user interface and functionality. Now more powerful and friendly than ever, Word 98 enables users to create a wide range of documents, from simple, one-page letters to complex multifile reports with figures, table of contents, and index to Web pages with hyperlinks and graphics.

Word 98 for Macintosh: Visual QuickStart Guide will introduce new and experienced Word users alike to the host of new features and improved Web integration and functionality. Using concise steps and numerous illustrations, the book covers everything from word processing basics and formatting fundamentals to desktop and Webtop publishing techniques. This is a comprehensive introduction to the powerful capabilities of Word 98.

260 pages • ISBN 0-201-35354-7 • $17.95

Excel 98 for Macintosh: Visual QuickStart Guide

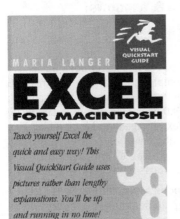

Maria Langer

Excel is the spreadsheet of choice for home users and business workers. With it you can create anything from a simple chart to an advanced worksheet with graphics and more, based on just about any data you can enter into a Macintosh. Excel 98 is the latest version of the most popular spreadsheet for the Mac. New features include the Natural Language Formula, Range Finder, and Formula AutoCorrect features to write and edit formulas; the free rotation, merge cells, AutoSize Text, and Conditional Formatting features; enhanced Internet features that let you include links in documents and convert Excel 98 documents to Web pages; and the new Office Assistant.

The fast-paced and easy-to-read *Excel 98 for Macintosh: Visual QuickStart Guide* helps both new and experienced Excel users get up-to-speed quickly on all of Excel's new and improved features. This book uses the power of pictures to guide readers through the software, with plentiful screen captures and succinct, to-the-point instructions. Numerous tips and tricks throughout the book make this an excellent reference to the versatility and power of the program.

262 pages • ISBN 0-201-35360-1 • $17.95

AppleWorks 5 for Windows & Macintosh: Visual QuickStart Guide

C. Ann Brown

With a simple name change and some modified screen elements, ClarisWorks 5 becomes AppleWorks, the integrated package that encompasses word processing, database, spreadsheet, graphics, and telecommunications modules, all of which allow users to create sophisticated documents quickly. Apple is so sold on its program that it has included AppleWorks on all new iMacs, the consumer Internet Macs for home, small business, and school, a market that has already embraced ClarisWorks. And what better match for an Internet Mac than a product rich with Internet capabilities and multimedia features, making it easy for users of all levels to add pictures, sound, and even QuickTime movies to their projects.

AppleWorks for Windows & Macintosh: Visual QuickStart Guide is a great tool for mastering the best of the "Swiss Army knife" applications. The Visual QuickStart Guide's simple-to-follow instructions, hundreds of screenshots, and loads of tips will help the beginner navigate Appleworks' many facets with confidence, and more seasoned users will value it as a useful reference.

224 pages • ISBN 0-201-35403-9 • $17.99

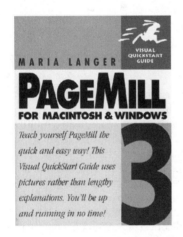

PageMill 3 for Macintosh & Windows: Visual QuickStart Guide

Maria Langer

With PageMill 3, creating Web pages has never been easier. No need to learn HTML or master complex applications—a WYSIWYG interface provides a familiar environment for creating colorful, dynamic Web pages. PageMill 3.0 uses drag-and-drop simplicity for adding and manipulating text, images, and hyperlinks. This allows for quick and easy integration with your current office and graphics applications. By taking away all the scary technical details, PageMill allows users to focus on content and design.

PageMill 3 for Macintosh & Windows: Visual QuickStart Guide is a richly illustrated, step-by-step guide that gets readers up and running quickly. In no time at all readers are designing and creating Web pages and effectively utilizing all the features of PageMill. Hundreds of screenshots accompanied by clear instructions and loads of helpful tips guide readers through basic editing techniques, applying styles, working with graphic images and links, and finally, to testing and enhancing their new Web pages.

253 pages • ISBN 0-201-35443-8 • $17.99

To order these and other Peachpit Press books, visit our Web site at http://www.peachpit.com/ or call toll-free 1-800-283-9444